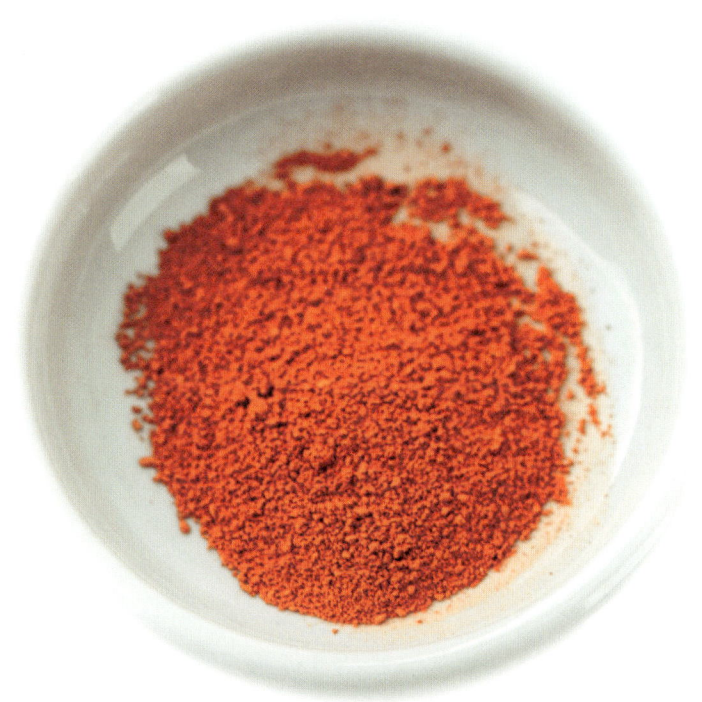

FOUND AND GROUND

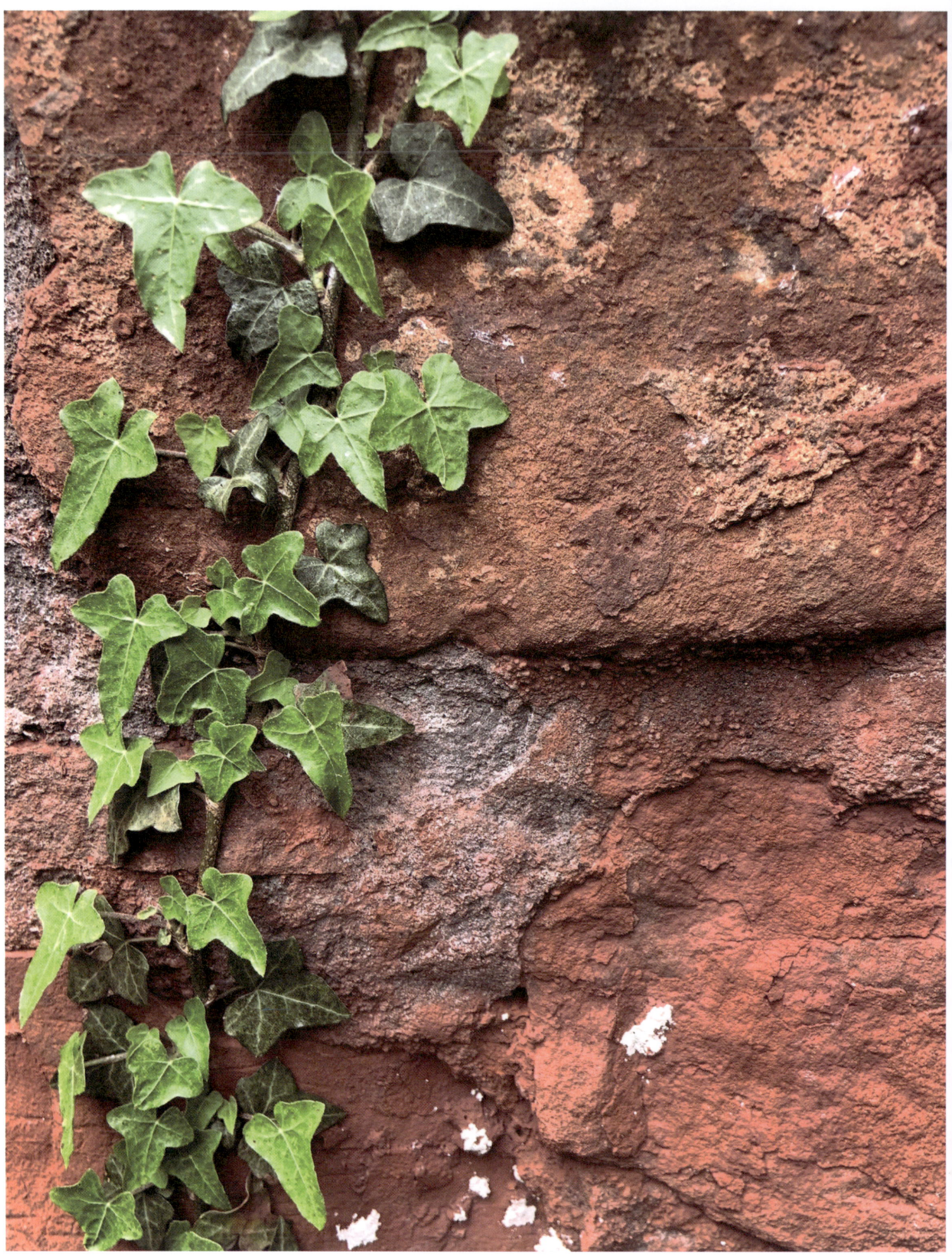

FOUND AND GROUND

A practical guide to making your own foraged paints

Caroline Ross

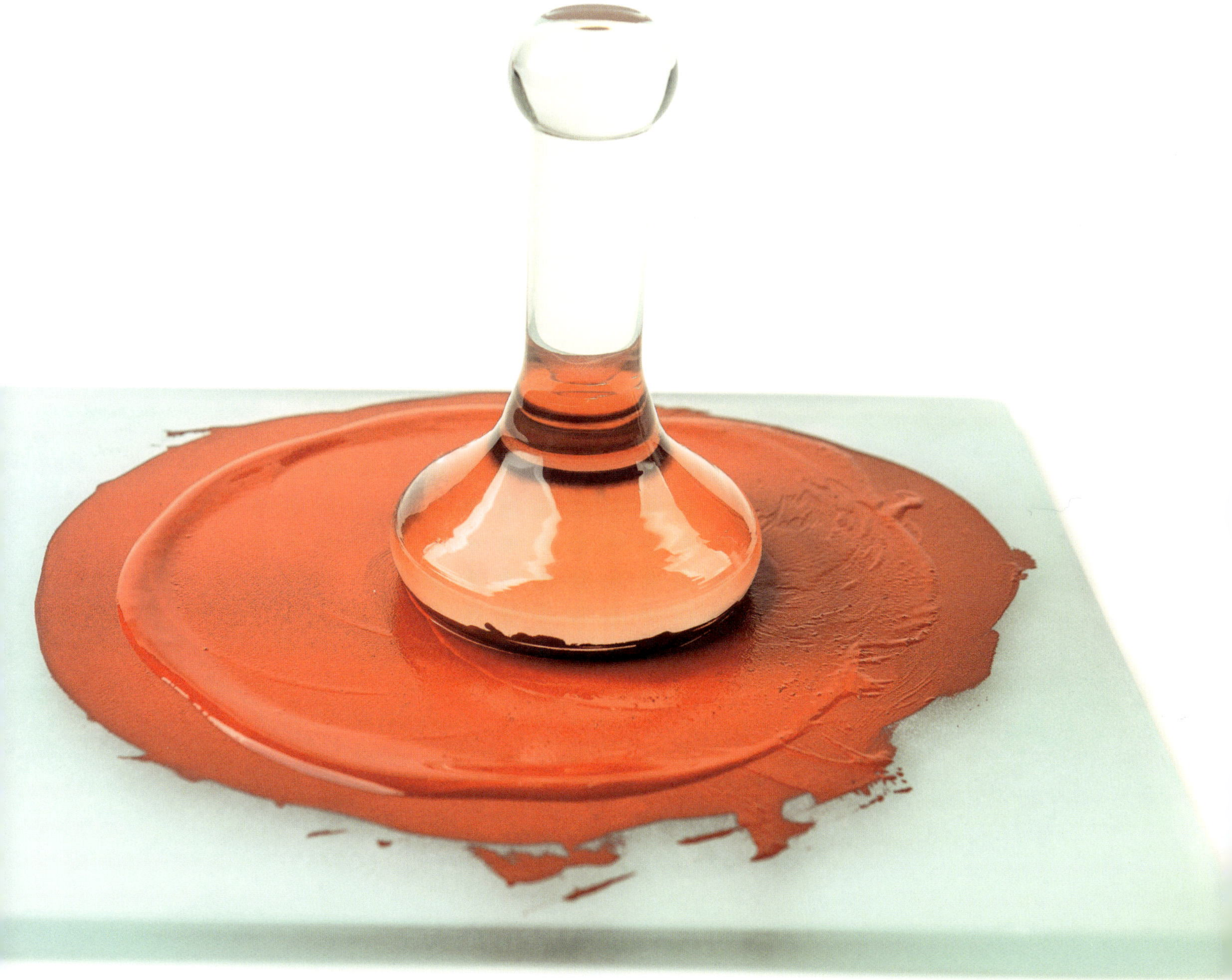

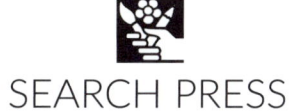

SEARCH PRESS

First published 2023

Search Press Limited
Wellwood, North Farm Road,
Tunbridge Wells, Kent TN2 3DR

4 5 6 7 8 9 10

ISBN: 978-1-80092-099-6
ebook ISBN: 978-1-80093-090-2

Bookmarked Hub
For further ideas and inspiration, and to join our free online
community, visit www.bookmarkedhub.com

Publishers' notes
Metric measurements are used in this book; the imperial
conversions are rounded to the nearest ¼in. Always use
either metric or imperial measurements, not a combination
of both.

The Publishers and author can accept no responsibility for
any consequences arising from the information, advice or
instructions given in this publication.

For errata, please visit our website (www.searchpress.com)
or the Bookmarked Hub (www.bookmarkedhub.com).

GPSR information can be found at www.searchpress.com
Printed in China, AP092025

You are invited to visit the author's website at:
www.foundandground.com

ACKNOWLEDGEMENTS

Many thanks to Tilke Elkins of the Wild
Pigment Project for her inspiring 'Guidelines for
Reciprocal Foraging'.

DEDICATION

To Mark Penson

CONTENTS

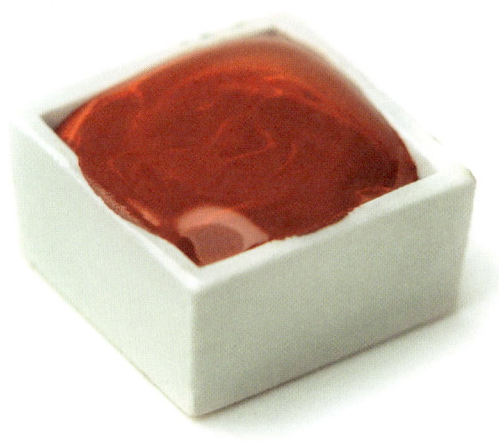

FOREWORD

by Paul Kingsnorth

Once upon a time I met a woman in a wood. The woman was carrying a basket. She told me that she wanted to show me its contents. I had never met her before, and didn't know her, but when this kind of fairytale-shaped invitation comes your way, you know you have to follow it where it leads.

In the basket were things of many colours. There were paints made from the earth itself: chalk, clay, charcoal, ochre. There were brushes and pens which were made of fox hair and swan feathers and twigs and twine. There was paper which looked like it had last been used to trial-run the Lindisfarne Gospels. It was a magical, medieval hoard.

It turned out that this basket had been at least partly inspired by my novel, *The Wake*, which was set in 1066, and written in a sort-of-Old English dialect which I had created myself. I had written that book to try and get as close as possible to the feeling of inhabiting the mind-world of Old England, as it was conquered and upturned by the Normans. I wanted to understand how the people felt, lived, wondered, worshipped and spoke. I knew that how they expressed themselves would be intimately related to – born from – their time and place. The Earth we stand on makes us all in slightly different shapes.

Caroline – for this turned out to be the name of the mystery basket-woman – had created her paint hoard in response to my book. My attempt to write like an Anglo-Saxon had got her wondering how the people of the time painted. What materials did they use? How did they make them? And how did those questions relate to their own place in the world? Most people might have just idly wondered about these questions, if they occurred to them at all. But Caroline is not most people. She responded by researching eleventh-century art materials, and then plunging into the undergrowth to find the materials to recreate them. Her magic basket was the result. Now the basket has become a book, and you can all rummage around in it, excited, as I did back then. You never know what you're going to find in here. But I can promise it will excite you. Caroline is no ordinary artist.

So I like the fact that my own work has played some small part in the genesis of this one. Since we first met in those woods many years ago, Caroline and I have become not only friends but collaborators. Caroline has used the contents of her magic basket to illustrate my novel (some of those images can be found in these pages), and we have taught together on many occasions, on courses which bring together writing inspired by the local landscape, and paints and inks literally made from it. The aim of those courses was the same as the aim of this book: to re-connect people intimately with the ground beneath their feet. To remind people that, wherever they come from or find themselves, the land around them is alive and singing; that even in the biggest city there are rocks, there is soil, there are feathers and there are leaves that can be hunted down and made into the tools with which the story you carry within you can be drawn out and recorded, as it has been for many, many generations of our ancestors.

All of this explains why I'm thrilled to see this book out in the world. Nobody knows more than Caroline Ross about the practice of connecting the hand, the heart and the ground. As I've discovered myself under her tutelage, you don't have to be any kind of trained 'artist' to make yourself a swan-feather quill, grind some rocks and then get going. But you will find that the very process of doing so will make you into one – and that this book is a unique and perfect guide along the path.

Paul Kingsnorth is the co-founder of the Dark Mountain Project and the author of *The Wake*, along with two other novels, two poetry collections and four works of non-fiction.

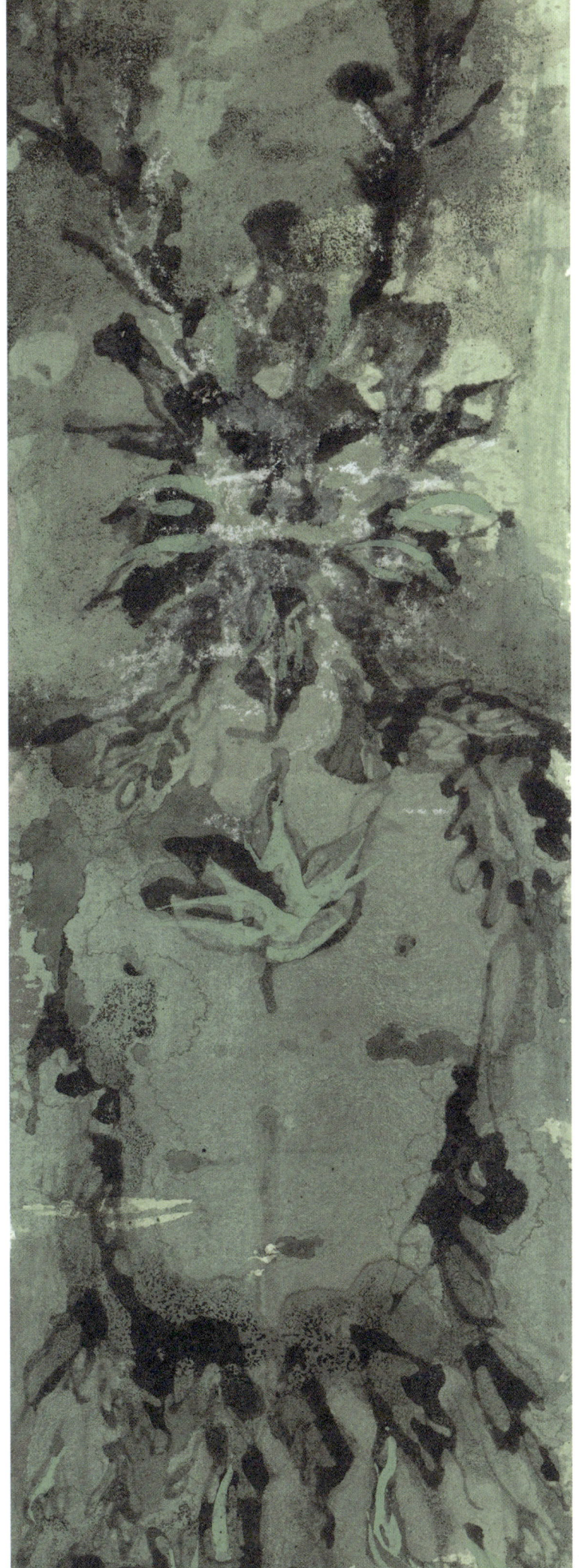

GREEN MAN
10 x 29cm (4 x 11½in)
*Handmade paints and ink
with chalk.
In the collection of
Paul Kingsnorth.*

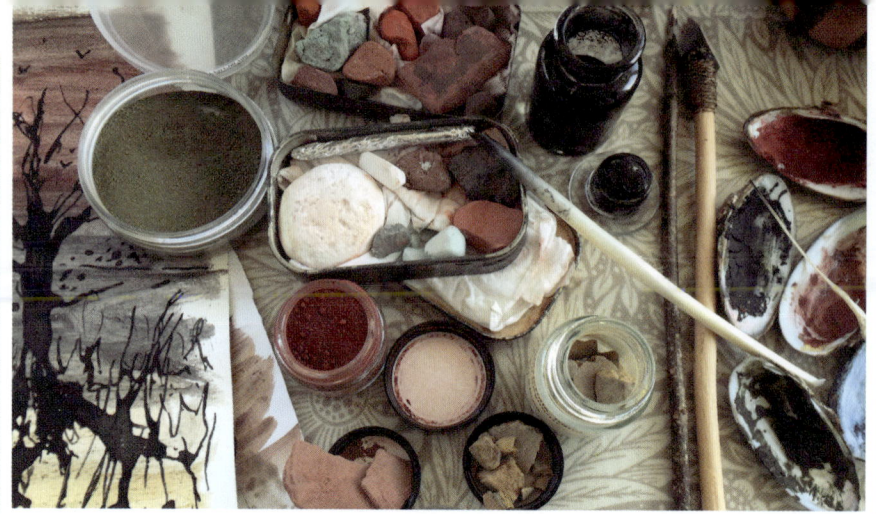

INTRODUCTION

―――――――――――――――

“ **The earth is alive, and we are part of it.** ”

This statement might sound radical – particularly if, like me, you are sitting indoors, at a table or desk with a screen nearby. Our current way of life represents just a tiny portion of how humans have lived and made art over millennia on this incredible planet.

Even relatively recently, a life spent closer to the land was the norm. In her youth in Scotland, one of my nan's tasks was to milk the cows. One particularly cantankerous beast head-butted her over the dry-stone wall into the deep brown peaty mud, which stained her clothes and got her told off. Nan also spoke about the white horse she'd see every day on the hill above her village as a child, how she loved it, as it made her feel at home. For many years I wondered how the same horse could always be up on the hill, until I finally visited Strichen and saw for myself the huge white chalk figure of the horse upon Mormond Hill!

The white of chalk against green grass is one of my earliest colour memories. The chalk of The Needles of the Isle of Wight are for me the same kind of 'home colour' as the incandescent glowing reds of the Grand Canyon are for some Americans, or the deep black sands of volcanic beaches are for Icelandic people.

In this book I invite you to explore, remember and appreciate the vast variety of colour that is there right under our noses, and beneath our feet. We'll learn our home area first, paying attention to what we often overlook.

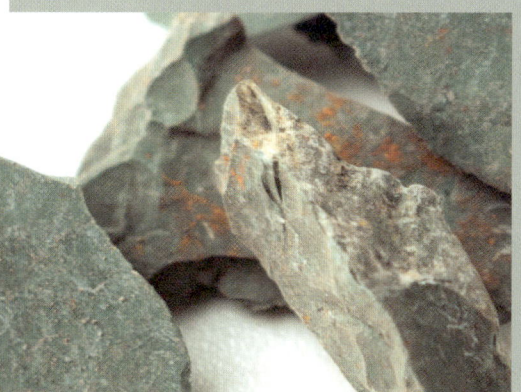
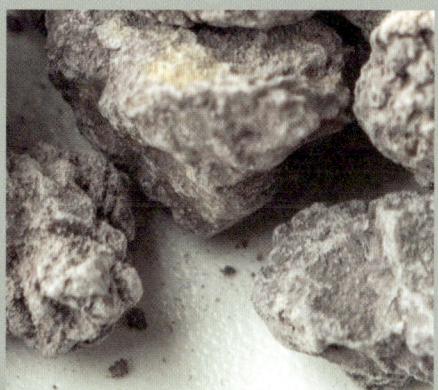
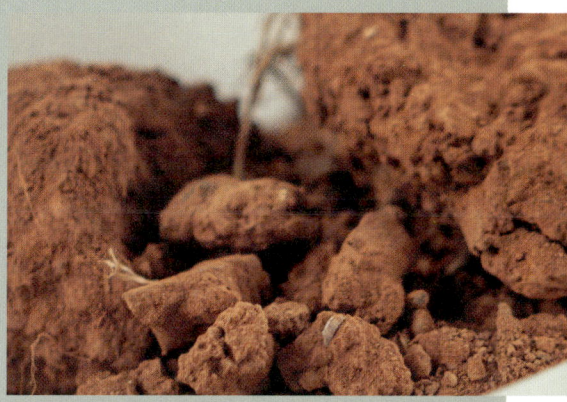

Possible pigment sources: from left to right, green rocks, lilac clay, red soil.

> ## Colour from the earth itself: rocks, clay, soil.

We are accustomed to a world filled with the polychromatic and highly-saturated rainbow of printed and painted colours that synthetic pigments allow. In adverts, books, and tubes of acrylic paint, almost any colour can be easily mixed or matched. But before the widespread use of petrochemicals, and the novel dyes and pigments they made possible, certain colours were extremely rare, difficult to obtain or expensive. Others were found only in one geographical area.

In limited ways, people synthesized colours for thousands of years – in antiquity, the vivid pigment we now call Egyptian blue was made from ground glass, for example. Besides these few exceptions, however, until the modern era, almost all colours used in art and crafts, from cave paintings to the ceiling of the Sistine Chapel, were naturally derived. Pigments and dyes can be obtained from a vast array of natural materials including plants, rocks, shells, animals, insects, gemstones, lichens and fungi.

In this book we'll concentrate on creating colour from the earth itself: the rocks, clay and soil in your locale. The palette you create will be unique to your area, your eye and your tastes, and won't look like anything you could buy off the shelf. I hope that, like me, you'll find exploring the world around you life-affirming and fascinating, as you gain new skills with your hands and take a closer look at what is just outside your door.

> ## The palette you create will be unique to your area, your eye and your tastes.

Why make your own paints?

It seems that every conceivable colour of paint is immediately available. Why would we go to the trouble of finding our own local colours and binders, or make our own? To answer that, take a moment to replace the words 'paint' with 'food' and 'colours and binders' with 'local produce and ingredients'. Many of us still regularly cook at least something from scratch, grow some of our own vegetables in a garden or allotment plot, or know someone who keeps chickens or bees – all because we want to know where our produce comes from. Perhaps we buy locally grown food, or forage for blackberries, apples, wild herbs or fungi because we can't get these unique flavours from mass-produced products.

> **Your local colour is unique to the land where you live.**

In the Slow Food movement, in traditional and regional cuisines the world over, and especially in winemaking, the idea of *terroir* is at the centre. The qualities of the soil, climate, geology and topography make the same grape varieties taste different. *Terroir* means that every bit of land is unique, and that a one-size-fits-all approach to agriculture, food production, land use and diet is neither wise nor desirable.

Similarly, pigments are not the same the world over. In this book I hope to inspire you to get to know your local earths and rocks, landscape and plants, and to see what unique shades are there, waiting, in the places near you that may already know and love.

There are other good reasons to make your own art materials.

Firstly, it is rewarding to create your art from paints you have made exactly to your own specifications and preferences. Secondly, you'll develop a deeper connection to your area, the land, and the seasons from foraging and preparing your materials. Thirdly, you'll be more self-reliant; less dependent on shops and fossil fuels. Lastly, you'll get to experience the tactile richness of a part of life little known to most urban, modern people. You'll get dirt under your fingernails, fresh air in your lungs – and, if you're lucky, a pocketful of colourful rocks.

Watercolour and other paints

Watercolour paints are made with water-soluble binders such as gum Arabic. This means that they can be used and thinned with water rather than the solvents necessary to thin oil paints. Watercolours are used on paper or other fine surfaces where they dry to a matt finish and are usually transparent, a quality that means underpainting layers remain partially visible. Gouache (poster paint) is a water paint with added chalk to give it 'body', making it opaque. Both watercolour and gouache are re-soluble, which means they can be reworked once dry. They can also be intermixed.

Some water paints use egg as a binder. Tempera uses the yolk, while glair uses a binder derived from egg white. These have a slight sheen when dry, and are not so easily rewetted. They are traditionally used on surfaces prepared with gesso, but can also be used on paper, where they make a good plastic-free substitute for acrylic paints.

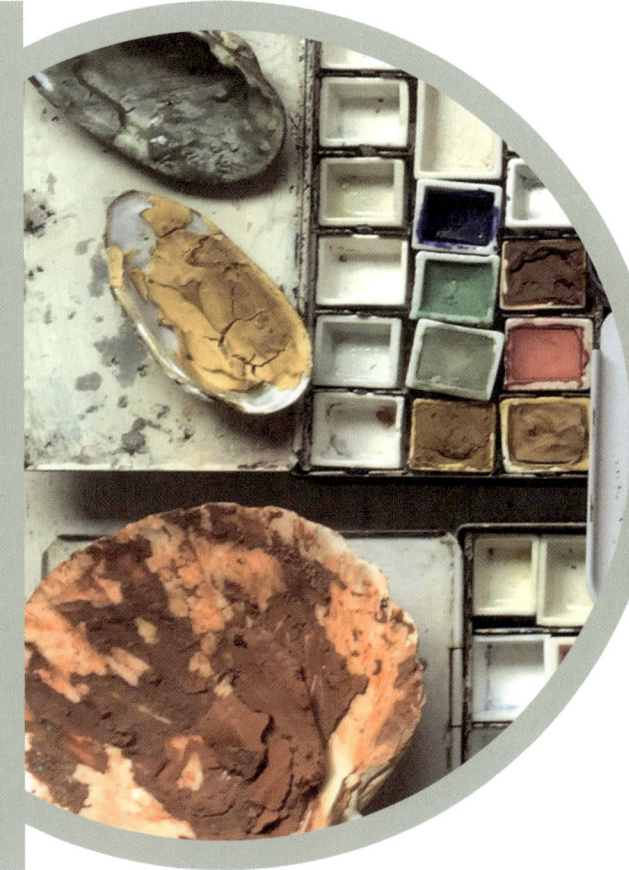

A selection of the author's handmade watercolour paints.

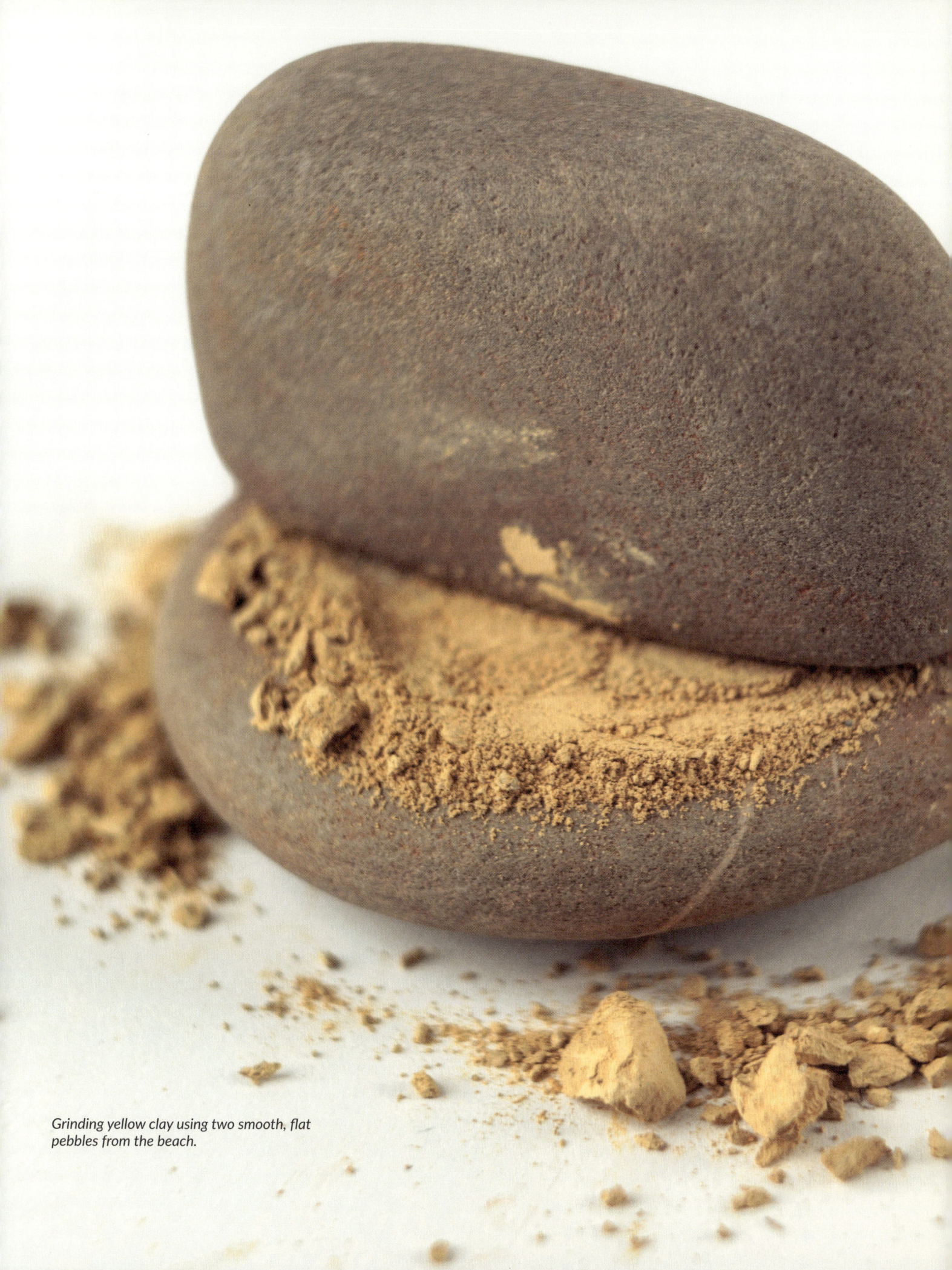
Grinding yellow clay using two smooth, flat pebbles from the beach.

I was always encouraged in my twin loves of drawing and science, both at home and at school, after which I pursued a traditional art education. For two years of foundation studies at Shelley Park in Bournemouth, England (once the home of novelist Mary Shelley and her son), I learned how to match, mix and use colour, alongside life drawing, photography, printmaking, textiles, ceramics, painting, sculpture and more. Sadly, foundation courses of this kind have all but vanished, and young artists must head to university or art college with few practical skills which my generation were able to learn in an extra year or two before our bachelor's degrees.

Even at our excellent college, full of great tutors, we did not learn how to make the paint, pastels, charcoal or grounds on which to work. Our materials were shop-bought and standardized; we did not know any other options existed. In ceramics our clay was pre-packed, and we did not learn how to identify, dig, clean, wedge and work with the raw natural material. Glazes were ready-mixed from a chart and the provenance of the contents were not discussed. In the sculpture workshops, factory-fresh sheets of wood and metal, as well as manmade materials and fixings, were on hand, but we were never told about how to use wild, foraged, recycled or found materials, traditional binding, gluing or joining methods, nor why we might choose to.

Over the last decade, and after a lifetime of foraging, experimentation and research on my own, I have had the pleasure of studying with the art materials experts and painters Daniel Chatto, at the Royal Drawing School for two terms, and David Cranswick, for a week-long intensive course in Suffolk. Their breadth of knowledge and skill were instrumental in helping me evolve my materials practice.

It is impossible to ignore our impact on the planet, or to notice how quickly things are transforming. Changing our usual art materials for ones that are earth-based, recycled, less toxic or plastic-free will not immediately halt the juggernaut of modernity; but by becoming more conscious of waste and careful in our choices, we can foster change and together have a much bigger effect than on our own. That has been my impetus behind *Found and Ground*: to show that we can make our art where the earth also matters.

"We can make art where the earth also matters."

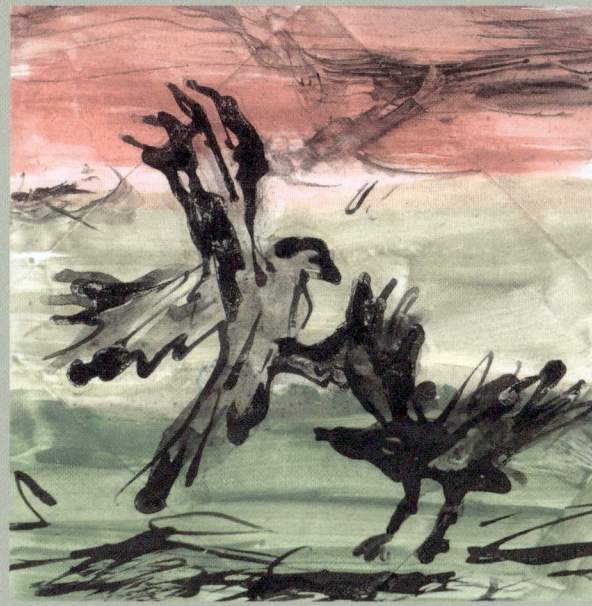

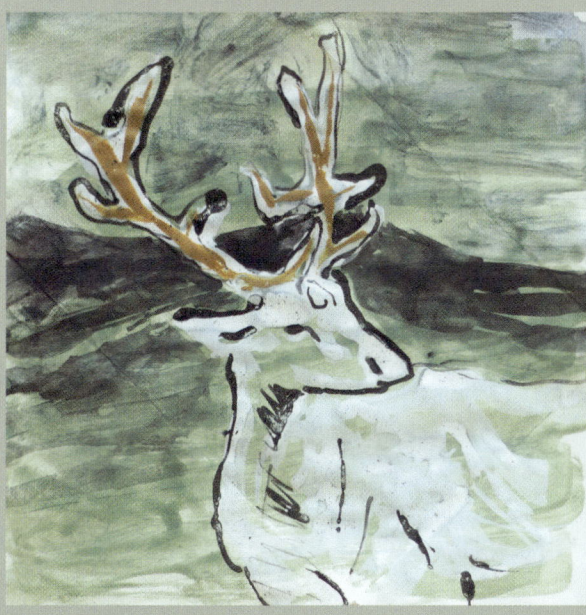

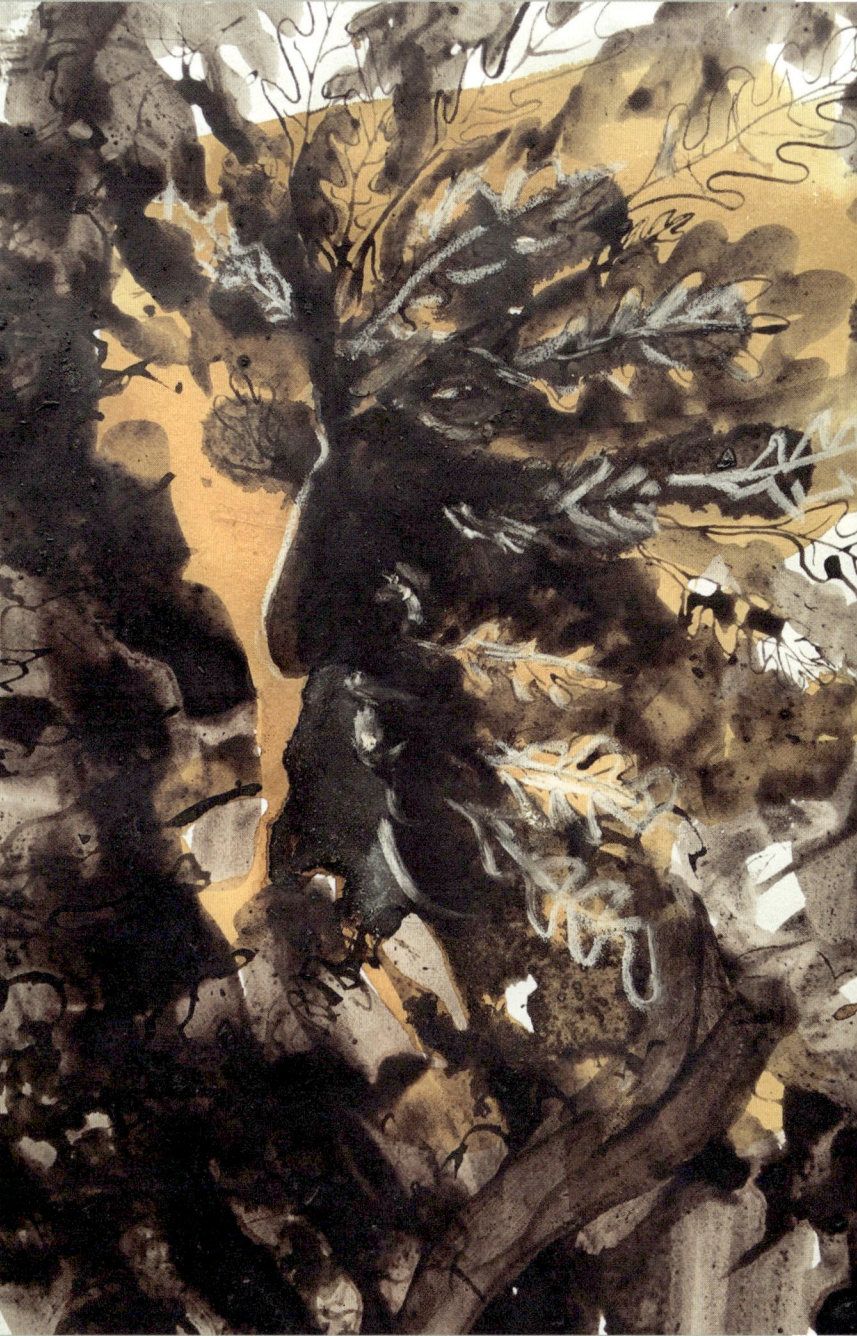

Top
HAWK AND CROW   21 x 21cm (8¼ x 8¼in)

Handmade watercolours of ochre, terre verte and madder, with iron gall ink, on a used envelope.

Above
THE STAG WITH THE GOLDEN ANTLERS
21 x 21cm (8¼ x 8¼in)

Handmade watercolour, gouache and iron gall ink on a used envelope.

GREEN MAN   30 x 42cm (11¾ x 16½in)
Oak gall and iron gall inks and chalk on paper.

The golden brown in the background of this painting is pure oak gall liquor, with no added iron. The dark sepia ink on top of it is the same liquid with iron added. So much variety can be made from these simple ink ingredients. The white highlights are drawn with a raw lump of chalk, straight from the earth.

In the collection of Daniel Slife.

What on earth..? Pigments and earth colours

Pigments are coloured substances that form the basis of paints. They may be derived from plants, minerals, animals or chemical processes. Earth pigments – literally, those made from soil, clay, mud, rocks and other minerals from the earth – remain at the root of some of the commonest commercial colours and are the focus of this book.

Earth colours have been so perennially useful and popular because, unlike many other natural pigments, they are stable, reliably lightfast and long-lasting. If you've ever primed metal or painted a garage floor, then you are likely to have used iron oxide red. This is the same hue we all know from rusty iron and 'red ochre' paint. 'Ochre' is the term for earth pigments that contain iron (Fe). These versatile pigments have been utilized worldwide throughout human history, for uses as diverse as cave drawings, medicine, sunblock, ritual and self-adornment.

Qualities of foraged earth paints

Humans have used earth colours for at least a quarter of a million years, so you are in good company as you set out to make your own. Here are some of the qualities you can expect, or need to consider, in your foraged paints.

Stability Earth paints on cave walls painted by our ancestors the world over are still bright and true, even on those painted on overhangs lit by sunlight. You can rely on the paints you make from earths to last more than a lifetime.

Granulation Ochres, earths and minerals are used in some of the smoothest, most opaque and beautiful paints – think of 'Titian red', for instance. When ground finely, your foraged pigments can handle as well as any others, and make great workable paints. Because we are not using machines to mill our colours to a specific particle size, you may find that watercolour washes granulate more or feel slightly rougher than their commercial equivalents. This is natural, and you may find you start to seek out these qualities in your paints.

Natural variation There may be slight variations between batches of your pigments or paints. This can be due to the site weathering between foraging trips, landfalls, contamination, or the way in which you process the earths for paint. Take notes to help you pinpoint gathering sites, and make your processing consistent. Alternatively, enjoy the inconsistencies! Even between batches of commercially bought ochres there are sometimes subtle variations. I tend to date my bought ochre swatches so I can track the changes from various suppliers.

Toxicity Although minerals like red ochre are used in many parts of the world ceremonially, as a traditional cosmetic, medicine or insect repellent, we cannot say whether any particular sample is 'non-toxic' without proper testing. Where we forage may be contaminated by traffic fumes, urban run-off, pesticides or micro-plastics, so we should be realistic, and not project ideas of pristine naturalness onto our creations. Wearing gloves and a mask while handling our dry powdered samples is always a good idea. Although ochres are commercially listed as 'non-toxic' pigments, I still handle mine carefully, as being low hazard but of unknown toxicity, for safety reasons.

Sourcing

When you want to supplement your palette (see pages 93–95), there is an abundance of naturally sourced pigment and paint available online. With just a little care and research, you can ensure you are supporting indigenous artisans, local artists and ethical businesses.

Pay due diligence to check where the supplier is sourcing their raw material. Reputable suppliers, big or small, are always happy to engage with customers, so ask about composition, ingredients, and sourcing.

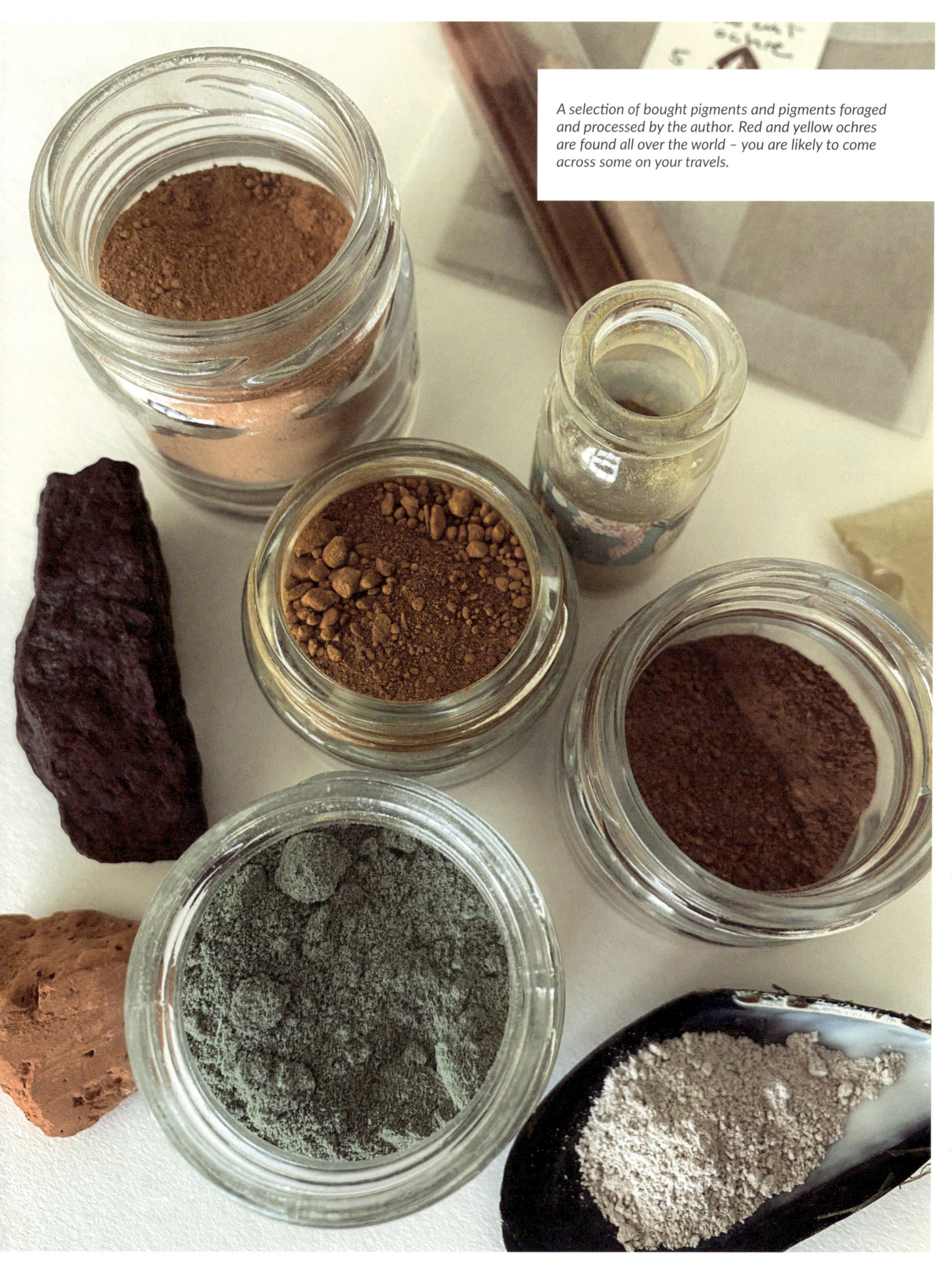

A selection of bought pigments and pigments foraged and processed by the author. Red and yellow ochres are found all over the world – you are likely to come across some on your travels.

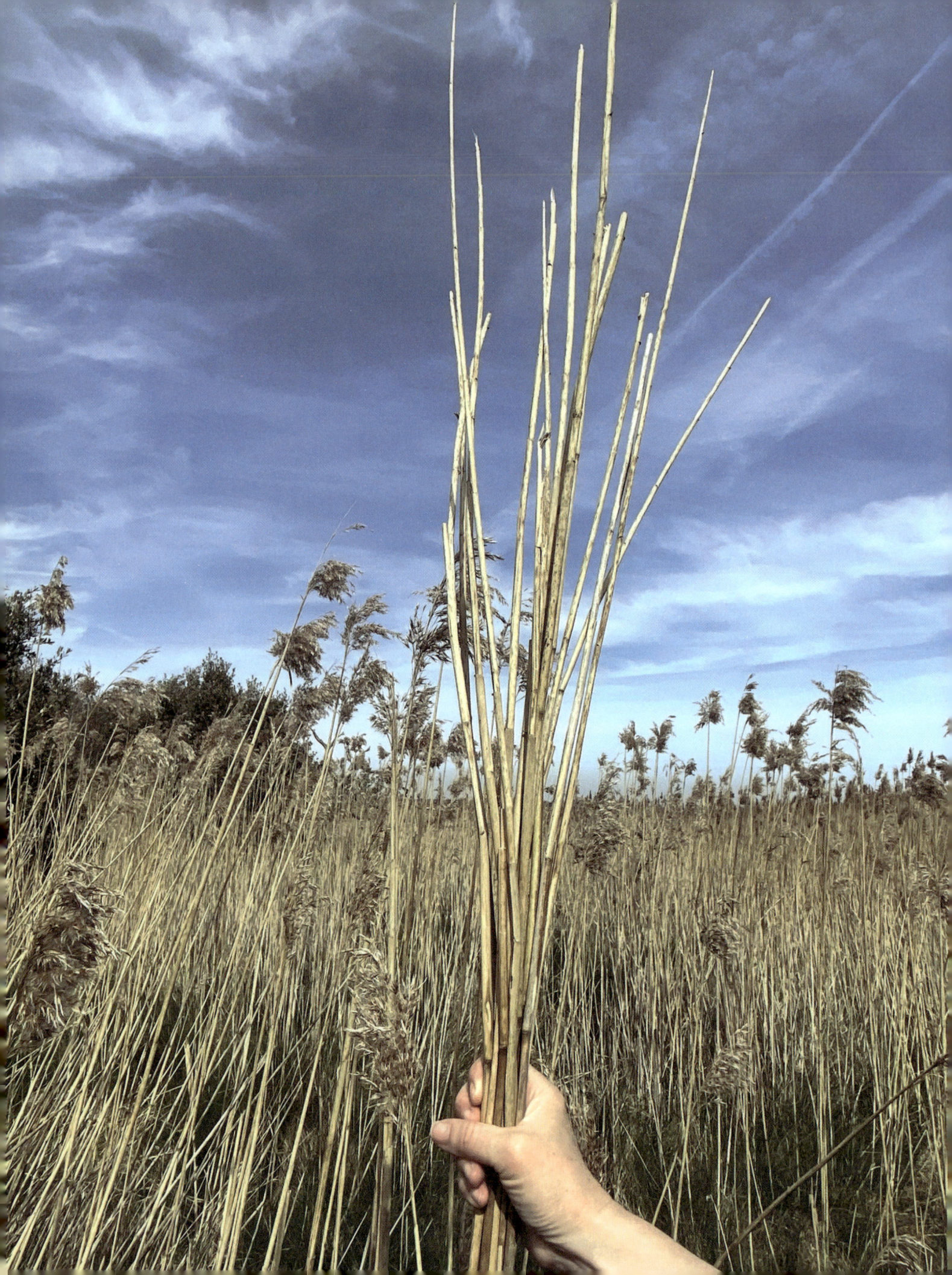

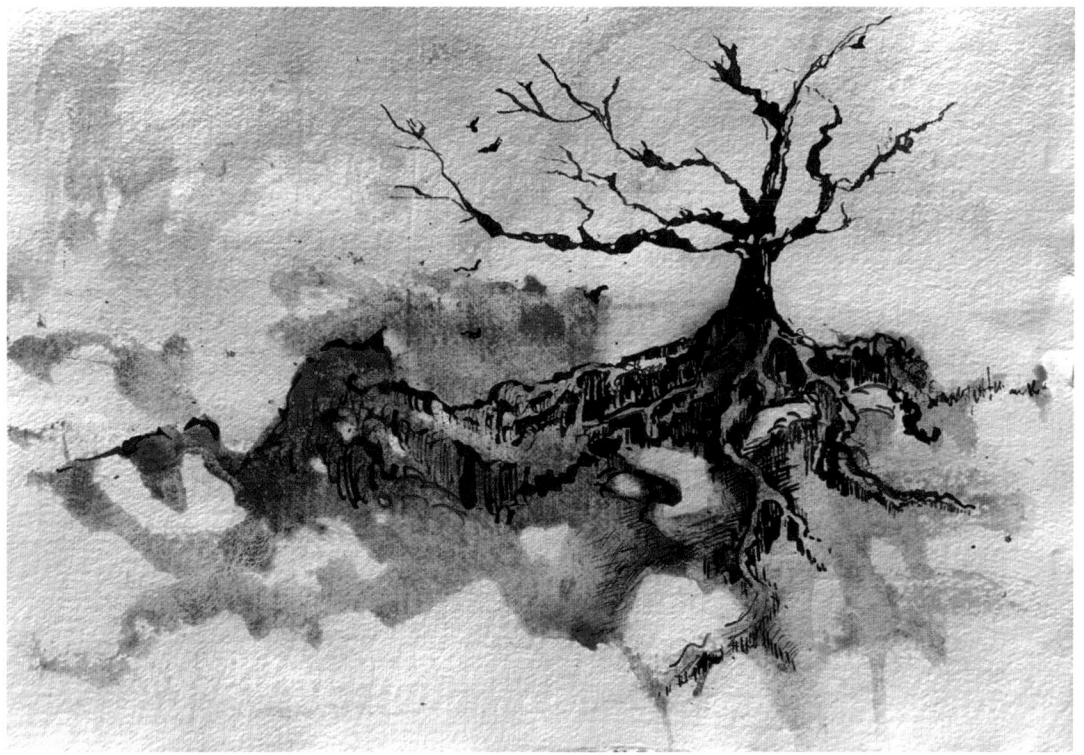

FORAGING

Drop your plans, expectations, assumptions, heavy bags, to-do lists, and any feelings that you can't do this.

Put on sturdy shoes and a coat. Take a small bag, an old spoon and a yoghurt pot, or a couple of old plastic bags. You might take a notebook and pencil if you like – or you can just walk out of the door as you are.

More important than any of these tools is to gather up your sense of adventure, ready your nose for sniffing out beauty, and open your ears to the rasping sound of gravel or the squishing suck of mud, as there might be colour out there.

> **What we are looking for is not a *thing*.
> What we are doing is finding a *way*.**

FORAGING PRINCIPLES

> ❝ **Land and people have been talking together since time immemorial; we just need to allow ourselves to relax and pay attention.** ❞

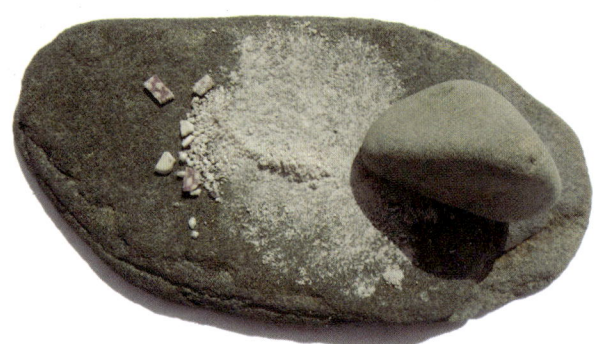

Keep an open mind

The beauty of foraging, whether for food or art materials, is never knowing precisely what you will find. To the modern mind, raised on clock-time and standardization, learning to enjoy and cherish uncertainty is a novel idea. With practice, a pigment-hunting walk can become a way to open our awareness and pay attention with all our senses. You may go out to find some beautiful coloured rocks to play with, but you may come back also having learned the spring calls of your local birds, the favourite tree of the neighbourhood squirrel, and the location of fruit trees from which you can gather gum. Those squirrel-eaten nut shells might make perfect little paint containers. 'Getting your eye in' may take a couple of forays. You'll know when it's happened as what once seemed like barren fields or uninteresting shorelines suddenly seem full of things that 'weren't there yesterday'.

Also useful are a sense of humour and imagination. Think like a magpie, turn things over like a beetle. Imagining that you are very small or flying up high can help you find all kinds of things.

Ethical, reciprocal foraging

People picked up rocks from the land to make colour in all times and places. It's a natural thing to do. However, the context in your country or region might vary widely from mine. My friend Tilke Elkins of the Wild Pigment Project has written extensive, clear guidelines for reciprocal foraging. They cover both the ethics of foraging and health and safety, and I encourage you to read them here:
www.wildpigmentproject.org/reciprocal-foraging

Guidelines to get you started

These brief guidelines will help you to get started, wherever you are in the world.

- Research the area where you plan to forage. Find out who owns the land, if it is a protected place, a National Park, cultural site, or Site of Special Scientific Interest (SSSI).

- If there are Indigenous or Traditional Owners of land in your country, then research and learn about the land and culture, seeking permissions to gather. We commit not to gather where we have been asked not to do so, for cultural, religious or historical reasons.

- Donate money or time to organizations protecting the land you traverse. I love Julian Cope's excellent advice in *The Modern Antiquarian* to carry a plastic bag in your sock so you can pick out any litter you find on your way.

- Gather only what is abundant, and just enough for for your artwork. Taking only what can be carried in your cupped hands is a good rule of thumb. We don't need to hoard, or collect for the sake of it.

- Never gather in contaminated areas such as old mines, very busy roads, or heavily sprayed agricultural areas.

- Wear gloves and a face mask unless simply picking up rocks in places that are not dusty.

- Give thanks inwardly and outwardly. Speak or sing words of thanks out loud. Worried what people will think, seeing you speaking to a rock? Don't be! Children do it naturally, and are always picking up treasures. Follow their lead.

- If you have a sense to not take something, despite seeming abundance, then listen to that urge, and move on. Sometimes leaving things be is the correct method. Appreciating things where they are cultivates a generous attitude rather than an extractive mindset.

- Lastly, make use of things other people discard. 'Single use' plastics, unwanted containers, and bottle tops can all be useful things when making or storing our paints and inks. We needn't be purists. If we can reuse or repurpose things that have already been made, we can prevent more things entering the waste stream.

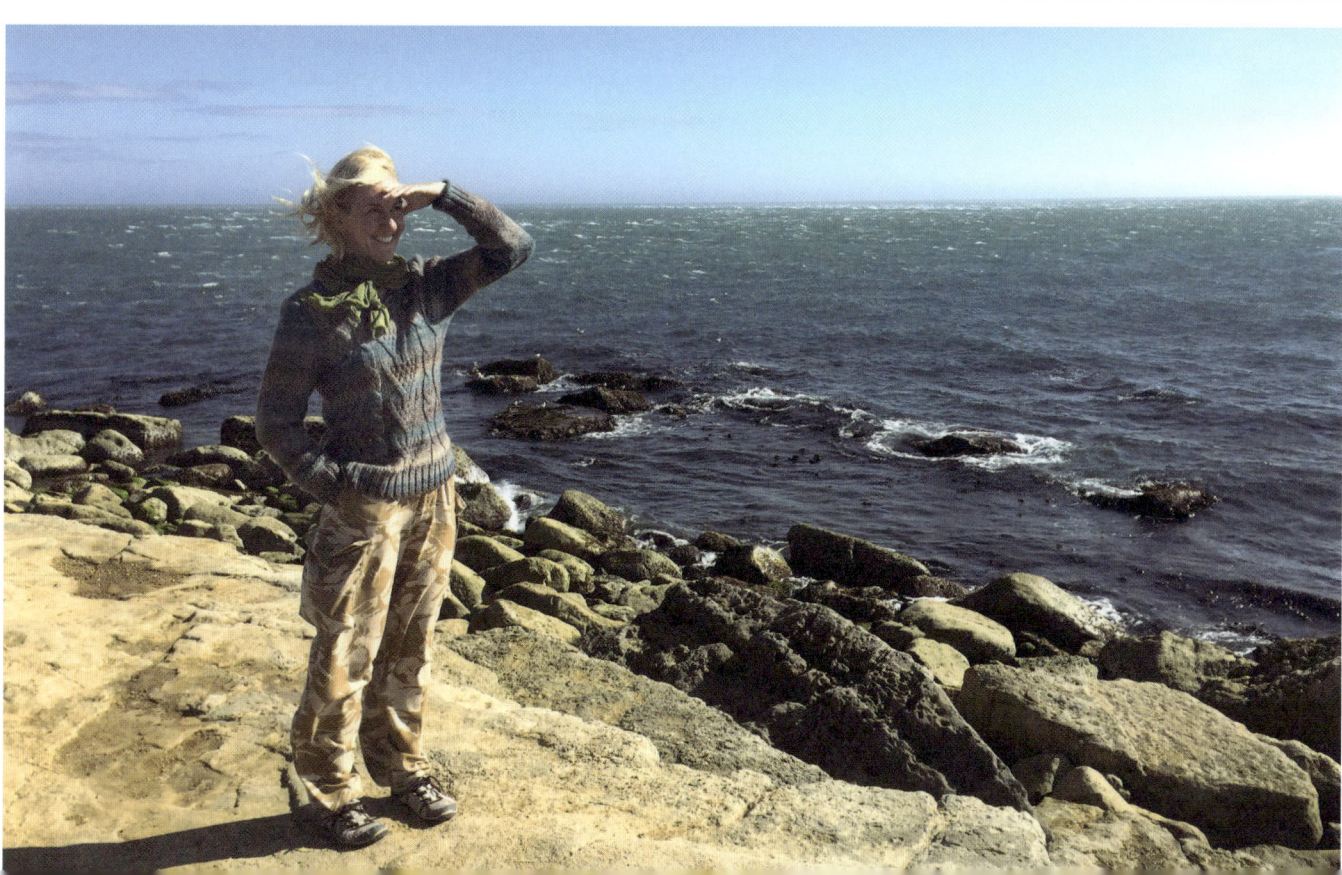

Abundance and scarcity

In consumerism, value follows scarcity. By instead becoming a connoisseur of the ordinary, we will find immense freedom. When foraging, you will discover favourite materials and places from which to gather them, and this relationship enriches both you and the place. We are far more likely to protect the places where we know something beautiful, useful, or dear to us resides.

Let's look at the wider context for our art. At the time of writing, the earth's polar regions are hotter than they should be by a huge margin, causing icecaps to melt. What was once considered freak weather is now a regular occurrence the world over. What has been in abundance in our living memory may soon be scarce, or conversely, some species, materials or foraging conditions may become more common. Things change, and we can adapt.

By applying the principles of taking only what can be spared, centring what is abundant, and leaving what is scarce, we can prevent harm to our environment from our paint making. By developing friendships and connections with other natural materials artists in our locale, region, or internationally, we can share and swap our ethically made pigments in person and by mail. By conserving and protecting the natural world in our region, and repurposing what we find in urban environments, we can make sure there are materials for future artists and habitats for other creatures. Sometimes, the right thing is to fill up our bag. At other times, we take only a longing glance.

Things that you can happily take without harm when locally abundant include: oak galls once the wasps have flown, shed feathers from the sea shore and river banks in the UK (your country may have differing rules), bright earths and ochres from highway spoil piles, and brick bits, charcoal, rusty nails and tree gum from urban settings where these things are already on the ground and will be swept into trash at some point. Waste-stream colours can be beautiful!

Direct your foraging towards sources which are locally common, paying attention to where things change: a landslide or a clearcut can change everything in an instant. Keep an eye out for neighbours having works done in their gardens, or for dug-up roads. Lumps of broken brick are future paints in hiding.

Trust practice, research, and intuition. As a teacher, rather than providing set rules, I encourage people to develop their sensitivity and skills and then to trust their own integrity.

> **The way to help prevent future scarcity is to take little, seldom, and only what's needed.**

Opposite:
Found in one foray; hazelnuts to eat plus acorn caps and knopper galls for inks.

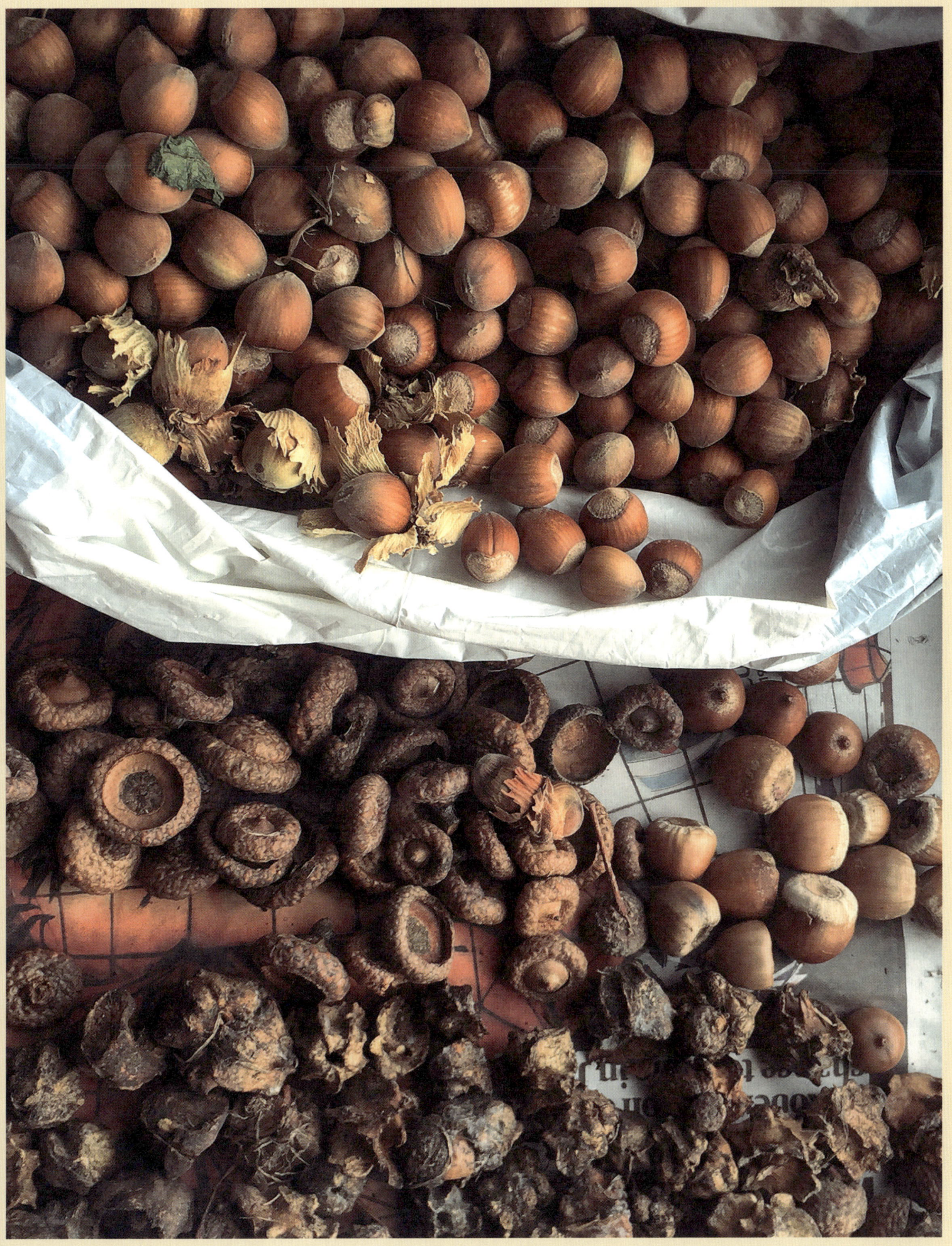

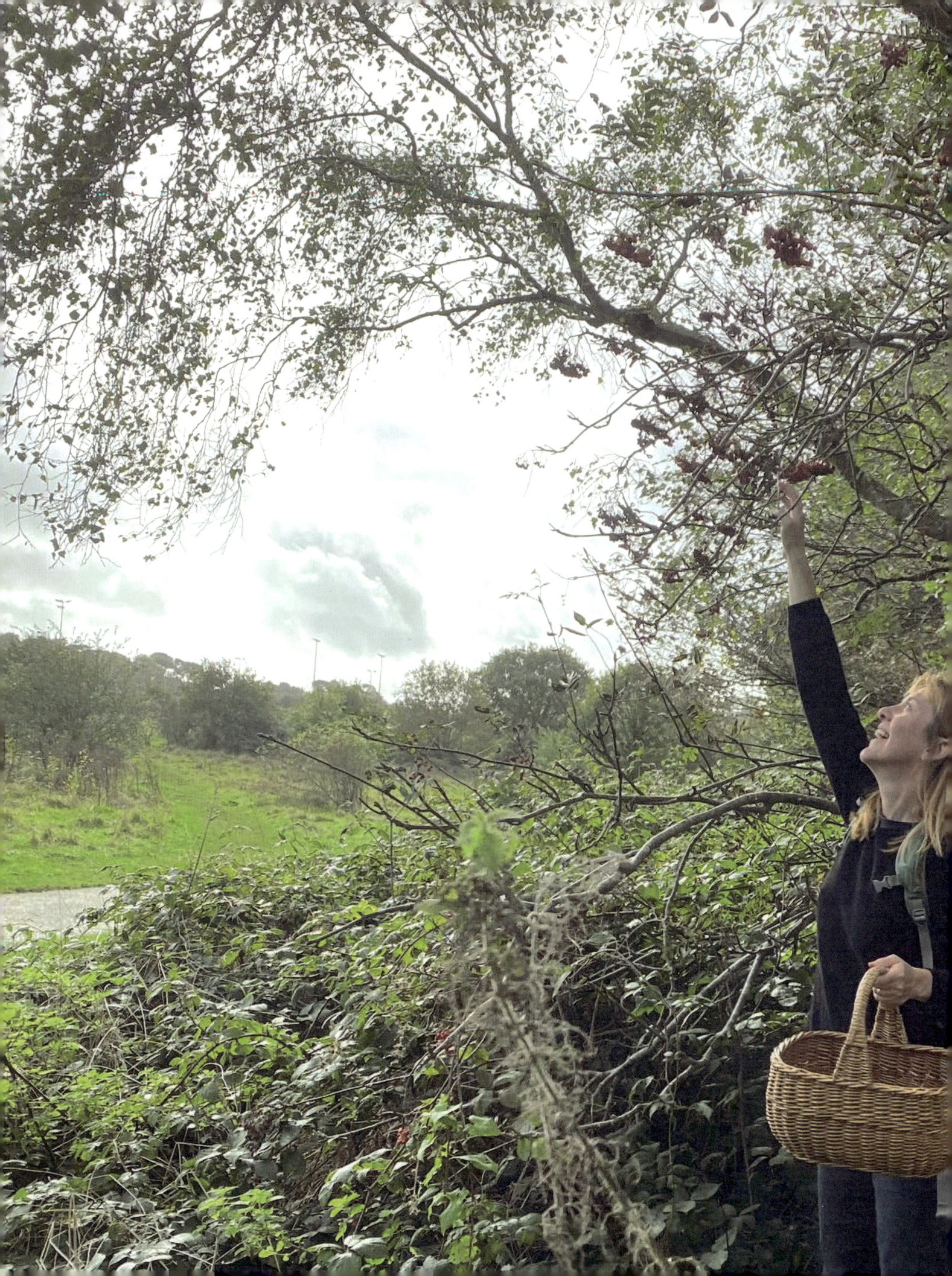

WHERE TO GO FORAGING

The best place to forage is wherever you happen to be. For years I lived aboard boats on the River Thames, and before that, beside the tiny River Graveney in London, and for six years, in a rural hamlet in the rolling hills of Aberdeenshire, Scotland. In each place I have been able to gather so many things that I need to make my art or crafts. You will be able to do this where you live, too.

Almost anywhere you can access can be a good place to start looking. When we start in places that are local and convenient, it removes the need for transport or detailed planning, which allows us to head out spontaneously when the weather and circumstances allow. Over this chapter we'll look in detail at various foraging terrains, and what makes them interesting to the pigment hunter.

Places to avoid include anywhere polluted by heavy industry; contaminated ground; and places where your foraging could disturb wildlife – and this might depend on the time or season: you might avoid an otherwise suitable area while ground-nesting birds are laying eggs, for example. Finally, it is important to avoid anywhere you feel unsafe.

Confidence and safety

Among my friends and family there are a huge range of attitudes regarding how confident they feel going off on adventures on their own. How you feel about foraging will be entirely personal, and there is no correct approach. If you'd like to walk with a friend the first few times you go to new areas, then do. Joining local walking groups and foraging as you go is a wonderful way to get started.

If you are on your own, it's good to research in advance what time dusk will fall, travel times for public transport, and good places to park if driving. You can let someone know where you're going and when you plan to be back. I use my phone as my camera to record great foraging places and keep it on 'airplane mode' when I don't want to be disturbed in nature – but it remains a great backup if necessary.

A change in perspective

Maps on screens and the buzz of everyday urban life make it easy to think of where we live as a grid, and ourselves as moving around a featureless flat surface. But that is the machine view. Although useful, we need to expand upon it and bring life back to it. On earth, all people live within a watershed on a landscape that, even if there are not mountains nearby, will have at least some undulations. If you usually travel by car or underground, it might take a moment to reimagine your locale as a three-dimensional territory rather than a two-dimensional map, and to sense how these two things are not the same.

I live in a coastal town, on the largest island of an archipelago of over a thousand islands, buffeted by the Atlantic ocean to the west, and the North Sea to the east. A short walk from where I write this, shimmers the Solent, part of the English Channel. That's the way I picture the British Isles.

> **Reimagine your locale as a three-dimensional territory rather than a two-dimensional map.**

Exercise:
Take a bird's eye view

Here's a fun way to experience where you live differently. You'll need a piece of scrap paper and a pencil.

Imagine you are a local bird – a crow, say, or a gull. You take off from where you are and fly up high enough to look down on your town or city. Can you see the nearest tall tree to roost? Mark where you are on the map and where the nearest tall tree is. Where is the closest river or stream (even if it is in a culvert or has been built over)? Draw this in, no matter how accurately.

Next, imagine flying to the nearest parkland or open ground and then sketch that in too. If there's a shoreline, a beach, a mountain or other large landform nearby, then add that to your map next. Mark on any abandoned or unused urban areas, edge lands, ponds or pathways.

Lastly, add anything else that is neither building nor road that you feel gives your area physical character: perhaps the highest and lowest places, local woods, a dock, the canal, cemetery or fields.

Have a look at what you've sketched from the bird's eye view. This will help you to make choices about where to foray first.

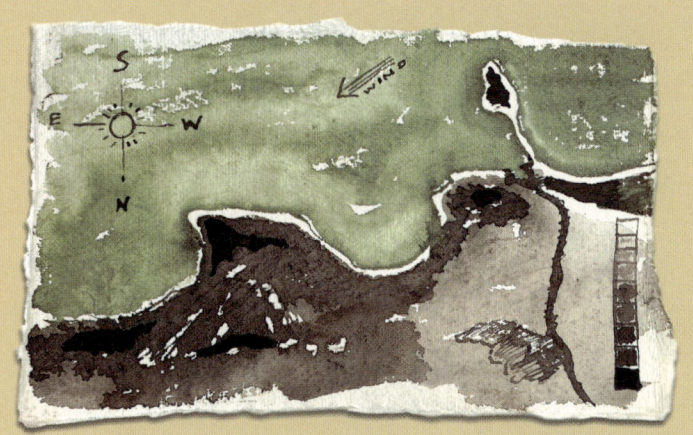

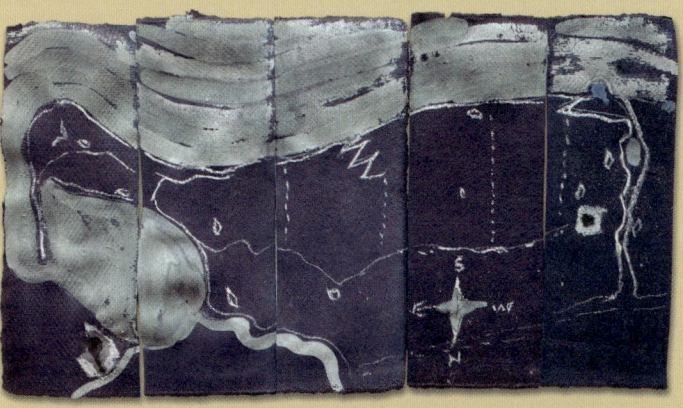

Sketched maps showing heights of a favourite local area and nearby foraging walks, made with mainly locally sourced materials.

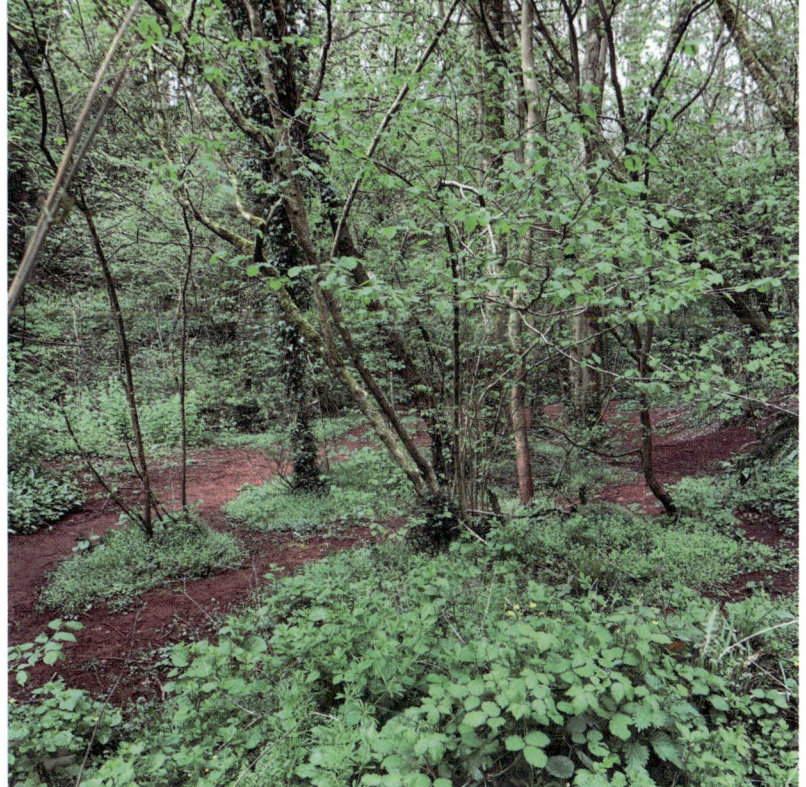

A country walk is full of promise for those with eyes attuned to foraging.

Foraging in your local area

How I gather at home is different from how I might do so as a guest abroad. Here, there is a very long history of ordinary people being displaced from the land by Acts of Enclosure. In England, for instance, we are permitted to roam over only eight per cent of open land, and three per cent of rivers; and the penalties got harsher in 2022. In Scotland there has been a right to roam since 2003 with no ill effect, and this sensible attitude is the norm in most of northern Europe.

I personally feel people should have the right to move freely on open land; assuming, of course, that they cause no damage to crops, livestock or property. I leave it to your own discretion to research who your local landowners are and whether you want to ask them whether you may pick up a small crumbly red rock or not...

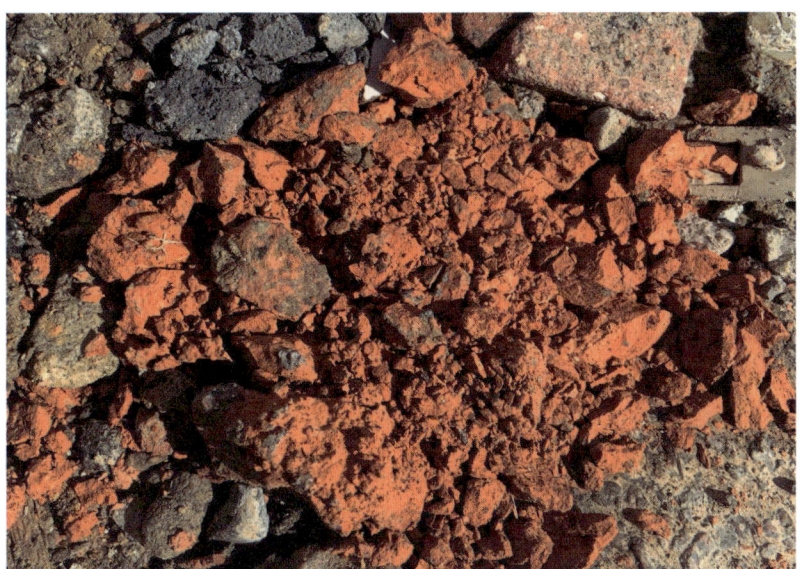

Soft bright red terracotta from old bricks near the Search Press offices, Kent, UK.

Foraging tools

A big part of the Found and Ground ethic is keeping things simple. I grew up picking blackberries along the alley by the railway with my brother, scrumping apples from hedgerows, and picking up cuttlefish bones from the beach for next door's budgerigar. I didn't think I was doing anything special, let alone 'foraging'. Often our equipment was little more than an old ice cream tub, a string shopping bag or, in an emergency, our pockets. More than once I have used the hood of my coat to carry home an unexpected haul of oak galls, or quickly finished a snack so that I can stash a lump of promising-looking colourful rock in the wrapper, to ensure it doesn't disintegrate in my bag.

I encourage you to use what you already have at home or in your shed, garage or attic. That old basket of your granny's? Perfect. Those ugly plastic food containers you've had for twenty years? Ideal. In fact, it is unlikely that you'll need to buy anything at all to forage and create your own paints in the way I am sharing in this book. If you do need to get the odd item, it'll be cheaply and easily available at a charity shop, thrift store, garage sale or household supplier. Here are the items that I find the most useful.

Trowel A standard small garden hand trowel.

Containers Clean used food containers with lids, such as yoghurt pots. A variety of sizes is useful.

Plastic and paper bags I wash, dry and reuse any plastic bags that come with food items many times before they get recycled. They are perfect for shells, clay, gum or other damp things we might find, as well as for collecting rubbish to take away. Paper bags are great for dry rocks, feathers and galls.

Basket or flat-bottomed strong bags Baskets with flat bases are the perfect way to carry what we find as we walk along, and are the traditional way to do so, the world over. If you don't have one, then a strong flat-bottomed 'bag for life' style shopping bag is a good alternative.

Spoon An old dessert or tablespoon is useful for collecting modest amounts of pigments, and has the advantage over a trowel of being a very small and ordinary thing to carry with you.

Scissors or a knife Most of the time we won't need these, but sometimes they are very useful. A small knife makes collecting cherry tree gum much easier, for example. Different countries and regions have widely varying rules about what may legally be carried, so it's worth checking the rules where you live.

Be correctly dressed

Consider your local climate. For me in Britain, dampness is never far away, and so sturdy boots and good waterproofs are the norm. Where you are, sunblock and a broad-brimmed hat may be the equivalent essentials for much of the year.

Other than this, whatever you'd normally wear for a hike is ideal for foraging. My foraging clothes always feature trousers with lots of big pockets. Army-surplus, cargo pants, or old workwear all do the job well and are much better than jeans, which are usually cut too tightly and hamper the constant squatting and straightening up.

To add to this I'd suggest:

Work gloves These make picking up rocks and rummaging through spiky plants a lot easier. I use rigger or gardening gloves, which are inexpensive and long-lasting.

Mask In dusty situations, you can wear a regular washable cloth mask that everyone seems to have these days.

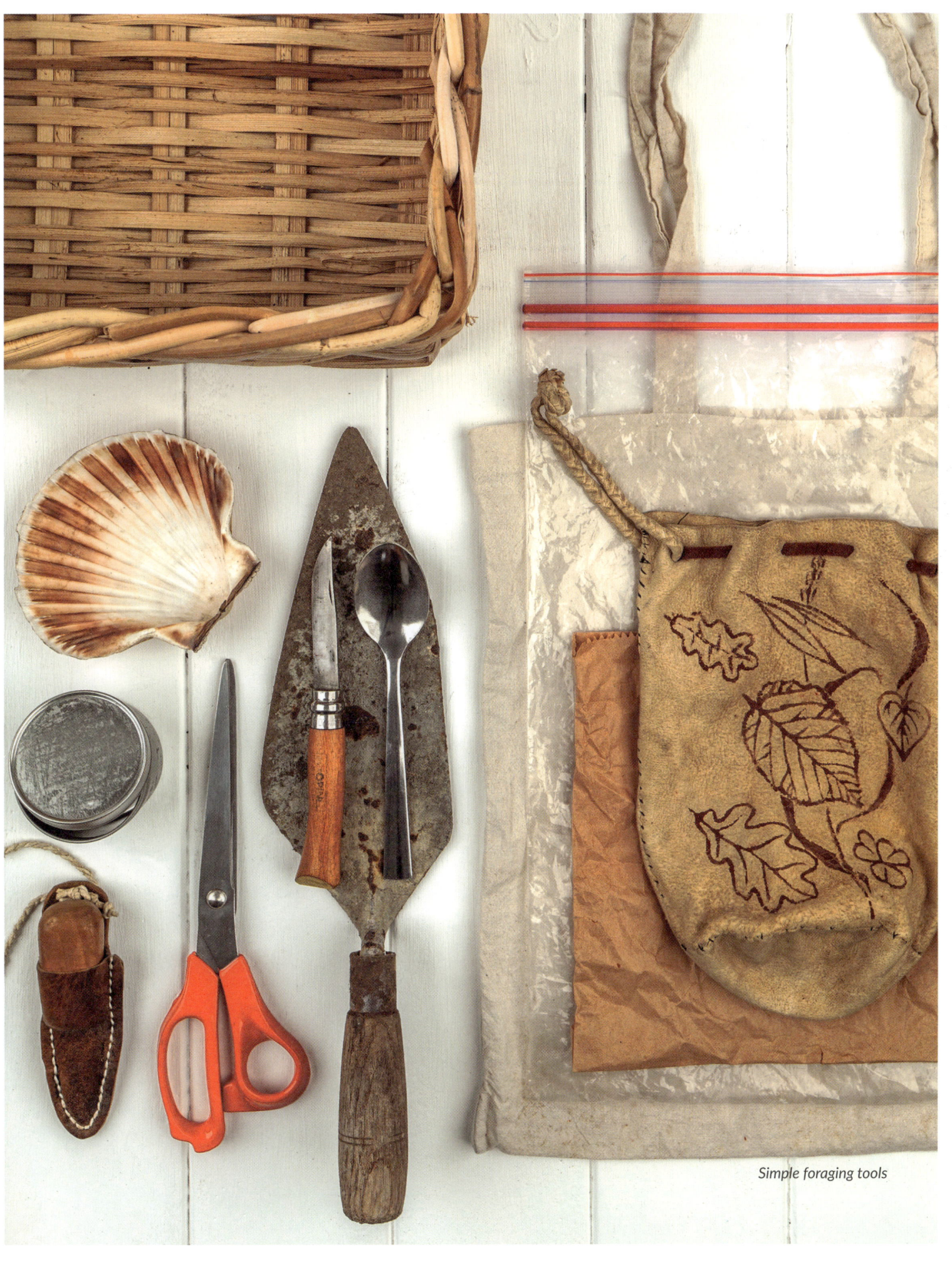

Simple foraging tools

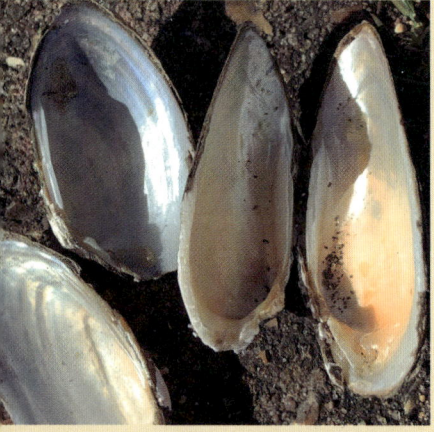

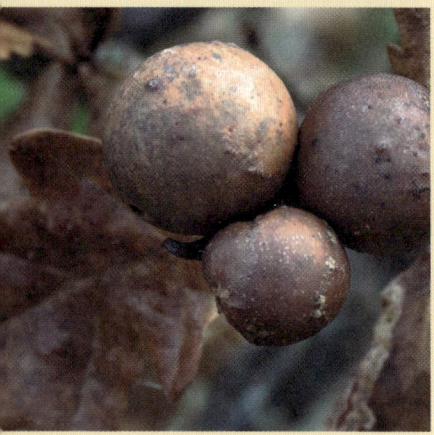

Seasonality

When we start foraging for natural colour, when to look is just as important as knowing where to look. With plants, seasonality is obvious, but it is more subtle for rocks and earth: it's much easier to find that first red clay puddle in the winter, when frosty paths are clear of crowds and the brambles have died back. Here is an overview with highlights of the seasons – but bear in mind that the opportunist forager is always ready to find something unexpected, no matter the season.

Winter This season brings bare trees and low vegetation. As the grass is short and tall weeds will have died back, winter is a great time to look for oak galls that we missed in the autumn, along with nails and old iron for the ink mordant pot. Fields may have been tilled, unearthing lumps of chalk or ochre – and it's also easier to see coloured rocks against bare ground. Just before the spring, many people have a clean-out of materials that can be useful to repurpose. Your neighbours might cut back their trees and hedges, giving a source of good straight sticks for brushes, and allowing access to the bark for gum. Winter storms bring shells and driftwood to the shores for palettes, and uncover fresh pebbles for colour.

Spring This is a great time to learn where local cherries or plums are, so when the sap starts to flow and the springtime blossom appears, you will be ready for gum-gathering. Longer days mean you can make more substantial forays than in winter, allowing you to gather earths and clays before they get smothered in weeds and grass. In spring I often find chalk in handy piles outside badgers' setts, left where it has been dug out.

Summer This time of year brings the moult for waterfowl, so along canals, rivers and waterways you can often find discarded flight feathers with which to make quill pens and brushes – the bigger the better. Freshwater mussel shells, plucked from rivers and dropped from a height by feeding birds, can also be found. I gather these, wash them and use them as the most traditional of palettes. Summer also sees oak galls forming on the trees – now is the time to notice this and make a note of where you see them, but not to pick them. Friends with laying hens might have an abundance of eggs to share, which means very good fresh paints for you. Being a source of calcium, the shells are also an alternative to using chalk for gouache.

Autumn Once oak galls have the tell-tale holes showing that the tiny harmless wasps inside have flown, you can gather them. Tree gums are abundant in the autumn and no longer flowing so fast, so you can carefully gather what you need. Many crops are now over, so you might ask permission from farmers to wander where you previously couldn't, due to crops or livestock. Reeds (and garden bamboo hedges) have finished their growing season by this time, too, making it a perfect time to gather a handful for reed pens.

Top to bottom:
Winter – ironstone on the beach;
Spring – cherry tree sap catching the light;
Summer – mussels by the lock;
Autumn – round oak galls.

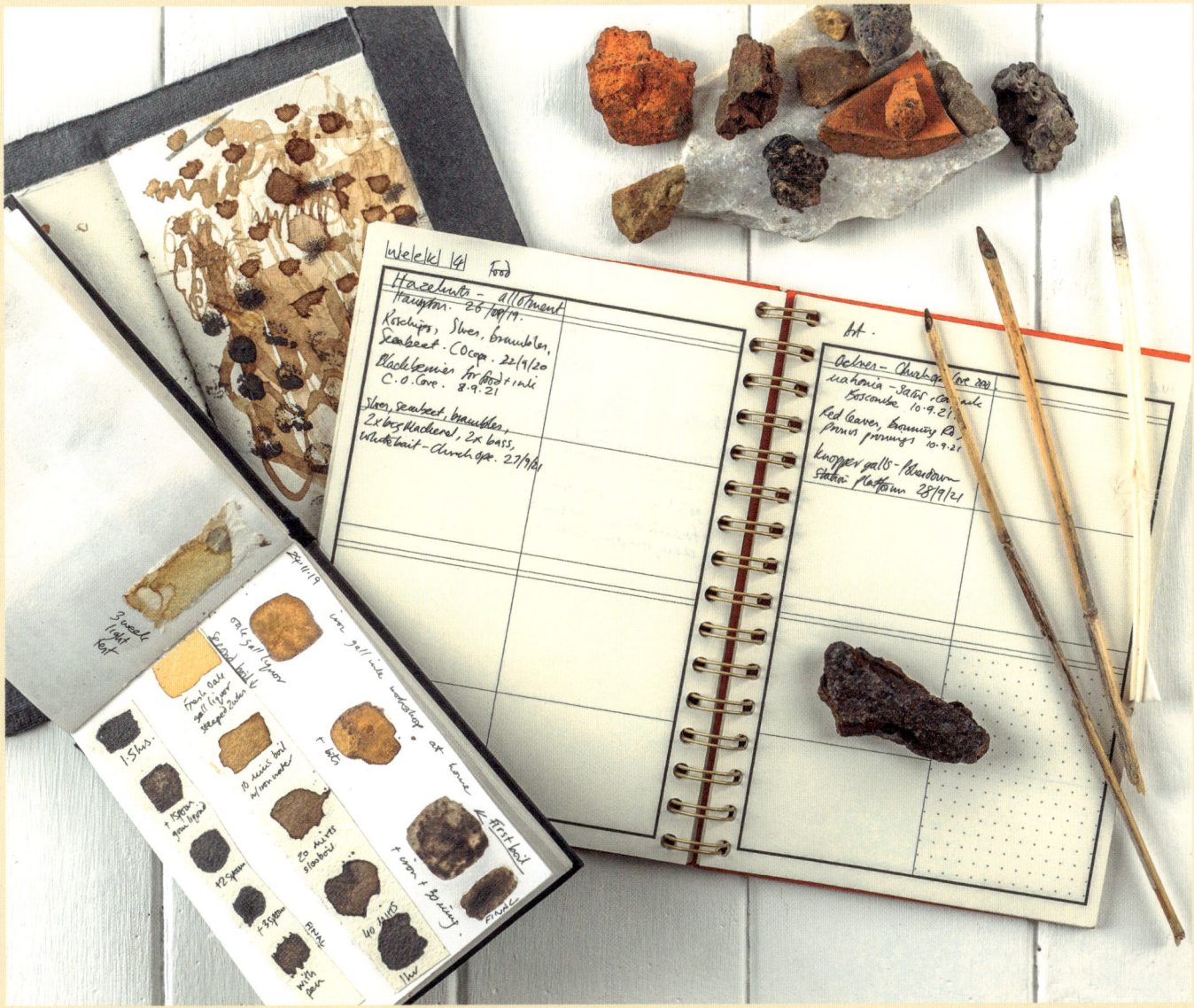

Foraging diary

I can picture specific young oak trees where I once found a glut of galls, and recall exactly where a fallen tree in Devon unearthed the brightest yellow clay. However, you don't have to keep the location of every find in your head. When I get home at the end of a day's foraging, I record the place, date and what I found in a spiral-bound perpetual diary which has spaces for writing the months and weeks for any year (a customized notebook would do just as well). I use the opposite page in the same diary to record food finds, as a day picking hazelnuts will, as often as not, also yield some ochre, galls, or feathers.

A foraging diary is a wonderful way to ease your way into the flow of the seasons if you feel a bit disconnected from nature. On a cold wet day, you can leaf through your notes and remind yourself of all the things you have found, and make plans to return to spots when the time is right.

Online map apps are useful for recording exact locations and details; I use What3Words, which also gives a three-word name to every three-metre square of the globe: useful to record parking places or hard to find spots in a big wood. I still write a diary by hand because a notebook full of nature notes is a joy in itself – and it doesn't rely on a phone signal.

Foraging in your house, your garden and street

Start where you are. Somewhere in your home, garden or street is a soft enough rock, or a colourful enough clay, a piece of terracotta or a blob of tree gum that's just waiting to become paint.

When was the last time you emptied your kitchen drawer? That jar of shells and stones – what's in it? Where's that worn bit of bright red terracotta plant pot that you found in the raised beds? The new gravel in the drive has really interesting green stones... take a closer look. There's claggy yellow clay in a pile from digging a pond at the bottom of your garden – take the brightest handful of that clay. The crumbling front yard red brick wall your neighbours are replacing, could you ask for a chunk from the rubble? The charcoal from the firepit is a lovely deep black, would that crush up into a nice pigment? That gooey gum on your Victoria plum tree needs collecting...

To test if something is usable, you'll need to get a few bits of scrap paper: strong cartridge paper is ideal, but a strong used white envelope will do well. You'll also need a hard stone, something not too shiny and smooth. Wash a big pebble or pale garden stone clean. If it's got a rough texture, even better.

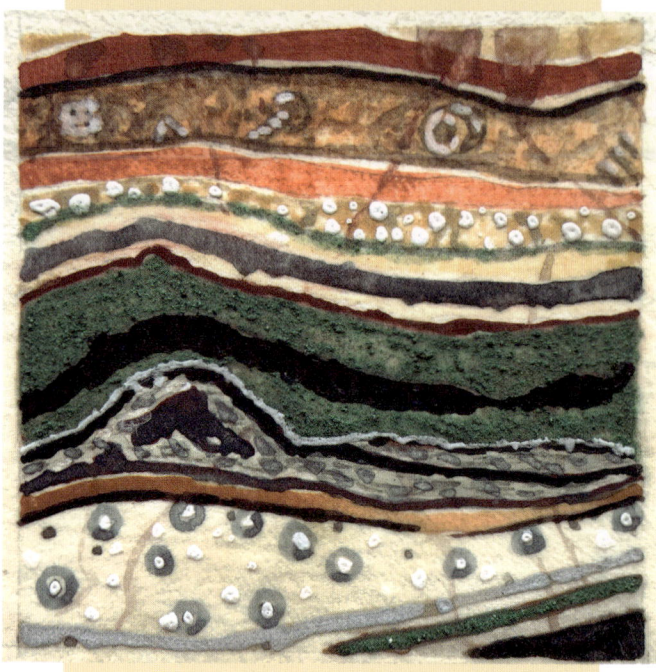

ANTHROPOCENE STRATA
10 x 10cm (4 x 4in)

Made for the book Dark Mountain – Sanctum, *this artwork reflects on what humanity is leaving behind us. Starting at home, we can reuse and reduce our footprints.*

Handmade paints on deerskin parchment.

In the collection of Candace Jensen.

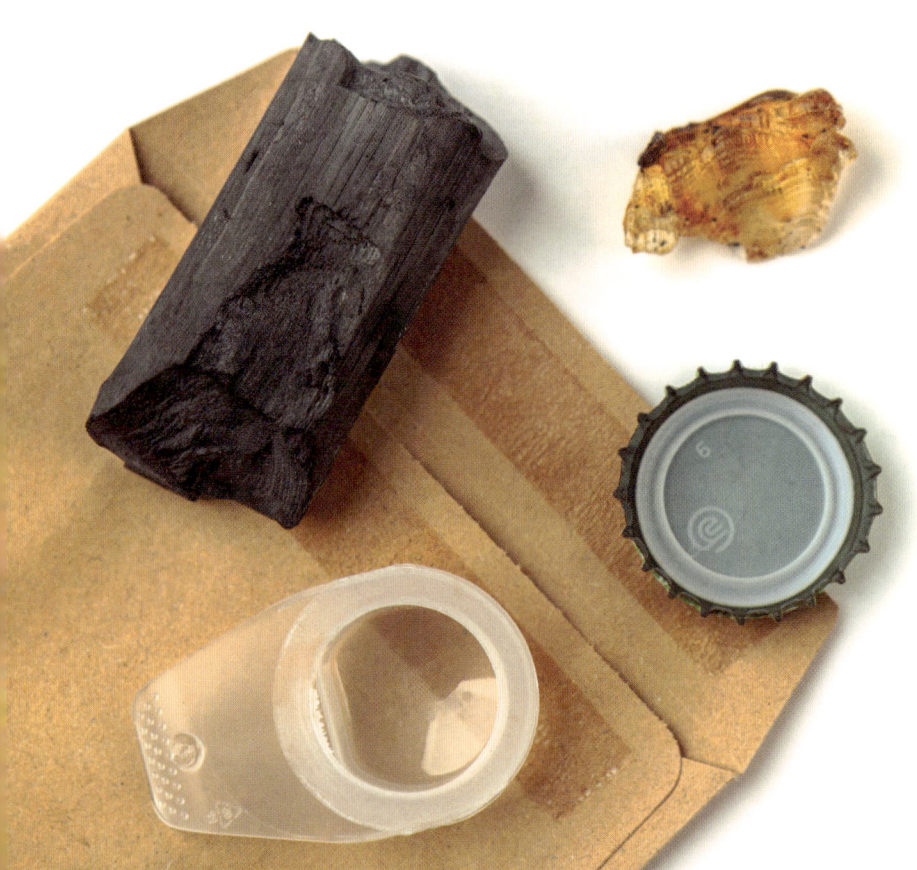

FORAGED FROM THE HOME

Charcoal, cherry tree gum, and envelopes; plus a contact lens case and bottle top – all useful for making or storing paint.

Exercise:
Rubbing objects on paper

With soft materials, such as charcoal, clay, earth, soils, peat, chalk or mud, all you need to test them is a piece of scrap paper, or a little sketchbook that's easy to carry on your travels.

Take a little of the material and rub it on the paper. Does it leave a mark? Get interested in the material and ask questions: What's the colour? Does it need wetting first? Is it scratchy or crumbly? Does it make hard lines or blend easily?

Use a pencil to make a note near the mark about what it is. If you like it, collect a little in the bag or tub you've brought. If not, leave it where it is and carry on hunting.

The material may be a bit hard for paper; tearing it, or not leaving a mark, like the third rock here. If it still shows promise, try the next test.

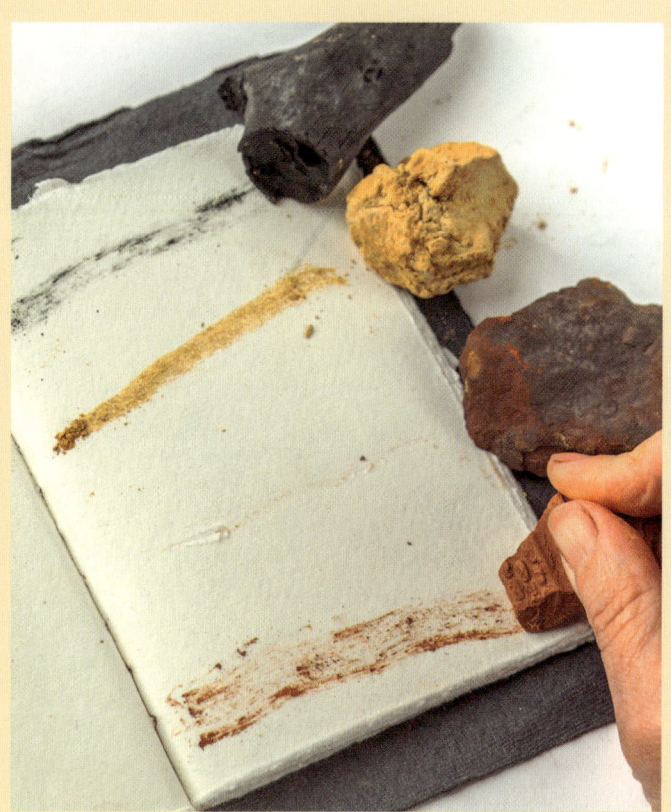

Top to bottom: testing charcoal, yellow clay, ironstone and terracotta tile directly onto notebook paper.

Exercise:
Rubbing objects on rock

Rub or scrape your harder material (such as a brick or stone) against the rock to see if it leaves a mark. If it leaves a colourful line, you might have something to make into a pigment. If it leaves no mark, it is too hard to process using the simple means we'll be utilizing.

Hard rocks often contain lots of silica, and generally don't produce a strong colour like the iron-rich rocks and ochres we hope to find. The advantage of having one testing stone is that you'll soon get to know how strong a mark needs to be to make a rock worth collecting to make pigment. The knowledge will be in your hands as much as your eyes – in the feel of the mark-making. Paint making usually engages all the senses, except perhaps for taste!

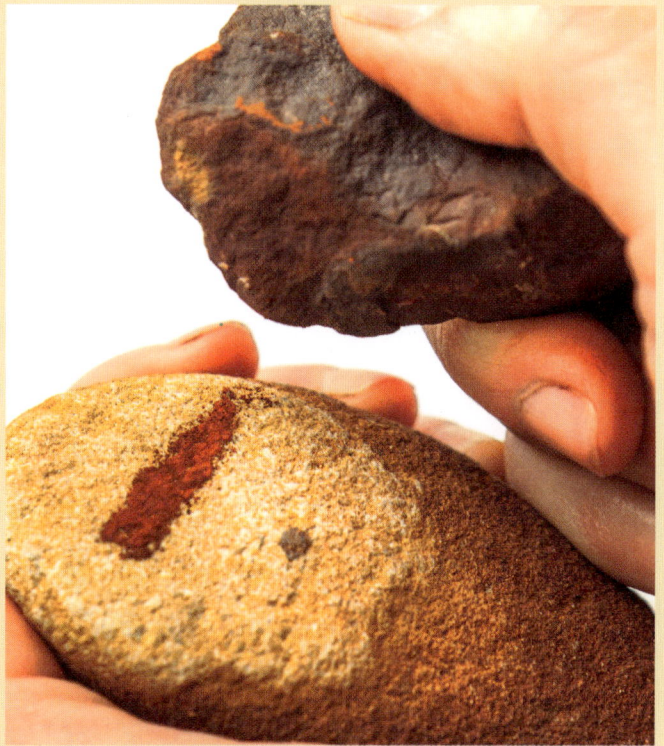

I use a favourite palm-sized textured stone I found on the beach at Burntisland, near Edinburgh, for my testing.

Foraging on the beach

Growing up by the sea, picking up shells, stones, driftwood, feathers and interesting flotsam has been a lifetime habit. Heading home with a pocketful of treasure (and sand in my shoes) is one of my earliest memories. Even today, when it's finally warm enough to take my light jacket out of winter storage, I find few impromptu pleasures outweigh finding that perfectly smooth pebble I stashed in the pocket last summer.

I mention these moments as part of consciously slowing down; a change in thinking of the natural world – not as a bottomless resource, but as a living store of delight, worthy of our time and all our senses. When we feel impoverished, we are tempted to buy more to fill that empty feeling. Watching the waves roll in, and seeing the multicoloured stones that wash up, we can feel replenished by something simple and free.

In the UK, we have a huge coastline in comparison with our small landmass. From high chalk cliffs to shale ledges, granite outcrops and sandy estuaries, there really is no end to what you might find. From bright red ochres and yellow clay lumps, pale green earths or soft weathered old brick, many coloured pebbles can be found along the foreshore. Test likely pebbles by scraping them on a harder rock, as described on page 31. You may also find soft chalk pebbles, green grey slate, or pinkish stones. Learn your local shorelines, if you have any, and become a beach bum or coastal connoisseur. In Ireland, my friend Shinehah Bigham found incredible green and yellow ochres on the west coast, some of the brightest shades I have ever seen.

Take only a pebble or two or a handful of each colour, as we do not want to diminish the beach or be greedy. Obviously, we do not take anything away from protected landscapes or Sites of Special Scientific Interest (SSSI) that we may pass through.

Tip

Find out if your local geological society runs beach walks.

FORAGED FROM THE BEACH

Driftwood; feathers for brushes or pens; and shells that can act as palettes or to store paint.

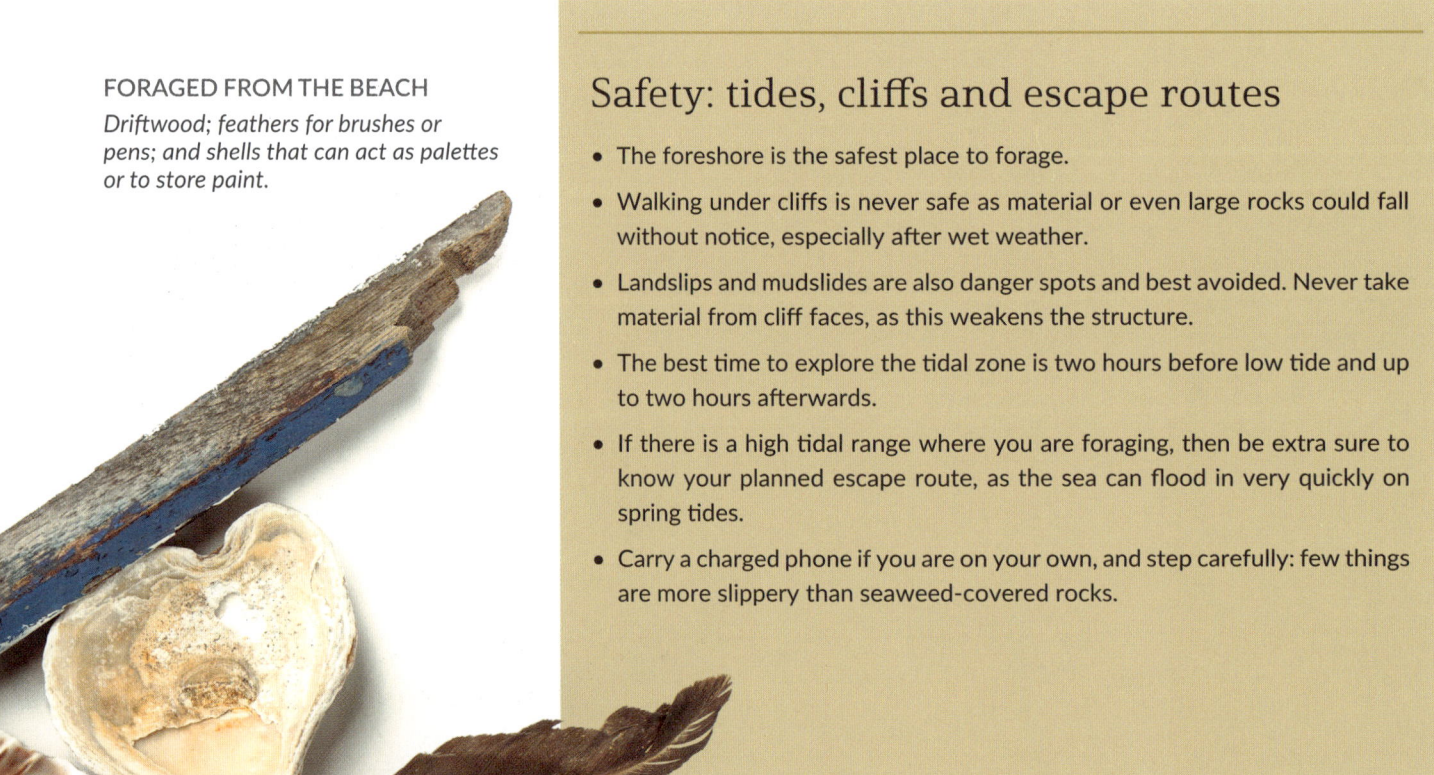

Safety: tides, cliffs and escape routes

- The foreshore is the safest place to forage.

- Walking under cliffs is never safe as material or even large rocks could fall without notice, especially after wet weather.

- Landslips and mudslides are also danger spots and best avoided. Never take material from cliff faces, as this weakens the structure.

- The best time to explore the tidal zone is two hours before low tide and up to two hours afterwards.

- If there is a high tidal range where you are foraging, then be extra sure to know your planned escape route, as the sea can flood in very quickly on spring tides.

- Carry a charged phone if you are on your own, and step carefully: few things are more slippery than seaweed-covered rocks.

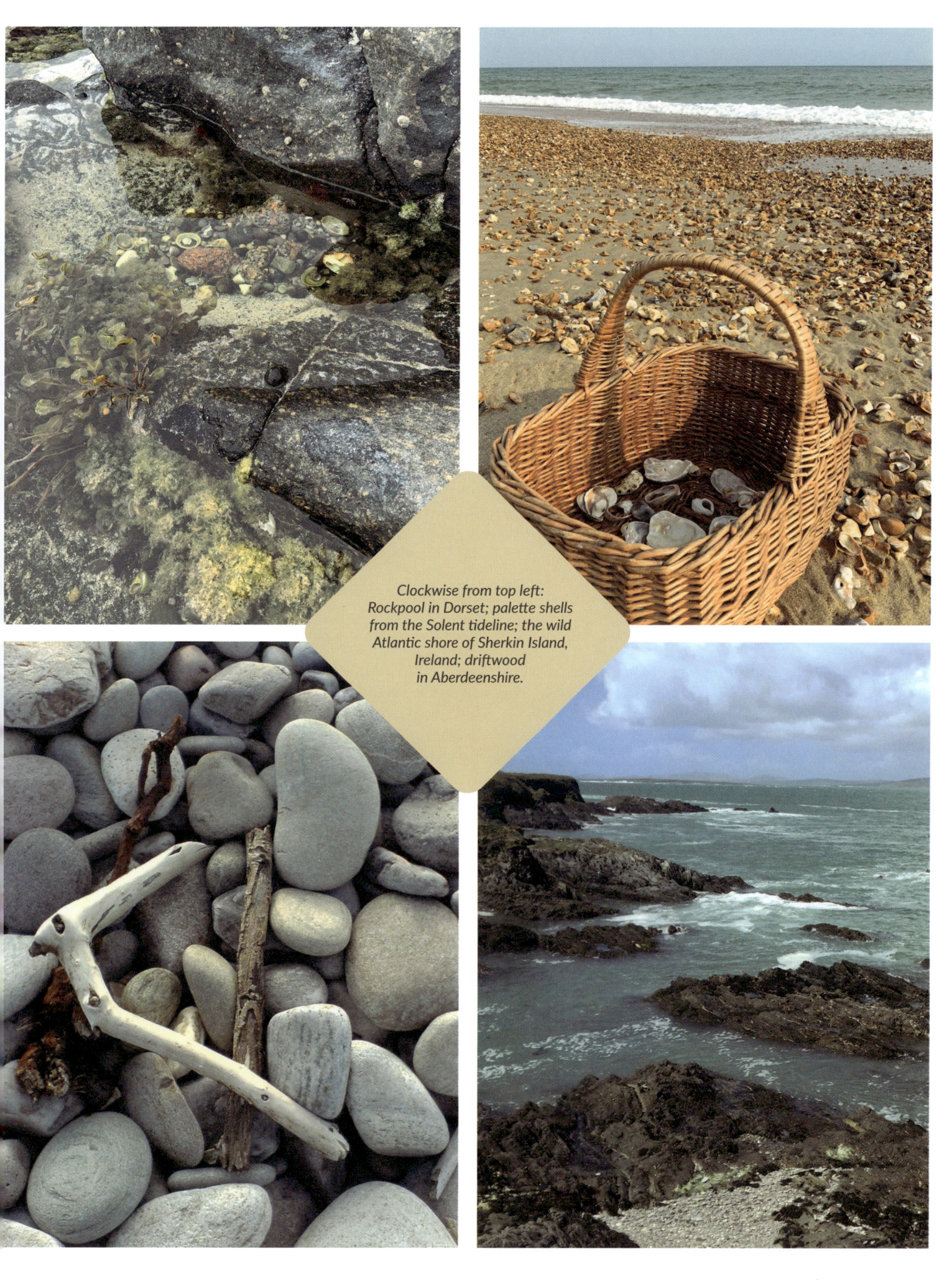

Clockwise from top left: Rockpool in Dorset; palette shells from the Solent tideline; the wild Atlantic shore of Sherkin Island, Ireland; driftwood in Aberdeenshire.

Colours from beaches

Here's what I foraged on my local beaches. You might find you can make a palette from what you can gather after just a few visits.

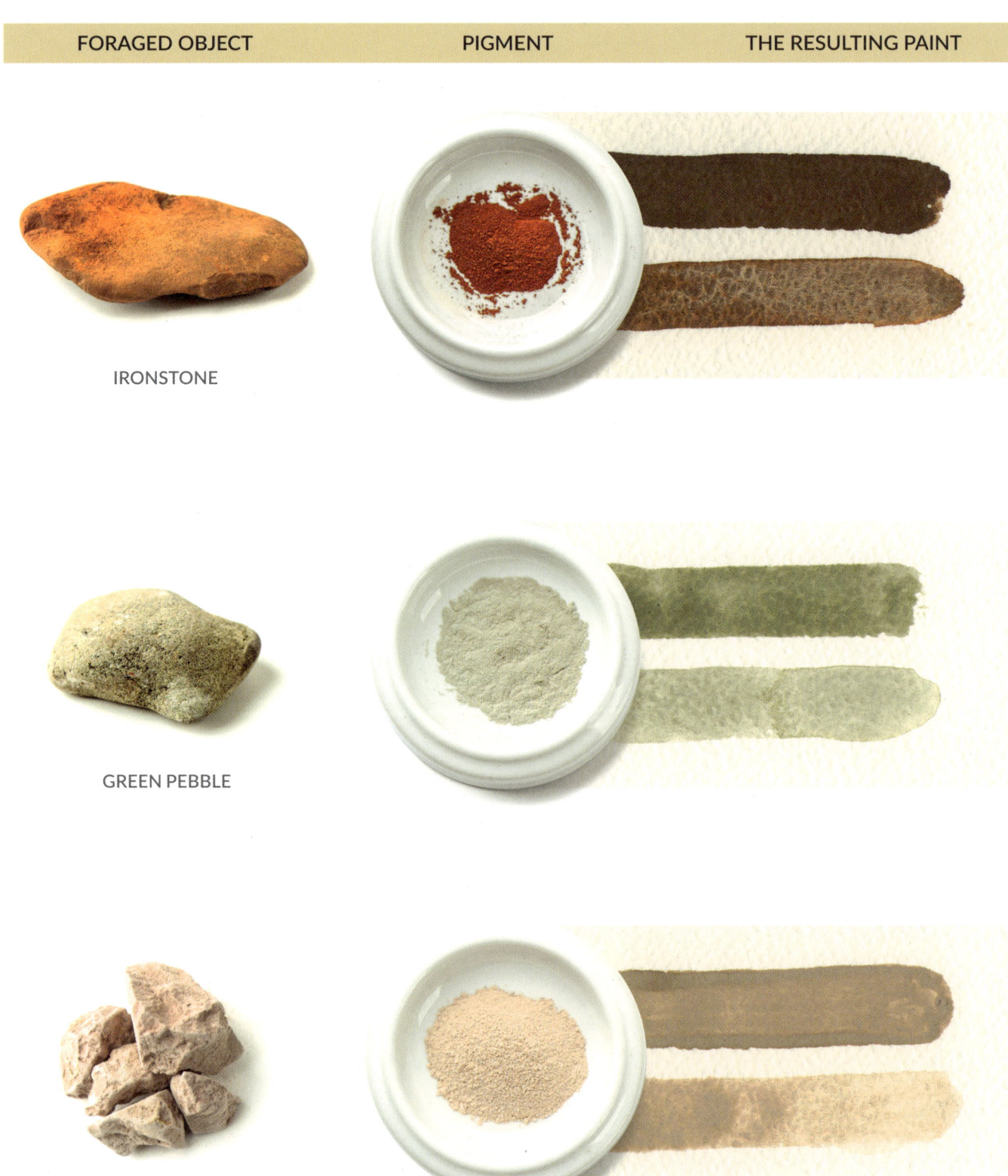

| FORAGED OBJECT | PIGMENT | THE RESULTING PAINT |

IRONSTONE

GREEN PEBBLE

PINK CLAY

Other tools to find

Like a detective, a forager also looks for what is 'out of place'. Once in St Magnus' Bay, Shetland, I found flint nodules on the beach. Knowing there was no flint-bearing rock nearby, I was perplexed, but my local friend explained how it once served as ballast, and was offloaded by traders centuries ago who had arrived from the south coast. Mysteries and questions are part of our bounty when we go on a foray. It is no coincidence that 'I gather' in English can also mean 'I understand'.

On the beach, look for gull feathers to make quill pens and brushes, driftwood to make brush handles, palettes and pens, rocks with multiple impressions that might make palettes for several colours. Mussel and scallop shells make good single colour palettes and ink trays. The gel found in some seaweeds can make a good impromptu paint binder, too.

On a safety note, never grind up shells without wearing gloves, goggles and a mask, as shellfish are bio-accumulators of heavy metals and other pollutants found in the sea, and these can be absorbed through the skin, lungs and eyes.

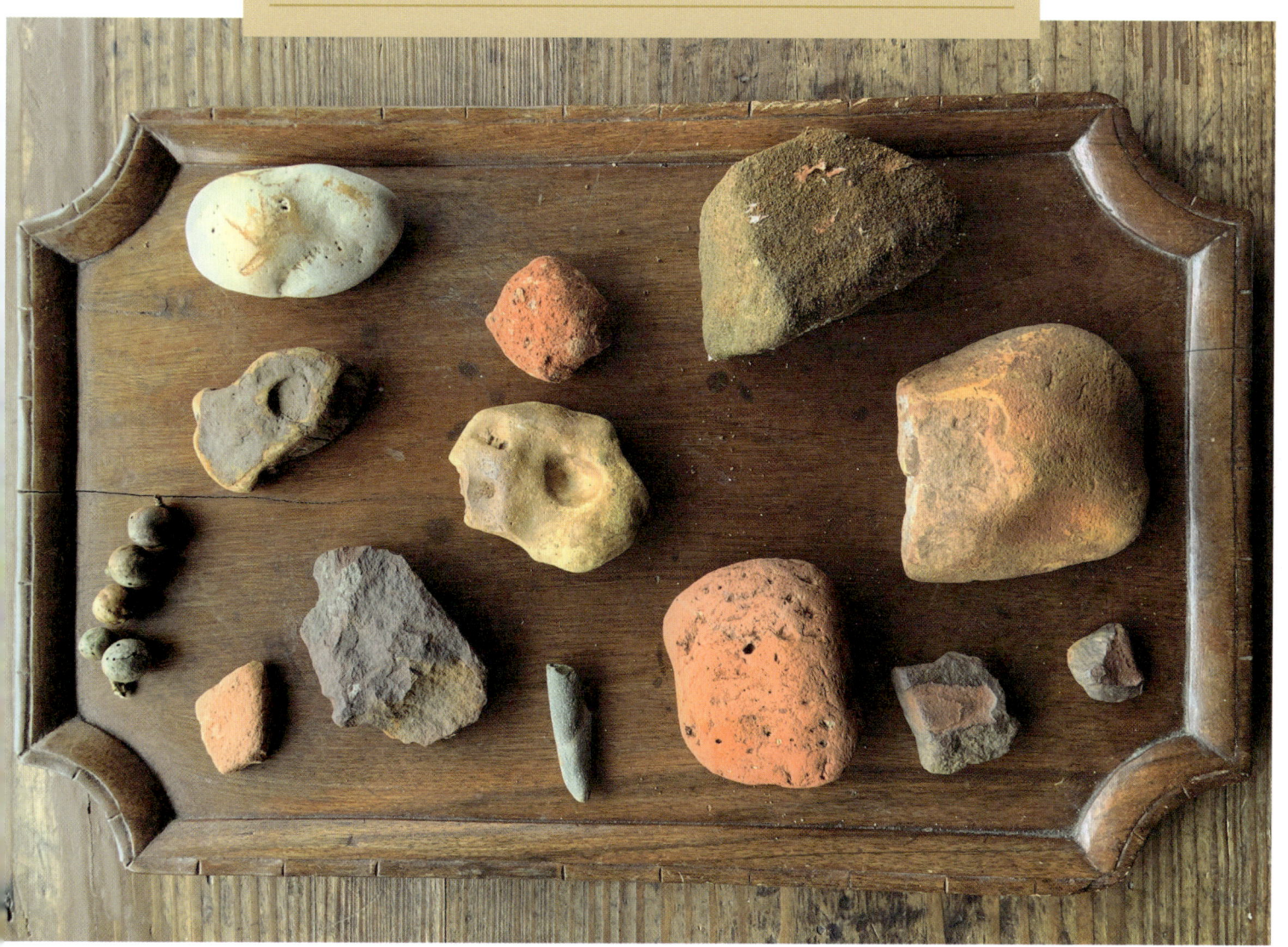

Foraging in the countryside

In the UK, 'countryside' usually consists of moors, heaths, farmland, hills, mountains, bogs, marshes, fields and field margins – the barrier zones between the farmland and the towns, rivers and woods that border them. Where you live, 'countryside' might be rocky areas, dry lands or even deserts, prairies, jungle, tundra or glaciers. What all these places have in common is their relative wildness.

When out and about in the wild, whatever that means where you live, there is even more reason to take care and hone your senses. Taking all the safety measures mentioned so far into account, it's also sensible to bring drinking water and a little food with you if you are going off the beaten track. Assuming you've packed everything you need, and dressed well for the terrain, what are you likely to find that can become art materials? Here's some of what I have found recently on my travels, as a jumping-off point for you.

Under a horse-kicked clump of heather, upturned on a heath, I found a little nugget of deep brown peat that made a beautiful sepia-toned paint wash. Bright golden ochre was nestling under a gravel path up a steep hill on a headland in Suffolk – and only spotted because a rainstorm had washed away the gravel and left a puddle of gold showing in the bright sunlight. Broken mauve-grey slate from an abandoned old croft in the Highlands of Scotland made a surprisingly good drawing material on thick rough paper, and an even better paint once ground up. Robin-breast red stopped me in my tracks at the edge of a field in Devon last year, when walking with a friend. I picked up a clod that had been dislodged by a tractor and it made the most amazing orangey-red paint.

Elsewhere in the world there are rightly famous deposits of deep red ochre, for instance in Iran, candy pink minerals in Greece and deep blue lumps of vivianite in the Pacific North West of North America. Where you live might be less dramatic geologically, but this is no cause for sadness. Subtle palettes are as much a delight as bold ones, so look closely at the natural variations in your local sources, and keep an open mind.

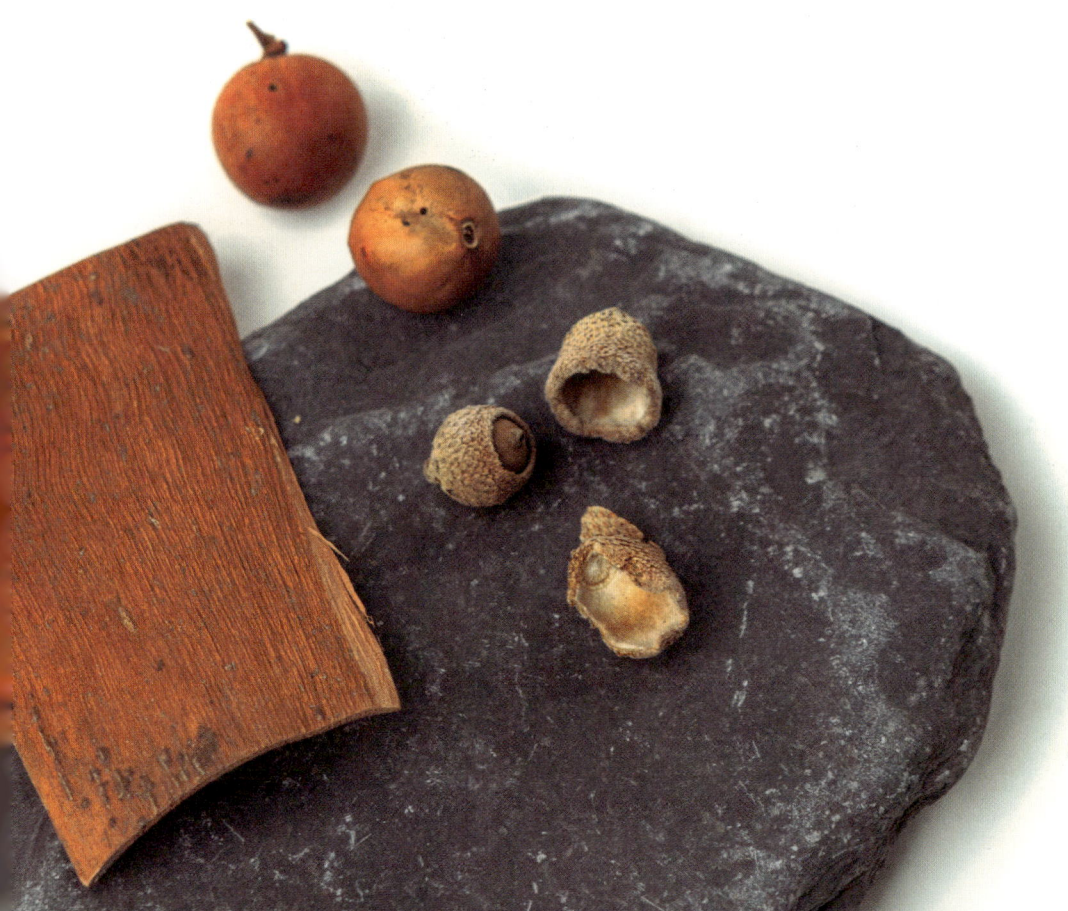

FORAGED FROM THE COUNTRYSIDE
Bark, oak galls and acorn shells for ink, plus slate for pigment.

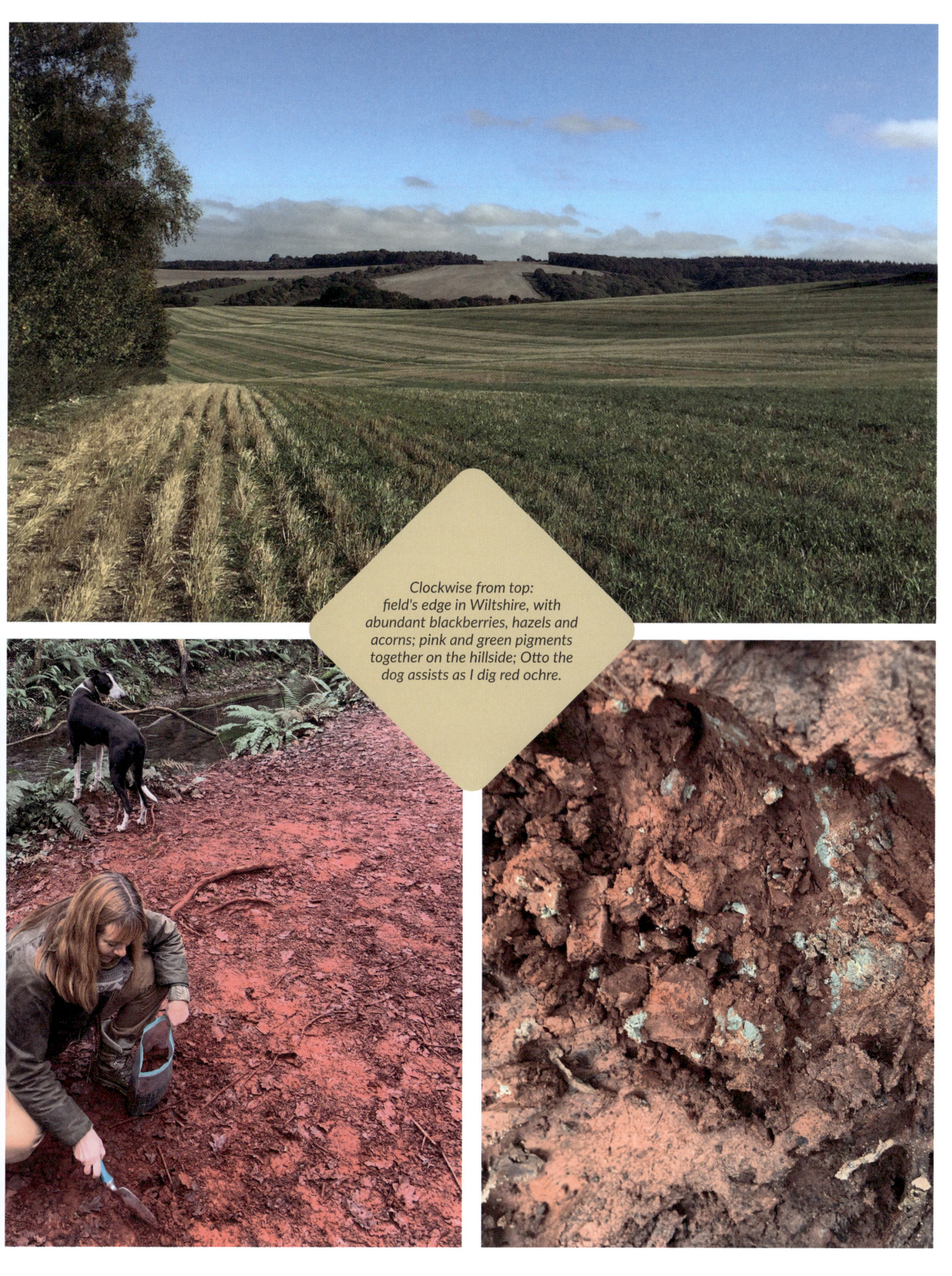

Clockwise from top: field's edge in Wiltshire, with abundant blackberries, hazels and acorns; pink and green pigments together on the hillside; Otto the dog assists as I dig red ochre.

Colours from the countryside

It's rewarding to take a palmful of crumbly red earth home from the countryside and within a few minutes make a simple paint swatch like these.

COLOUR TESTING, opposite

Keeping a record of earths, paints and inks is a great way to remember what you've found. It's also good to make a lasting note of gift-ochres foraged by friends, as in these examples.

FORAGED OBJECT	PIGMENT	THE RESULTING PAINT

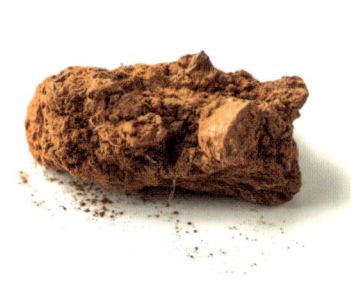 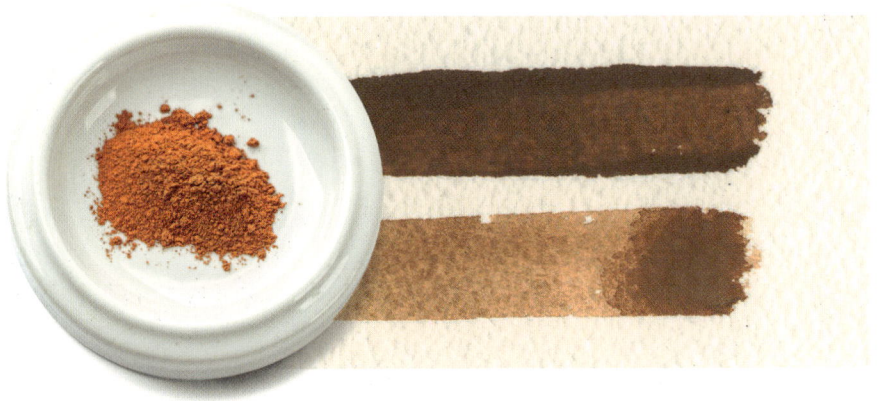

SOFT RED EARTH

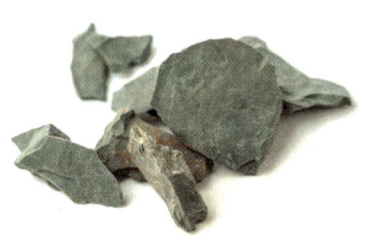 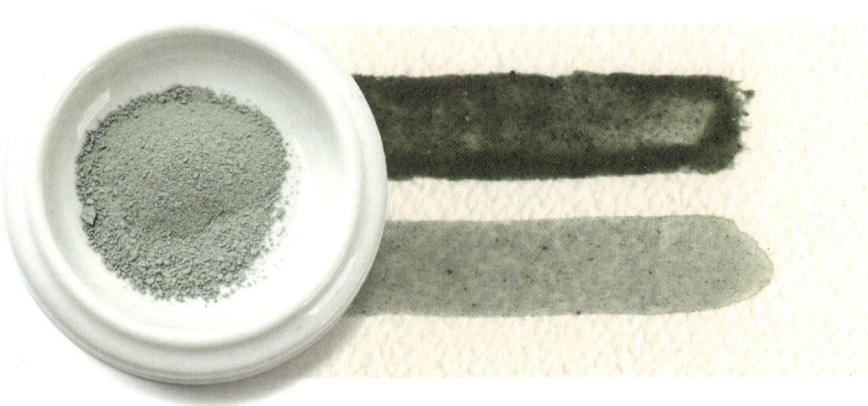

SHALE

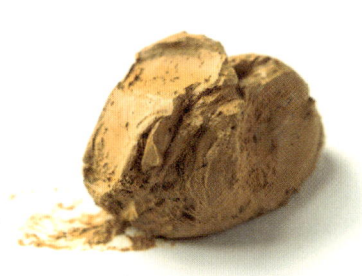 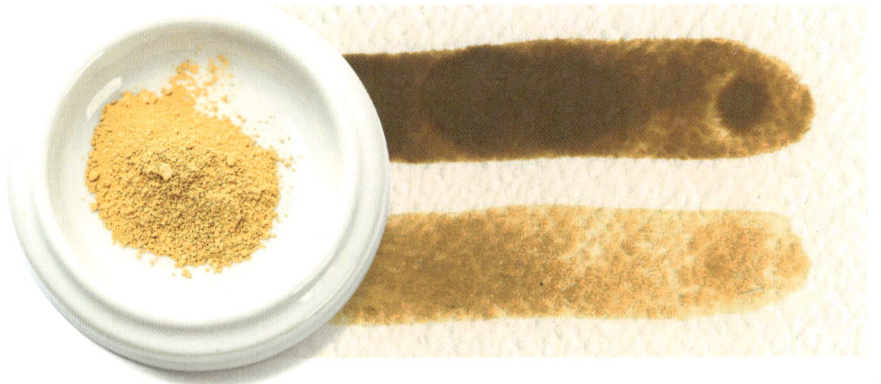

YELLOW CLAY

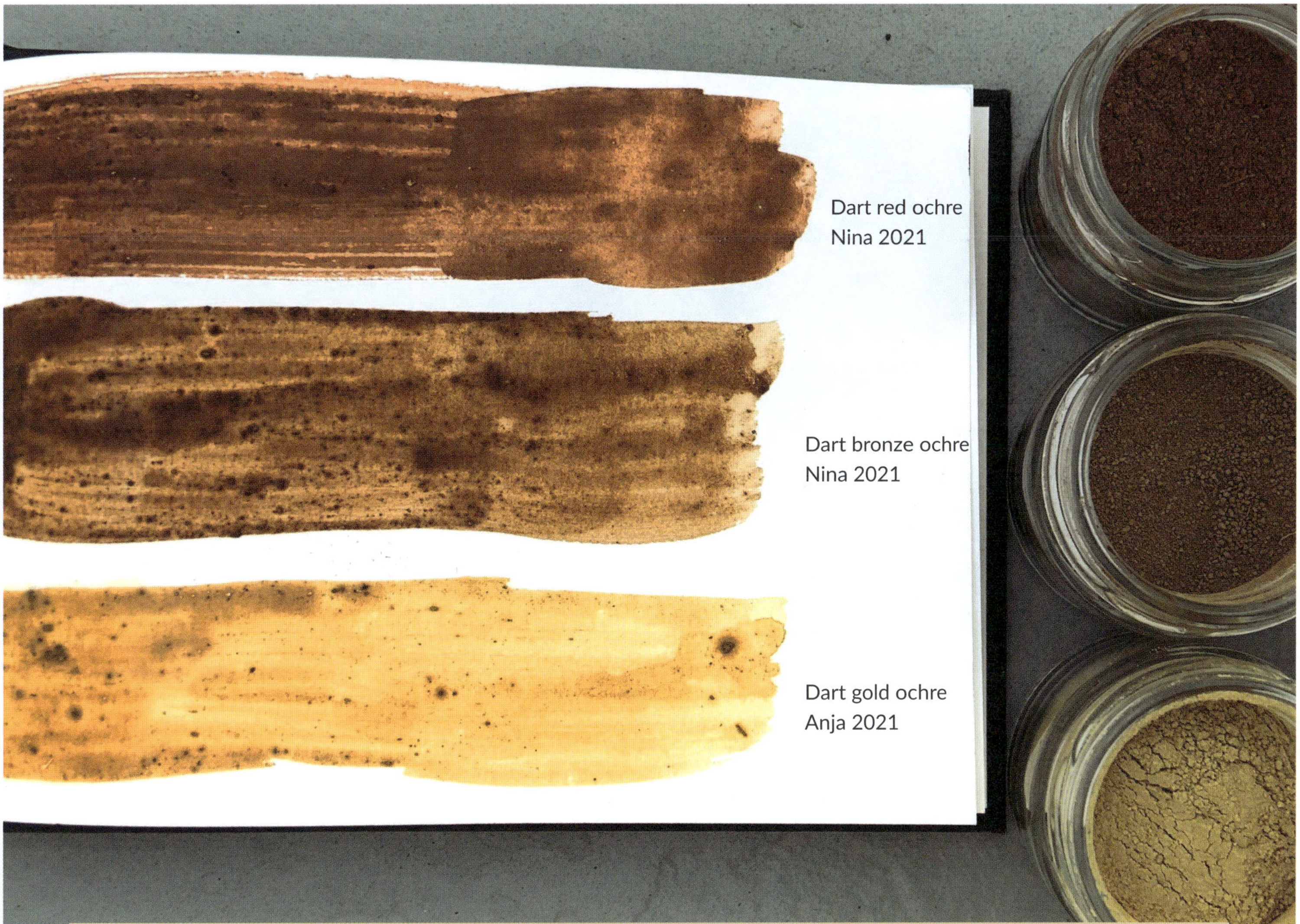

Dart red ochre
Nina 2021

Dart bronze ochre
Nina 2021

Dart gold ochre
Anja 2021

Colour tests from rubbing plants

As you forage, test leaves, petals and fruits on a page in your sketchbook. Although outside the scope of this book, plant colour holds a vast rainbow of shades that can make ink, lake pigments, dyes and paints. Though not as permanent as earth pigments, they are beautiful in their own right.

Make notes as you go beside purple elderberry smears, yellow streaks from gorse and dandelion, green lines from grass, red blurs from rosehips, and the short-lived blue of forget-me-not petals. This additional colour-finding practice will help on those days when the stones elude you but there's lots in bloom. Also, in making work with your paints later on, you can incorporate the marks made by plants growing beside your rock finds. If kept in a closed sketchbook, rubbed plant colours can last surprisingly well.

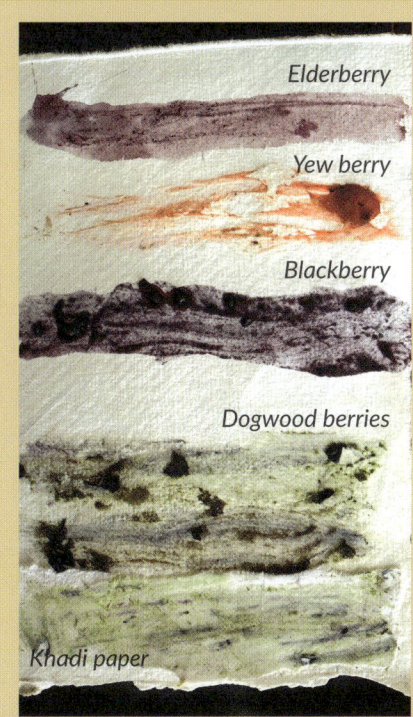

Elderberry

Yew berry

Blackberry

Dogwood berries

Khadi paper

Foraging in woodland

The woods – forests, orchards, plantations, spinneys, coppiced groves, indeed, wooded places of all kinds – are at the heart of natural colour practice. The environments that trees create are rich in goods for our wild inks and paints, tools and materials. Here are some of the things I find in woodlands.

Oak galls These harmless growths, common on oaks, are where the larvae of gall wasps grow and mature, finally making a hole and escaping in the autumn. After late summer, when the escape holes are visible, they can be harvested to make the basis of oak gall ink (see page 114), which has a wonderful tannin-rich brown colour. Collect at least enough to fill your cupped hands; twice that amount is better, if abundant.

Chalk In some Wiltshire woods there are many badger setts. For some reason the badgers do not like the chalk or flint nodules in their homes and dig them out, leaving them in handy piles beside their entrances. At dawn and dusk these almost glow in the dark woods, and all I have to do is collect the unwanted chalk in bags. I use larger pieces to draw and crush smaller pieces into powder for thickening gouache and making paler-tinted paints.

Clay It's always worth looking under the root plate of upturned trees; you never know what you'll find. In the upturned roots of a fallen tree in Devon I first saw the bright yellow clay that is one of my favourite pigments. Rain collects in the depression left where the roots once grew and here a pool of clean sticky golden pigment collects, washed off the roots. I just spoon it out into yoghurt pots.

Birch bark Birch tree bark is full of natural oils and has many fire-craft and handicraft uses, such as the beautiful, lidded tubs common in Scandinavia. It's also great as an alternative surface to paper and is ideal as a wrapper for your pigment finds. If you first make some cuts, the bark peels off easily from fallen dead birch trees, both in papery layers and in sheets. It curls up quickly, so once back at home, slightly dampen the bark before placing it under a heavy object to flatten it. Don't remove bark from living trees.

Sticks There are so many art uses for the humble stick. Sharpen it to a chisel point like a fountain pen and you have a simple pen. Elder twigs are hollow on the inside – insert some charcoal, chalk or ochre and you'll have an instant pencil that's much easier to handle than fiddly bits and pieces of pigment. Likewise, you can use sticks of culinary species such as hazel, willow, chestnut, ash, apple, or maple, to make a paintbrush – see page 120 for how to do so.

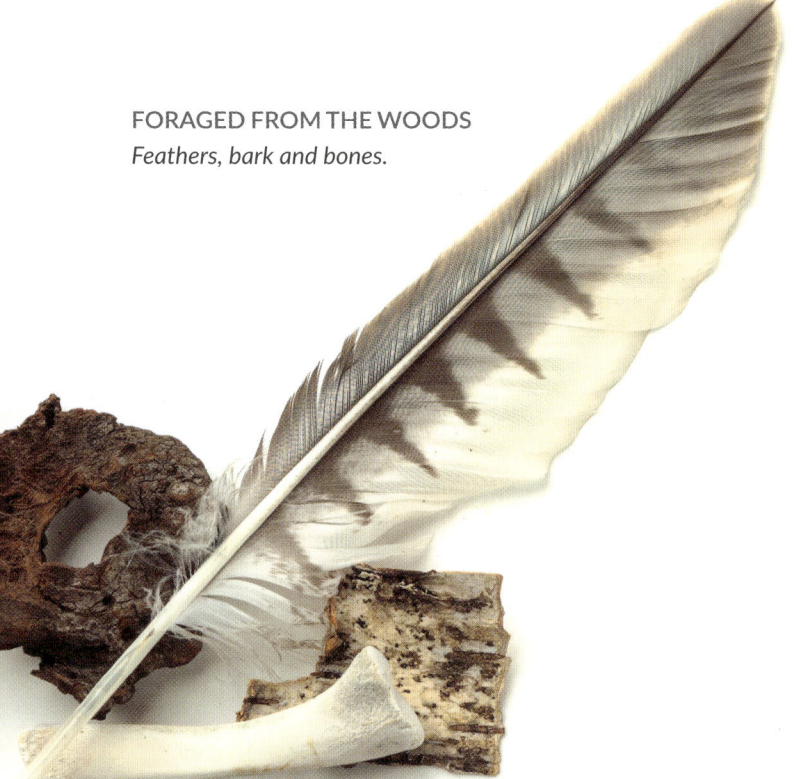

FORAGED FROM THE WOODS
Feathers, bark and bones.

Alternatives to galls

If you can't find oak galls where you live, then you can collect bark from freshly fallen or cut wood. Avoid bark that has been lying around, as rain washes away the tannins which give the colour. Acorn caps are another alternative tannin source. Though galls, acorn caps and bark all give different tones, they will all produce good dark inks for the recipe later in this book.

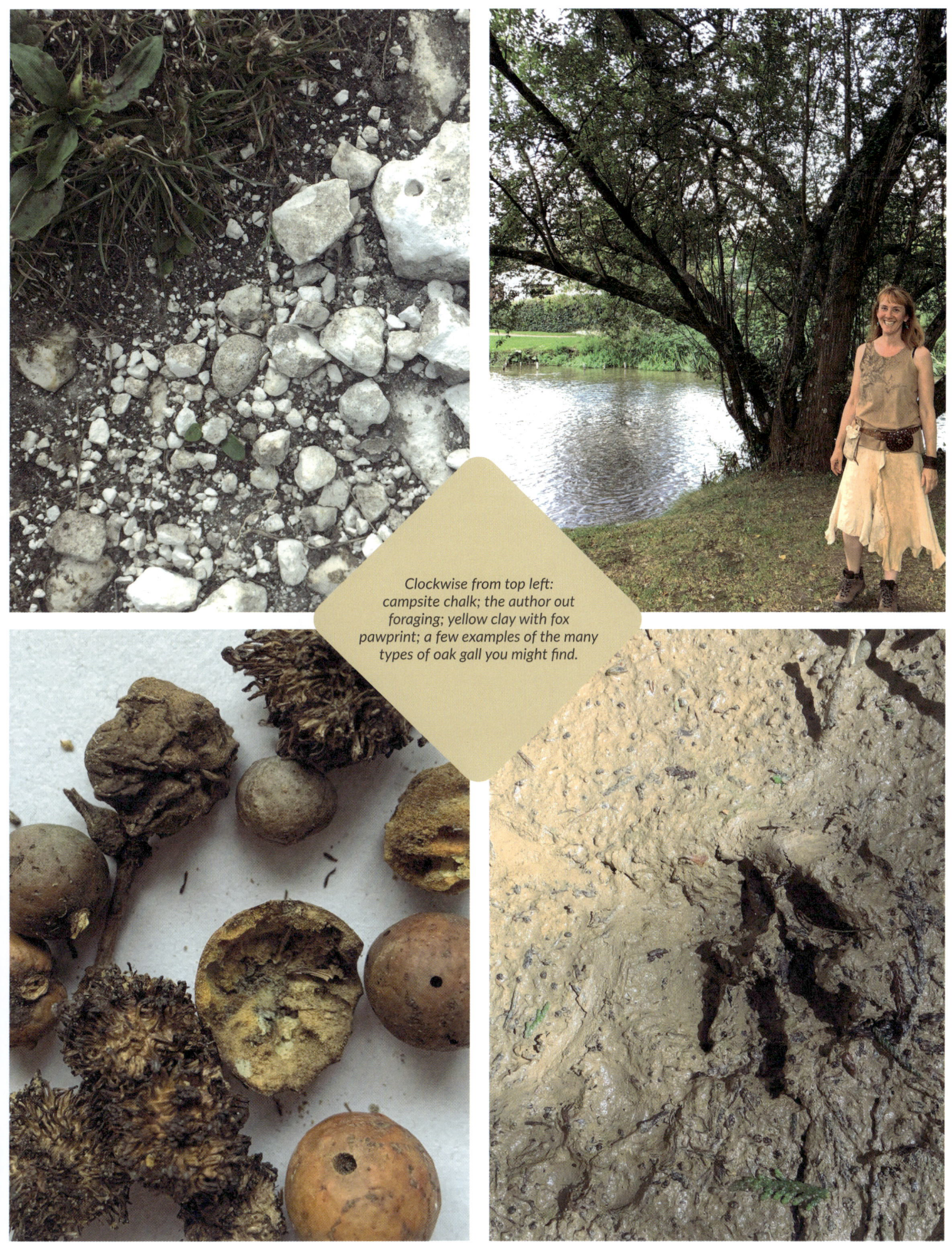

Clockwise from top left: campsite chalk; the author out foraging; yellow clay with fox pawprint; a few examples of the many types of oak gall you might find.

Colours from the woodland

Few things are as relaxing as foraging in dappled woodland light.
Amongst the leaves and fungi there is also hidden colour.

FORAGED OBJECT	PIGMENT	THE RESULTING PAINT

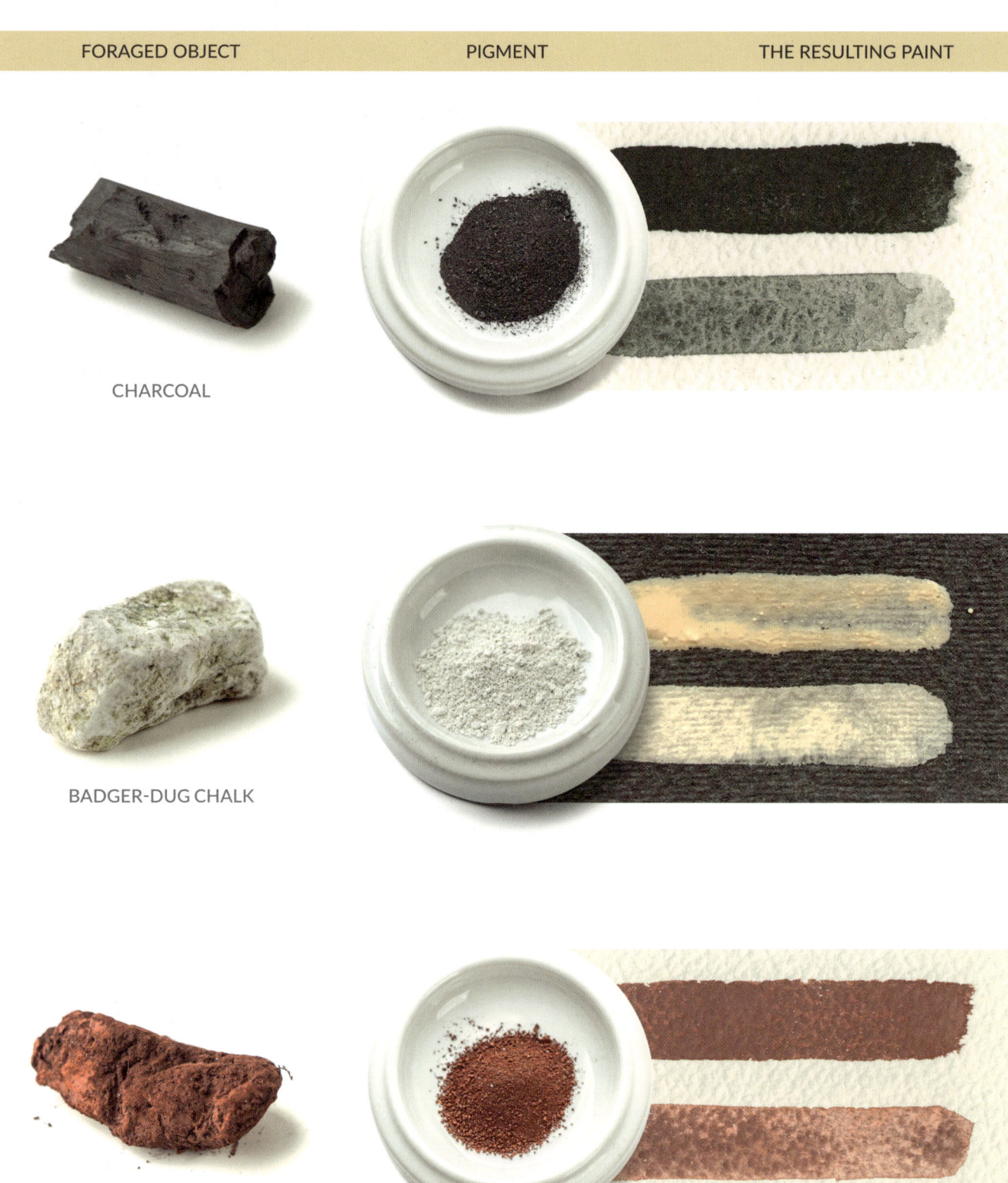

CHARCOAL

BADGER-DUG CHALK

HAEMATITE

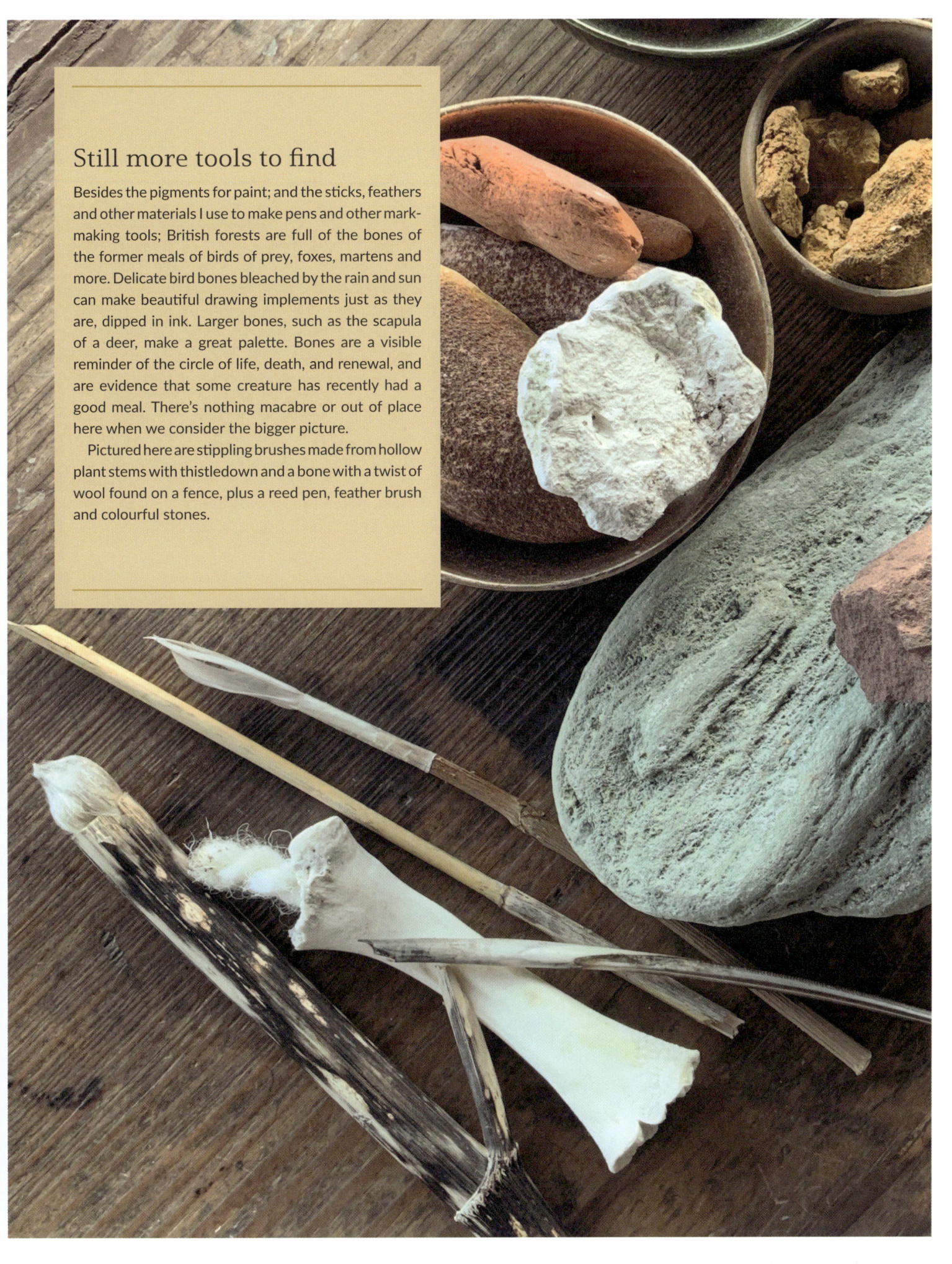

Still more tools to find

Besides the pigments for paint; and the sticks, feathers and other materials I use to make pens and other mark-making tools; British forests are full of the bones of the former meals of birds of prey, foxes, martens and more. Delicate bird bones bleached by the rain and sun can make beautiful drawing implements just as they are, dipped in ink. Larger bones, such as the scapula of a deer, make a great palette. Bones are a visible reminder of the circle of life, death, and renewal, and are evidence that some creature has recently had a good meal. There's nothing macabre or out of place here when we consider the bigger picture.

Pictured here are stippling brushes made from hollow plant stems with thistledown and a bone with a twist of wool found on a fence, plus a reed pen, feather brush and colourful stones.

Foraging on rural roads and paths

There are many quieter rural roads, footpaths, bridleways, green lanes, holloways and farm tracks where I live. Holloways are roads so ancient that they have been worn down into the landscape and the trees have grown over to form a magical green tunnel with the gnarled roots of trees forming the sides. Along most paths and hedgerows, you can find lots to make paint and brushes. Unless it's the middle of the day, consider wearing bright reflective clothing (like a cyclist), as narrow lanes can have reduced visibility.

Hollow sticks for brushes Collect elder sticks at any time, or, in the autumn, dry stems of alexanders, fennel, or hogweed. These cut easily into sections and make ideal holders for brushes.

Wool, fur and livestock hair These are found on fences everywhere in the British countryside, and wherever animals are used or farmed. Barbed wire and thorny hedges hold countless tufts of wool, while gates gather hair from cows' tails and horses manes. I've found piles of fluffy feathers and perfect rabbits' tails by fence posts where a buzzard has sat and eaten its dinner. All these are worth collecting to make a selection of wonderful paintbrushes and mark-making tools, once home.

Thistledown and seedhead tufts If you prefer to avoid animal products, the plant kingdom also has a wealth of fluffy brush options. In the spring, willow catkins are ready-made little felt tip brushes, perfect to dip in ink. In late summer many abundant species produce big fluffy seed heads with downy threads or silky fibres. I gather these to make very soft brushes that create stippling patterns rather than fine lines. Wild cotton, which grows in warmer climates, also makes a perfect instant brush tip.

Cherry plum and damson sap Hedgerows along country lanes are often full of useful culinary Prunus species such as cherry, cherry plum, damson and gage. All of these give excellent sap that exudes from cracks in the bark (a phenomenon called 'gummosis') and dries into lumps. Without cutting into the bark, remove the gum and take it home to dry. It is a traditional alternative to gum Arabic (from Acacia species) and although it is not as sticky or glossy, it makes a great paint binder. Warmer countries may have acacia or eucalyptus family trees which also yield gums that can make great paint binders.

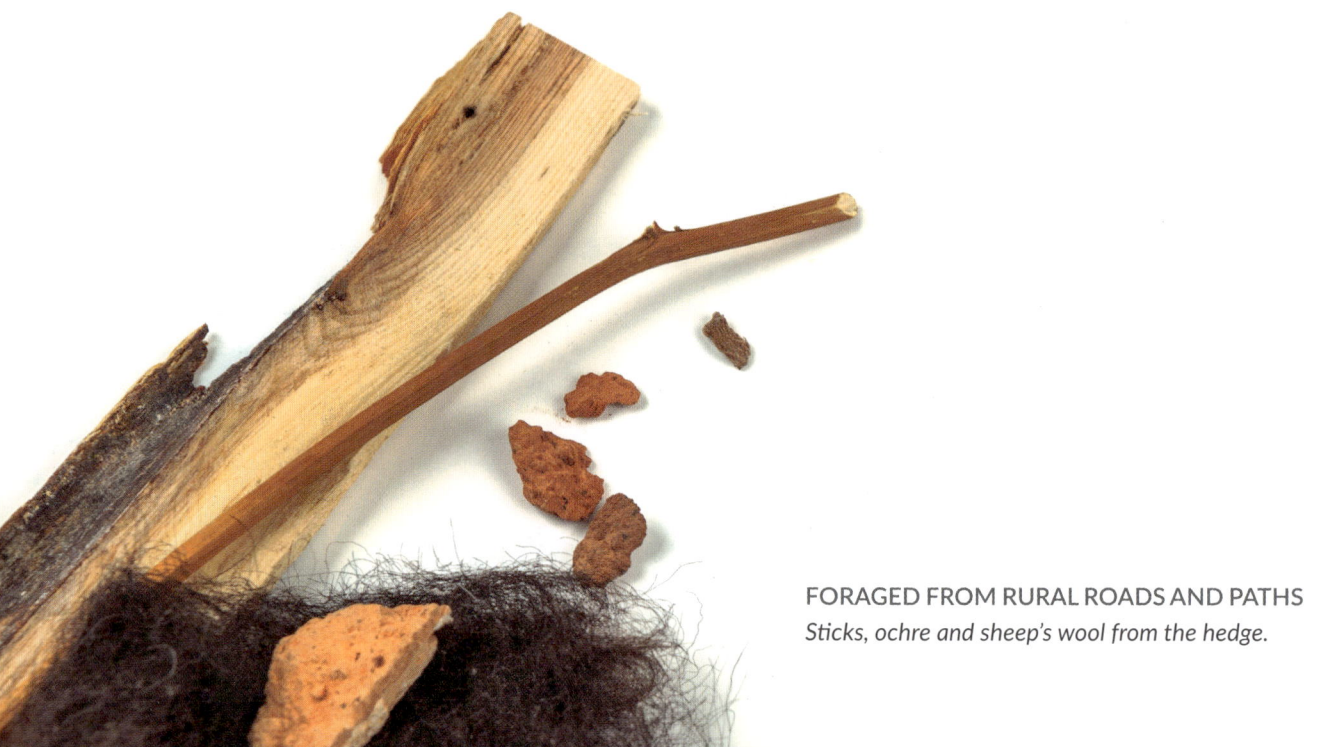

FORAGED FROM RURAL ROADS AND PATHS
Sticks, ochre and sheep's wool from the hedge.

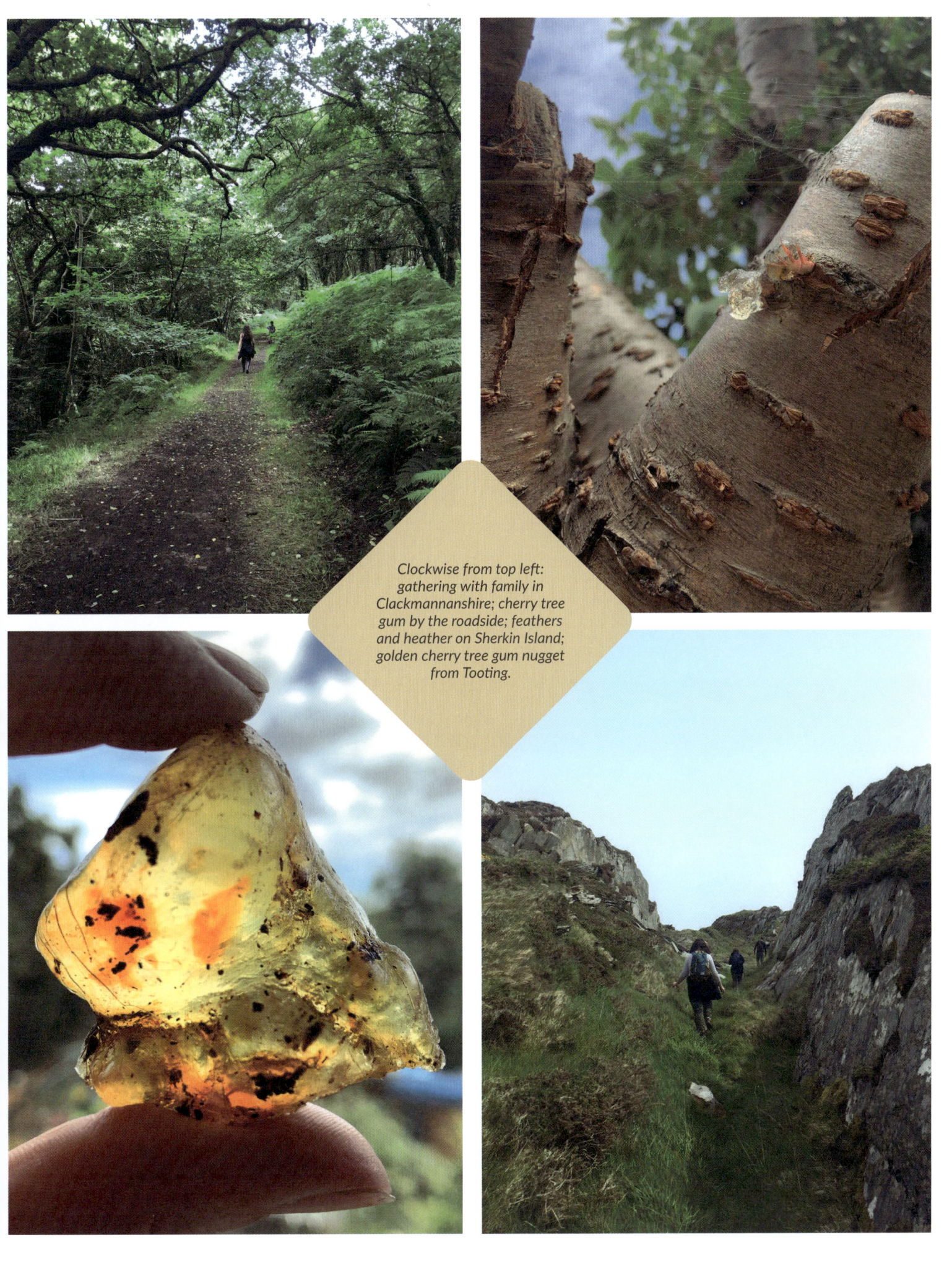

Clockwise from top left: gathering with family in Clackmannanshire; cherry tree gum by the roadside; feathers and heather on Sherkin Island; golden cherry tree gum nugget from Tooting.

Colours from rural roads and paths

Shown opposite is distinctive red earth that I found on a riverside walk near Bath. Rural roads and pathways are a visceral reminder that colour is always around us; right beneath our feet.

FORAGED OBJECT	PIGMENT	THE RESULTING PAINT

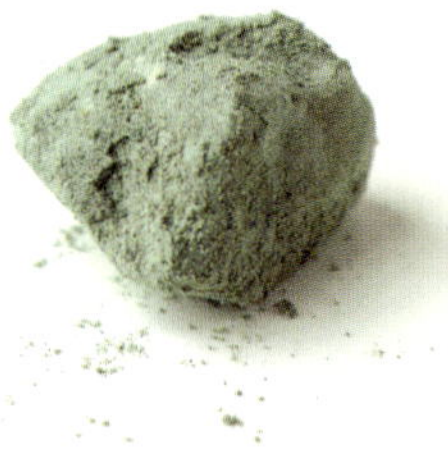

SOFT GREEN ROCK

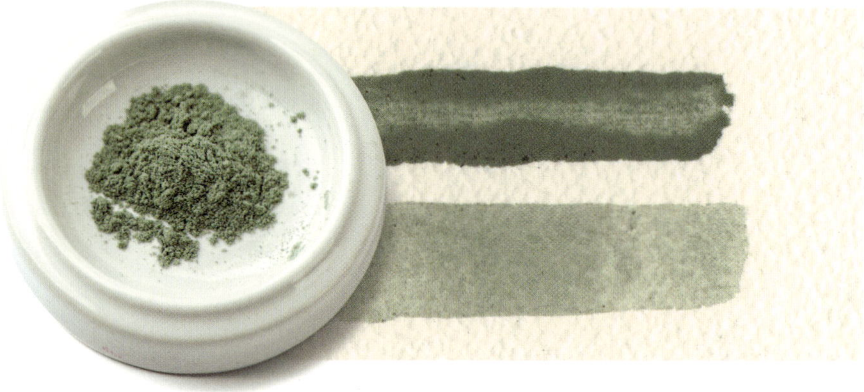

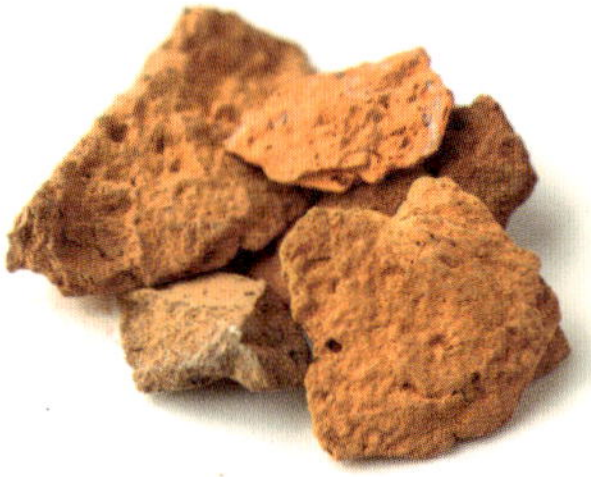

MEDIEVAL TILE

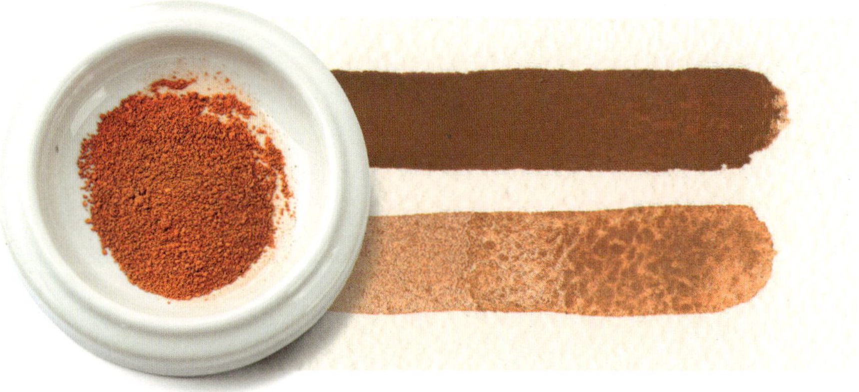

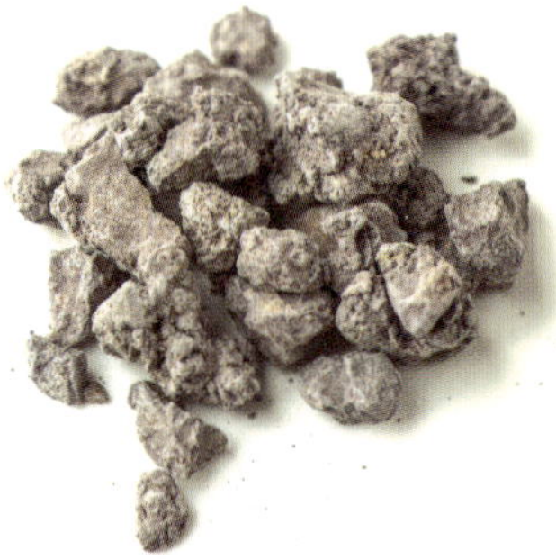

LILAC CLAY

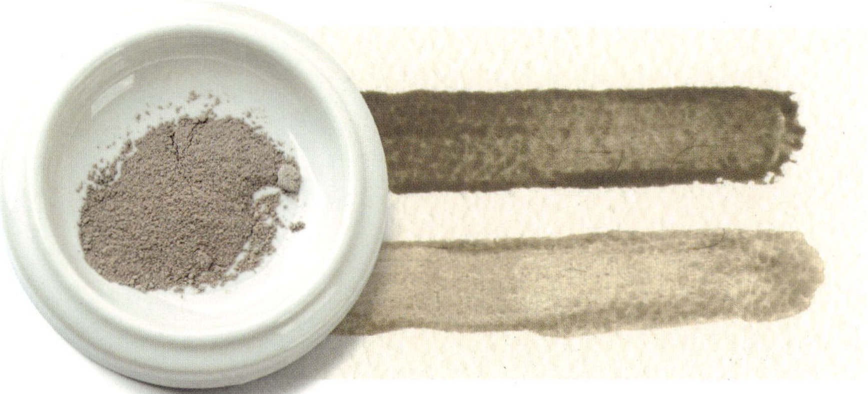

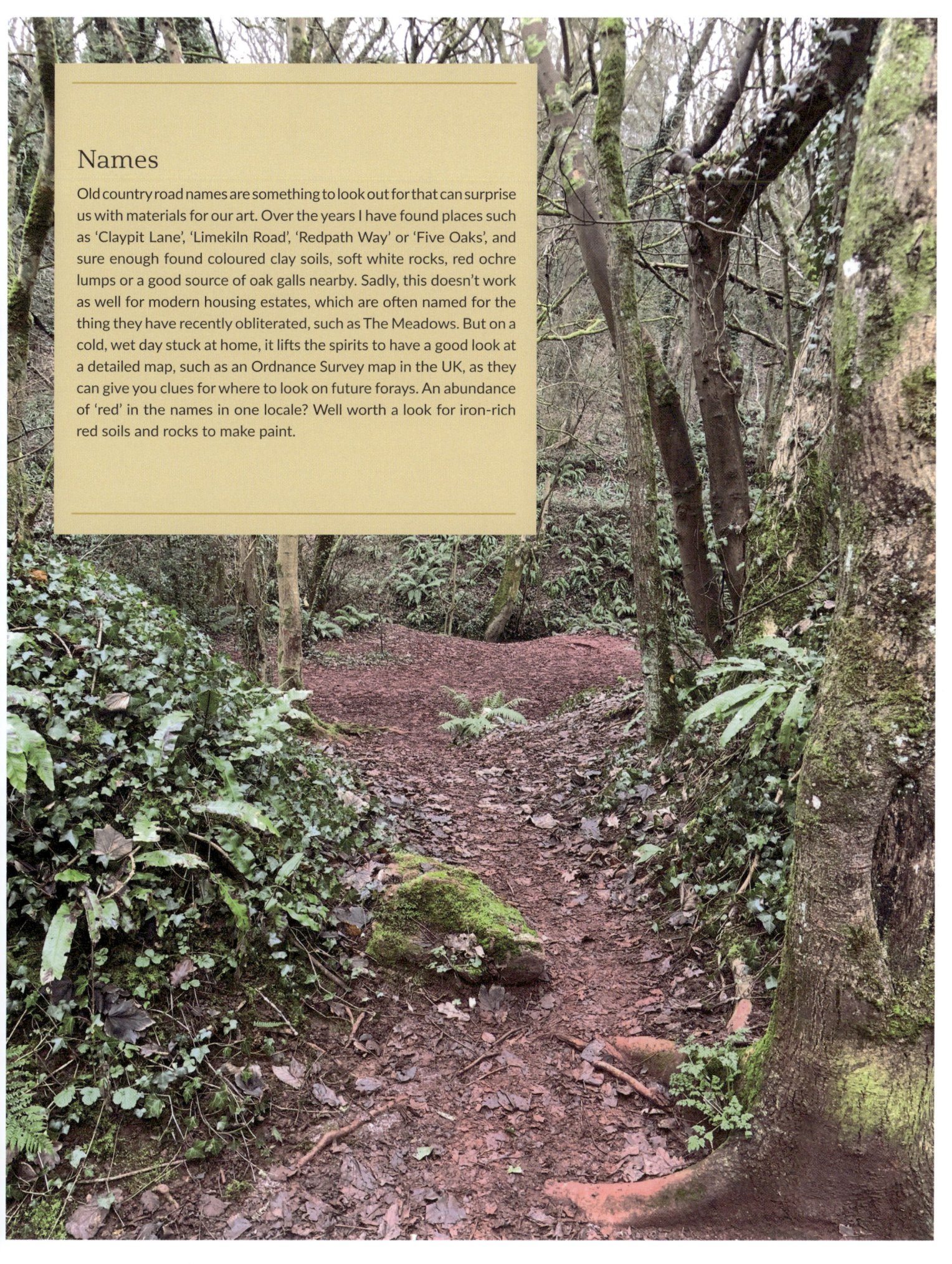

Names

Old country road names are something to look out for that can surprise us with materials for our art. Over the years I have found places such as 'Claypit Lane', 'Limekiln Road', 'Redpath Way' or 'Five Oaks', and sure enough found coloured clay soils, soft white rocks, red ochre lumps or a good source of oak galls nearby. Sadly, this doesn't work as well for modern housing estates, which are often named for the thing they have recently obliterated, such as The Meadows. But on a cold, wet day stuck at home, it lifts the spirits to have a good look at a detailed map, such as an Ordnance Survey map in the UK, as they can give you clues for where to look on future forays. An abundance of 'red' in the names in one locale? Well worth a look for iron-rich red soils and rocks to make paint.

Foraging in edge lands and waste lands

By now you'll have got the idea – almost anywhere can be a great place to forage for pigment and natural art materials. Think of it as learning to be a bit more like a fox or a magpie; finding what's useful amongst what seems of no use. Waste lands, edge lands, urban, suburban and semi-urban places can be like this. Ignored and passed by most people, you can find tree gum, old iron for your rust plant (see page 114), soft crumbly brick for reds, and nice bits of scrap wood on which to paint. Where roads are being dug, there are often spoil piles, and new cuttings are just as full of surprises. If you can safely park up, or walk near, then foraging a little of what has already been dug by others is a very good idea, and a way to reduce your own impact. Mole hills are great for this too; natural diggers, if you find them on good pigmented soil, their little spoil heaps are ready dug and ready to bag.

Don't forget to explore your friends' places, next time you pop by for a coffee. Friends have been amazed when I've pointed out cherry tree gum, colours in their gravel paths or oak galls on their trees that they didn't know they had. No one has yet refused me a little bagful of goodies to take home. Remember your childhood haunts, and favourite parks of your youth. If possible, re-explore them with a pigment hunter's eyes, but with the same sense of adventure you once had.

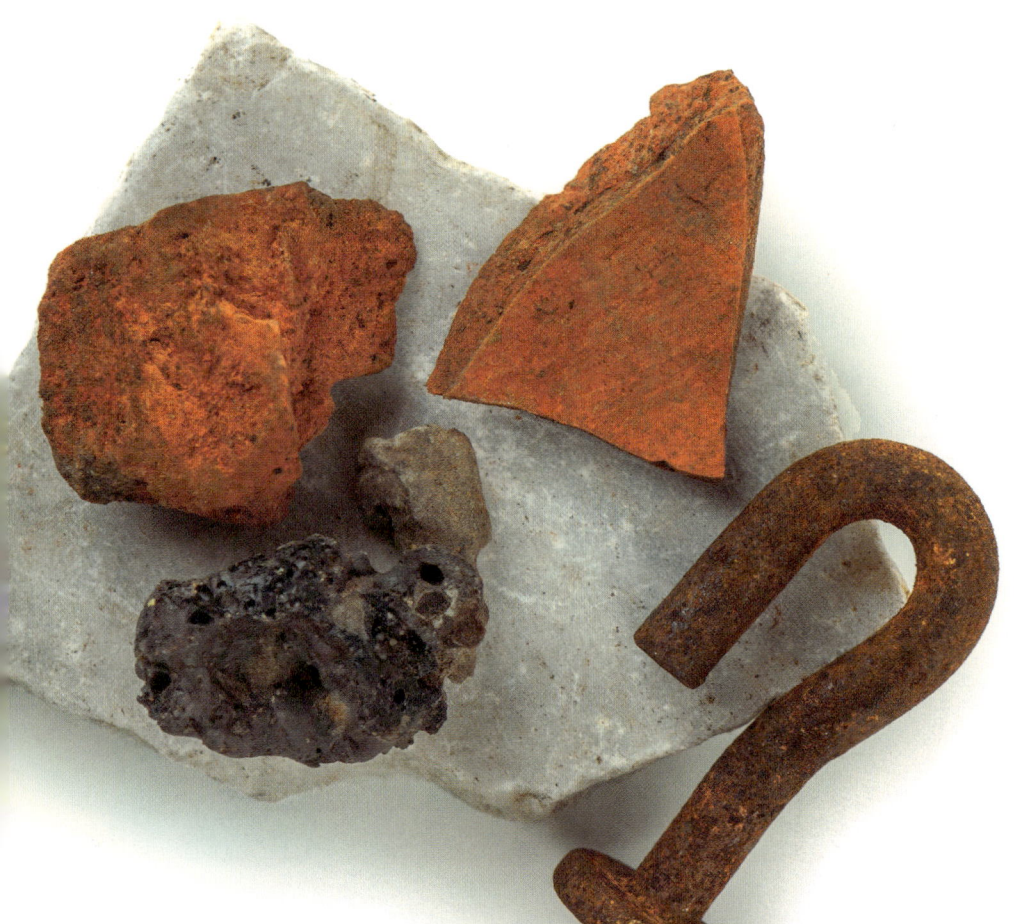

FORAGED FROM EDGE LANDS AND WASTE LANDS

Marble, rusty iron, kiln slag and fired terracotta from a Tunbridge Wells worksite.

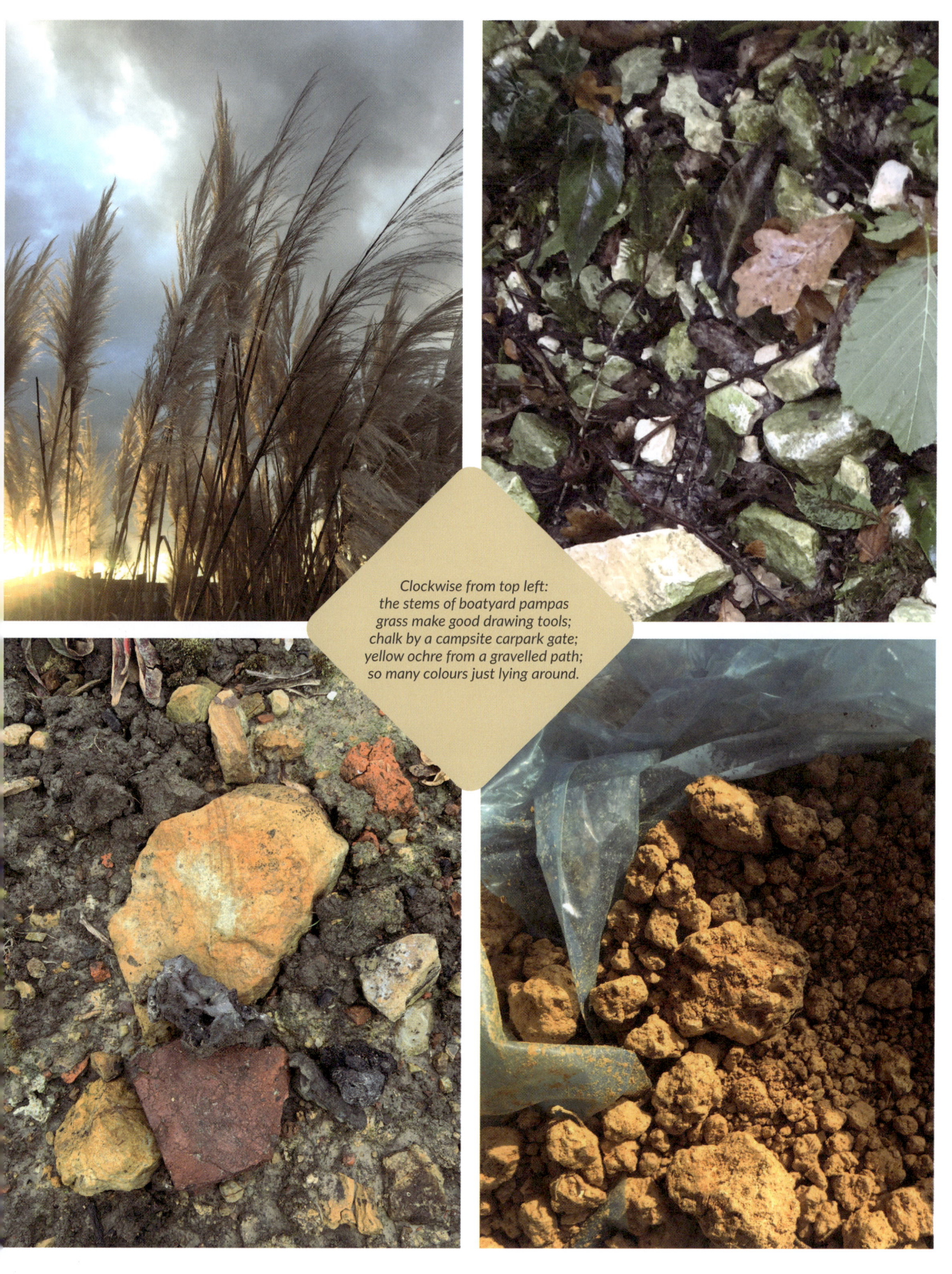

Clockwise from top left:
the stems of boatyard pampas
grass make good drawing tools;
chalk by a campsite carpark gate;
yellow ochre from a gravelled path;
so many colours just lying around.

Colours from edge lands and waste lands

'Waste' lands might be a misnomer – value is in the eye of the beholder. With a little knowledge, these liminal zones between countryside and urban or semi-urbanized areas can provide the forager with rich pickings, such as the examples shown below.

FORAGED OBJECT	PIGMENT	THE RESULTING PAINT

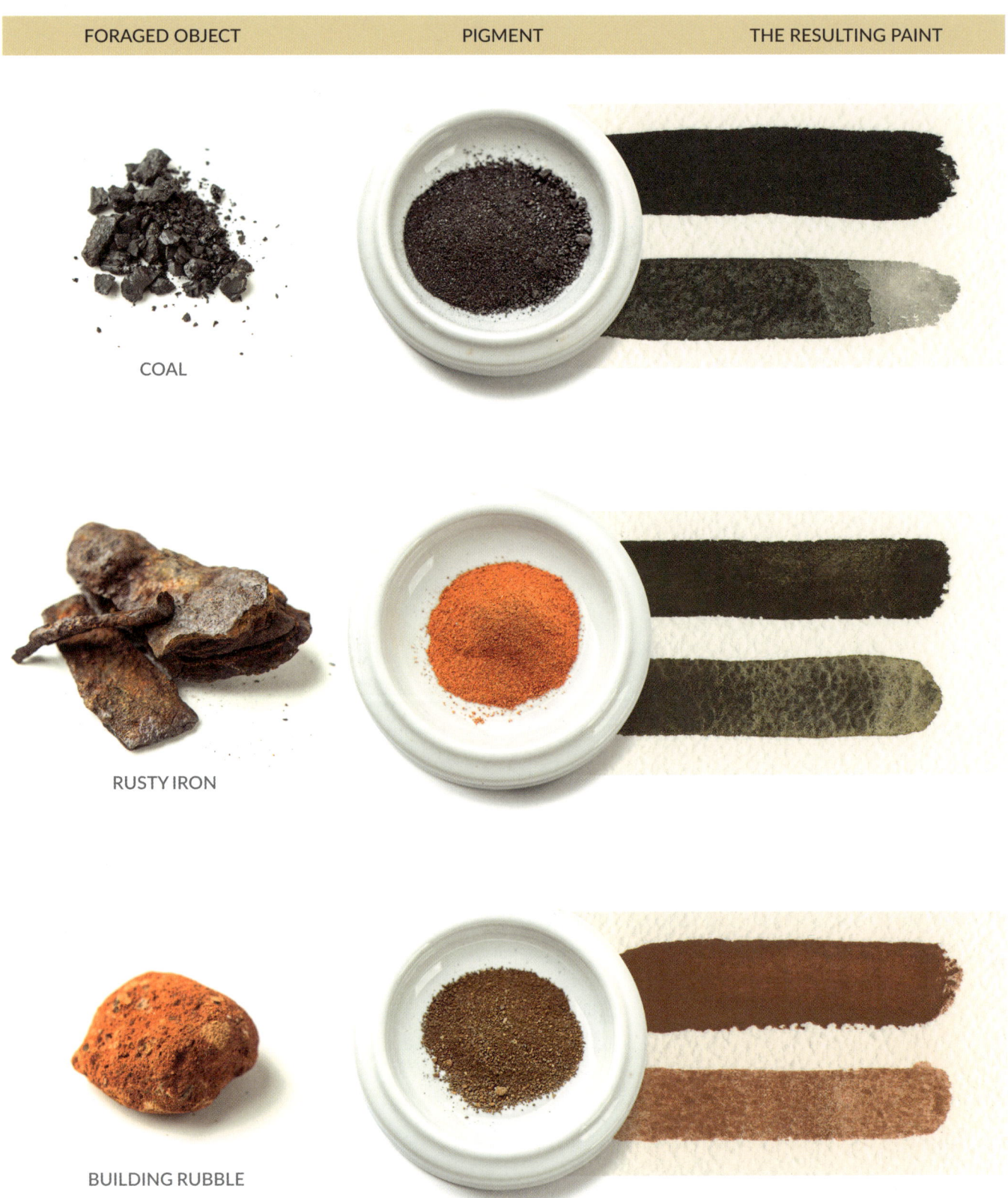

COAL

RUSTY IRON

BUILDING RUBBLE

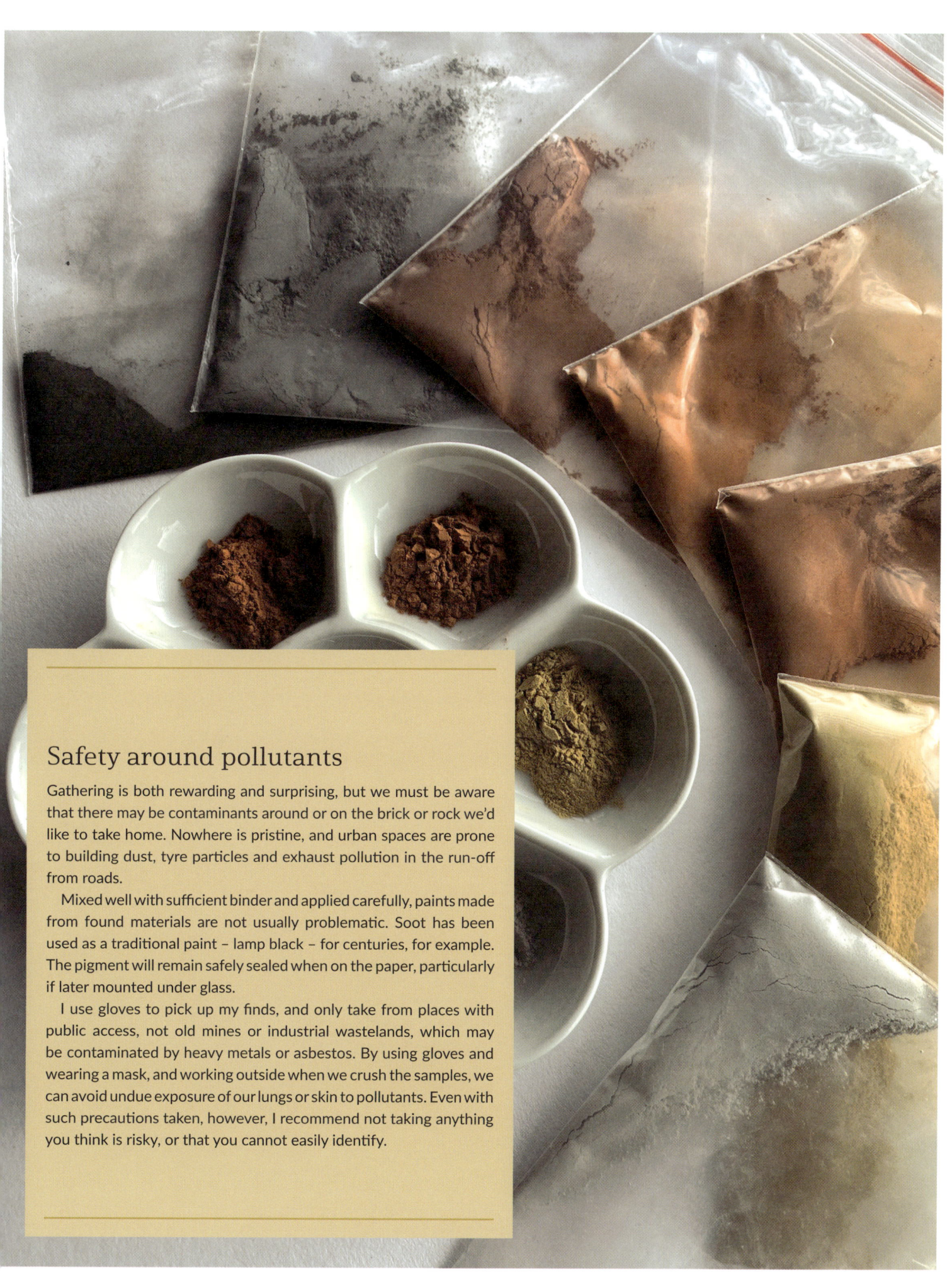

Safety around pollutants

Gathering is both rewarding and surprising, but we must be aware that there may be contaminants around or on the brick or rock we'd like to take home. Nowhere is pristine, and urban spaces are prone to building dust, tyre particles and exhaust pollution in the run-off from roads.

Mixed well with sufficient binder and applied carefully, paints made from found materials are not usually problematic. Soot has been used as a traditional paint – lamp black – for centuries, for example. The pigment will remain safely sealed when on the paper, particularly if later mounted under glass.

I use gloves to pick up my finds, and only take from places with public access, not old mines or industrial wastelands, which may be contaminated by heavy metals or asbestos. By using gloves and wearing a mask, and working outside when we crush the samples, we can avoid undue exposure of our lungs or skin to pollutants. Even with such precautions taken, however, I recommend not taking anything you think is risky, or that you cannot easily identify.

Foraging near fresh water

Freshwater features such as lochs, fjords, lakes or ponds, riverbanks and canal sides each have their own treasures. Safety around water is important, especially near deep or cold water, so be aware of any risks in terrain or weather.

Gently shelving edges down to lakes are great places to find small stones of the local geology and to test them against harder rocks. Ponds often form in clay areas, and some clays can give beautiful hues with which to make paint. Clay needs little work to turn into pigments as the particle sizes are already very fine, and just a little sieving or washing can be enough. Coloured clays are some of the earliest paints and body adornments humans used. Even other creatures love to be covered in mud: pigs, hippos and elephants share our love of a clay skin bath. Feeling the silky texture of clays between your fingers when you dig a little for paint is not to be missed.

Along rivers and streams in or near cities there is sometimes pollution, so it's important to do a little research or a recce first of all. River banks are good for finding unusual stones, interesting objects with which to make palettes or brushes. I collect most of the goose and swan feathers I use for quill pens along the upper reaches of the Thames and the Stour when the birds moult in early summer. The long flight feathers are best for this. I also find mussel shells for palettes.

In many places there are no specific rules about finding things on the banks of a river. On the tidal Thames in London, however, 'mudlarking' is regulated, and you need a permit. Mudlarking is the name given to the ancient and ongoing practice of searching the Thames foreshore for items as varied as garnets, flint, old clay pipes, coins, even Roman roof tiles, still bearing the thumb prints of their maker.

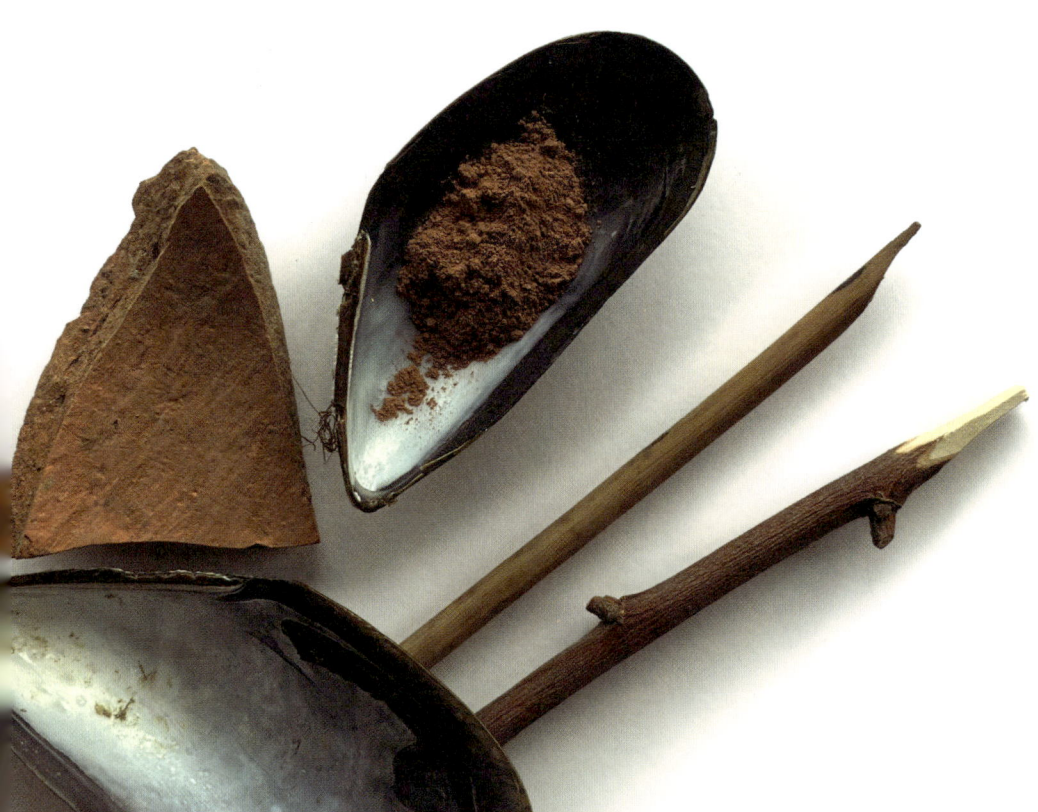

FORAGED NEAR FRESH WATER

Sticks and reeds for pens, mussels for palettes and a potsherd – the pigment from the potsherd is shown in one of the mussel shells.

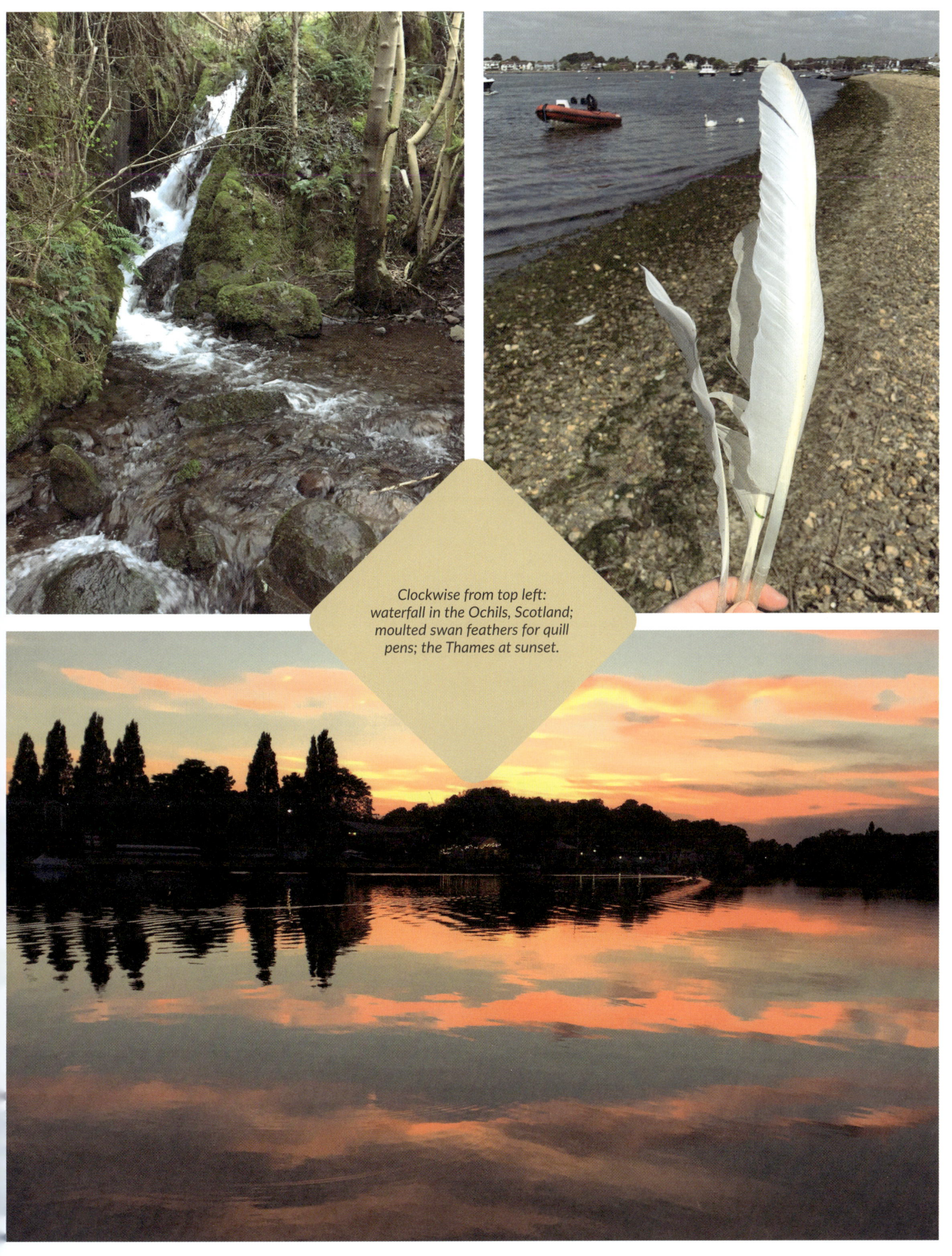

Clockwise from top left: waterfall in the Ochils, Scotland; moulted swan feathers for quill pens; the Thames at sunset.

Colours from fresh water

Besides offering an abundance of riches in terms of colour, you'll have great river- or lakeside scenery if you like to paint and draw from life. Painting a landscape with the materials that make it is always rewarding.

FORAGED OBJECT	PIGMENT	THE RESULTING PAINT

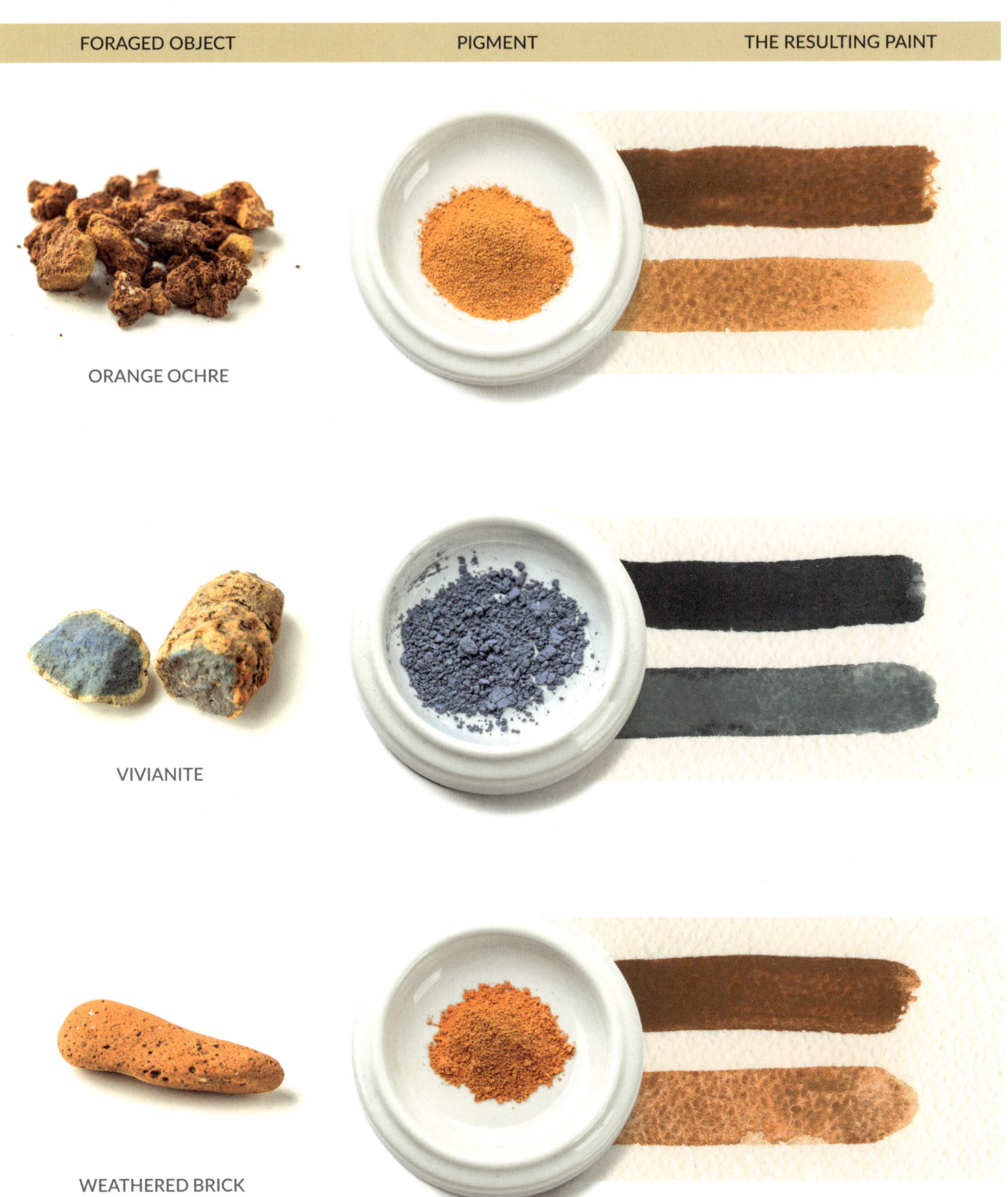

ORANGE OCHRE

VIVIANITE

WEATHERED BRICK

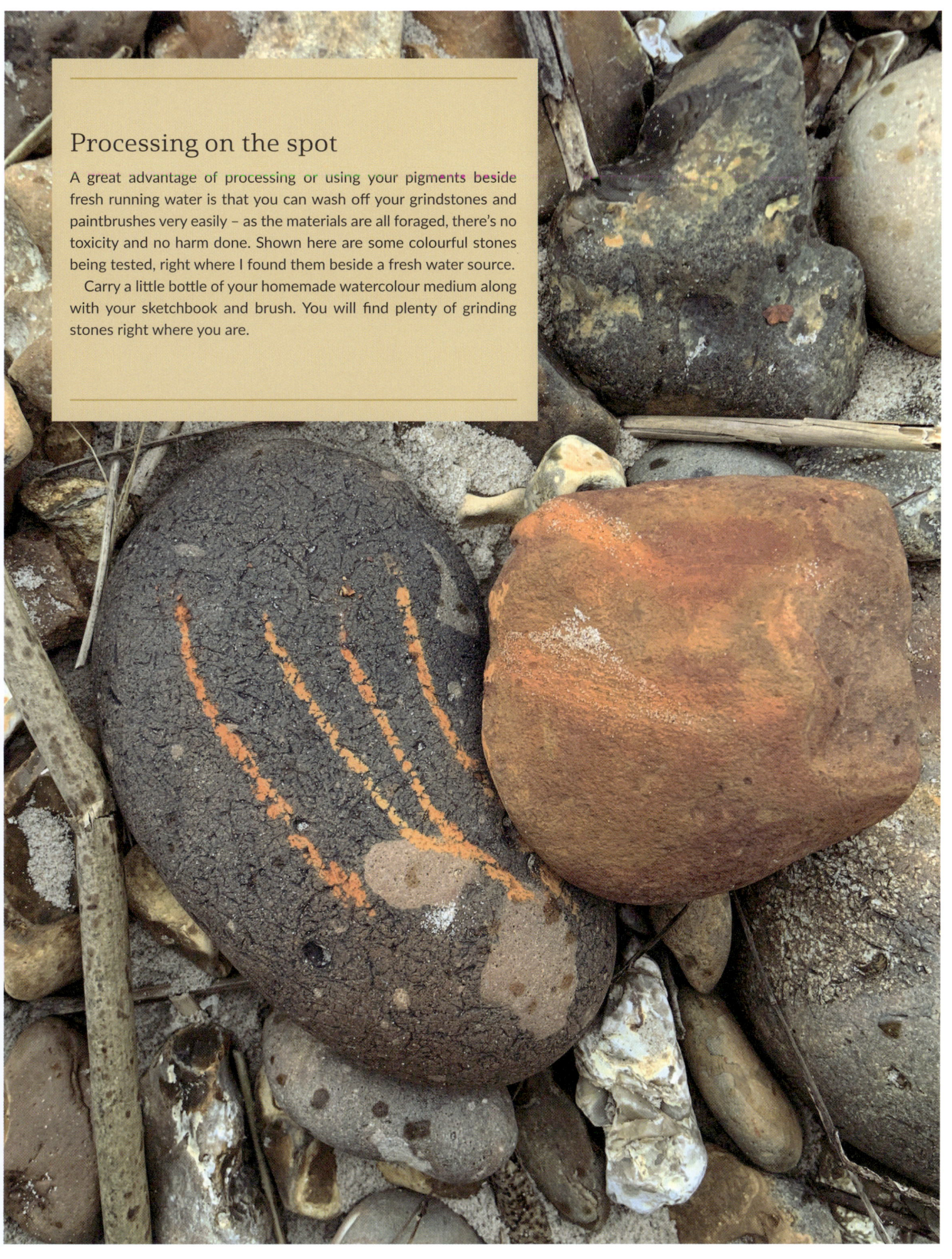

Processing on the spot

A great advantage of processing or using your pigments beside fresh running water is that you can wash off your grindstones and paintbrushes very easily – as the materials are all foraged, there's no toxicity and no harm done. Shown here are some colourful stones being tested, right where I found them beside a fresh water source.

Carry a little bottle of your homemade watercolour medium along with your sketchbook and brush. You will find plenty of grinding stones right where you are.

Store cupboard

Before rushing out to the shops to buy a few things we might need to make paint, it is worth looking in our food cupboards to see what's already there. Many of the natural basics of good paints are the same ingredients that people have used to bind or thicken foods for thousands of years. For the watercolours we'll be making in this book, you can use some of these things from your kitchen stores.

Eggs Egg yolk can be used to make tempera paint, a glossy, versatile, long-lasting, traditional European paint; ideal for use on gesso panels and other hard surfaces, but also adaptable to good-quality medium to heavy-weight paper. Egg whites can be used to make glair, a matt, transparent medium that is great for use with our earth pigments – and, if sprayed with a diffuser, also an excellent natural sealant for pastels and other looser media. I use organic and free range, or eggs from my friend's hens when I can get them, along with a little vinegar. Egg shells can be washed, ground down and used as a beautiful natural white, a little less bright than chalk or marble dust, but they make a good addition to other colours to create paler tints.

Vegan alternatives to eggs include all the 'bean waters' and aquafaba which is the cooking water of chickpeas or any white beans, such as cannellini, haricot or butter beans.

Gum Arabic A common ingredient in cuisines from across India, parts of Asia and the Middle East as well as being used by western confectioners, this is an almost colourless gum derived from acacia trees. Gum Arabic thickens sweets, makes glazes and emulsifies mixtures. Sold as 'gum gar goond' or 'char goond', gum Arabic can be inexpensively bought in powder or lump form online or in specialist shops. Artist's quality gum is supposedly paler and finer, but I have found no such difference myself in use.

Milk, plant milks, cheese and curds All produce great wall paints, casein paint, and washes. Regular flour can make wheat paste paints, and several other starchy flours can too. Gelling ingredients such as cooks' gelatine, agar gum and other vegetarian jelly powders can create wonderful binders, printing ink bases and more. I forage for common edible seaweeds such as carragheen, and, once dried, if they have been a little too long in my cupboard, they migrate to my art shelf where they are boiled to extract a clear gel for paint, so that nothing is wasted.

Tallow, lard, deer fat and other hard white fats These parts of the organic meat and wild game which I eat become the most traditional paints of all. Mixed with ochre and used on rock or hard surfaces, these are truly the nearest we get to 'cave paint'.

Isinglass This fish air bladder glue is commonly used by home-brewers to clear wines and beers but was also used by illuminators of manuscripts for over a thousand years as a fine, clear paint binder.

Edible drying oils These include linseed (flax) oil and poppy seed oil. Although the culinary product is lighter, more fluid, and obtained from different varieties than specially produced oils for artists, they are still useful in recipes for the thrifty foraging artist.

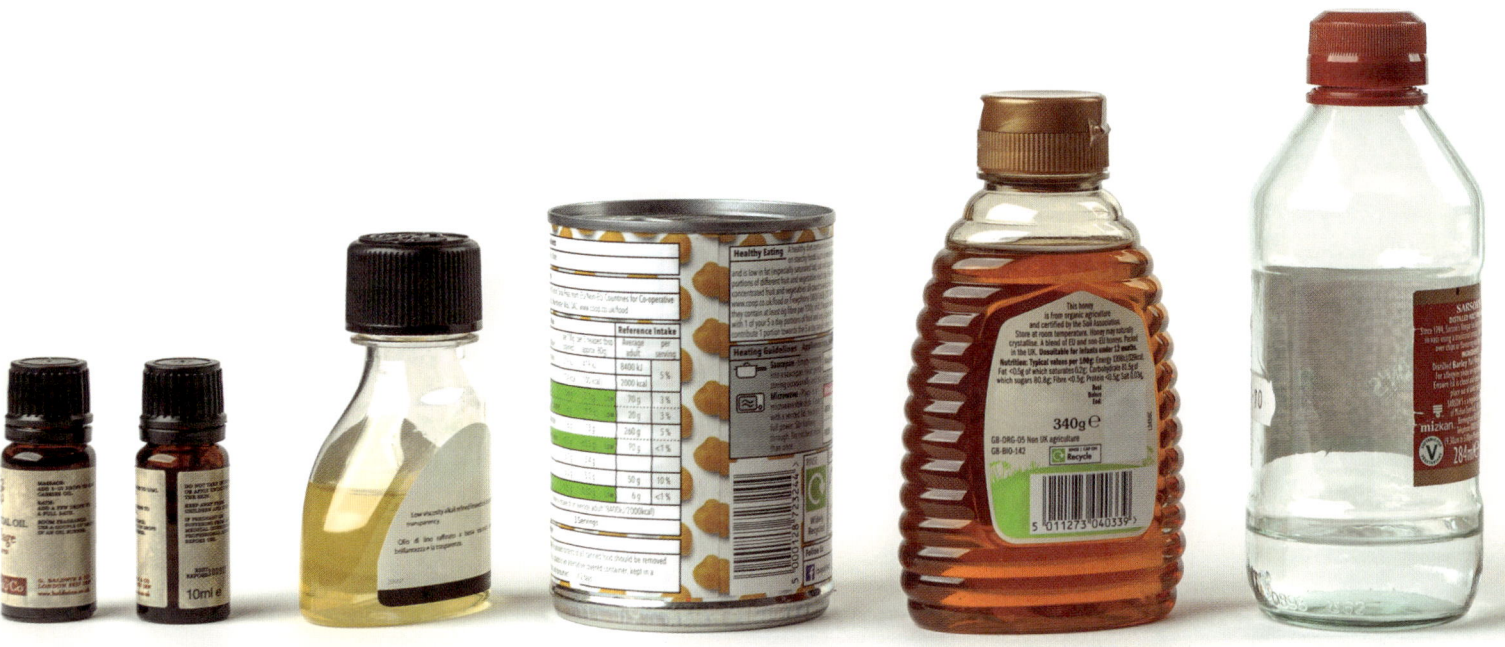

Runny honey This wonderful ingredient makes a good paint medium with water in its own right, but when mixed with gums to make watercolours, it allows re-wetting of the paint, so that you can return to your dried pan of paint, add water, and paint another day, without having to scrub away with a brush.

Vegan alternatives to runny honey include agave syrup, which is pale and runs just like honey; sugar syrup, a clear colourless confectioner's product; and plain sugar itself, whether granulated or fine powdered. These will all help with re-wetting the paint.

Some honey comes with cut comb in the container, which looks lovely but is often wasted. I wash and save any wax comb from gifts of local honey I buy, to melt it down to make a variety of art painting media, as a resist on paper for watercolour washes, and for wax crayons. It's worth noting that I never forage honeycomb in the wild if I see it – bees have a hard enough time as it is, so I like to leave their tree stump homes intact.

I hope this inspires you to explore your own traditional cuisine, and your home store cupboards, with fresh eyes, as you may find a smorgasbord of rarely used, back-of-the-pantry ingredients that could make great paints, and which now won't go to waste.

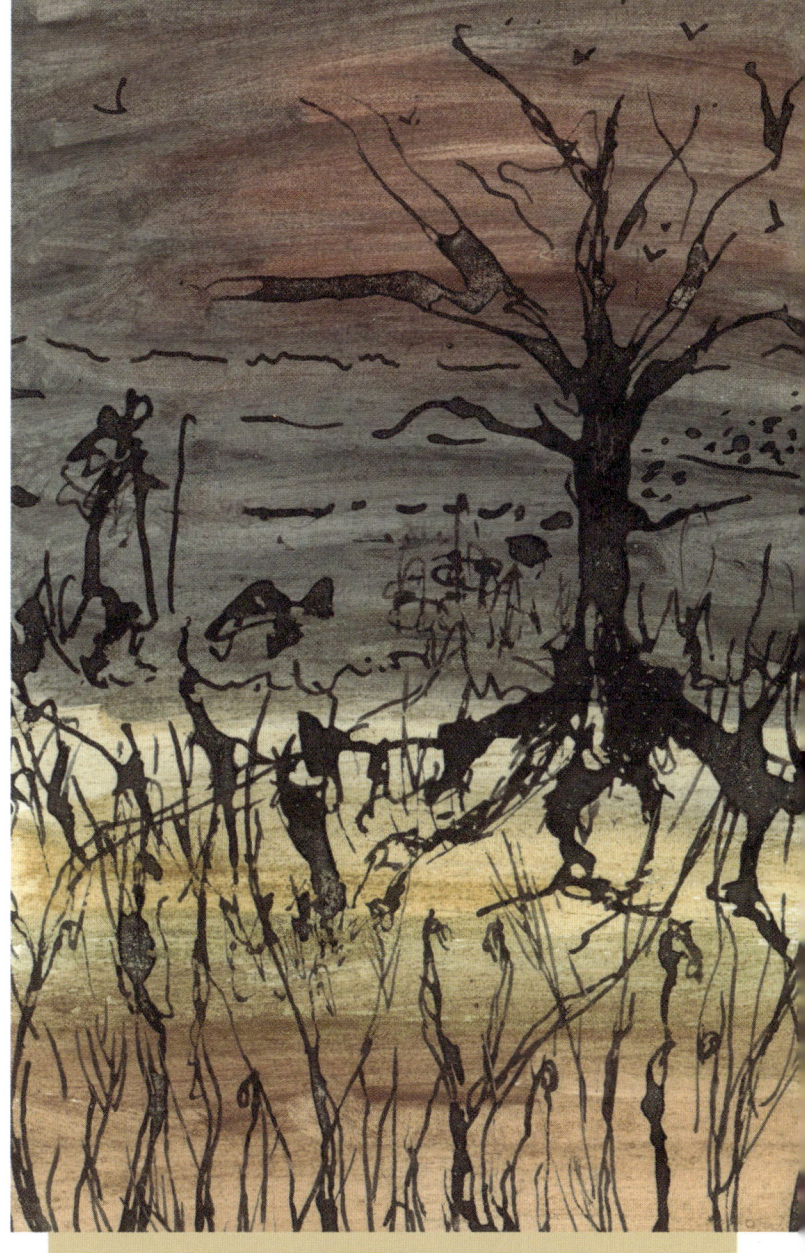

THROUGH THE FENS AT SUNSET
20 x 28cm (7¾ x 11in)
Ochre watercolours and iron gall ink.
The ochres for this painting were mixed with gum Arabic, honey and water to make very simple washes as a background for the black ink drawing, made with a quill pen.

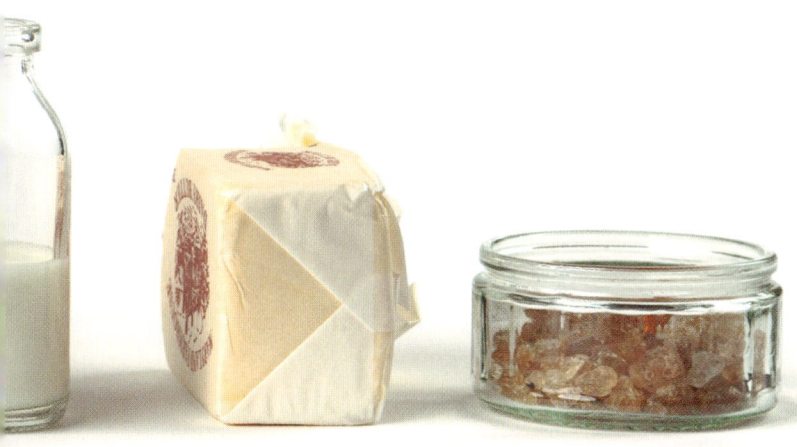

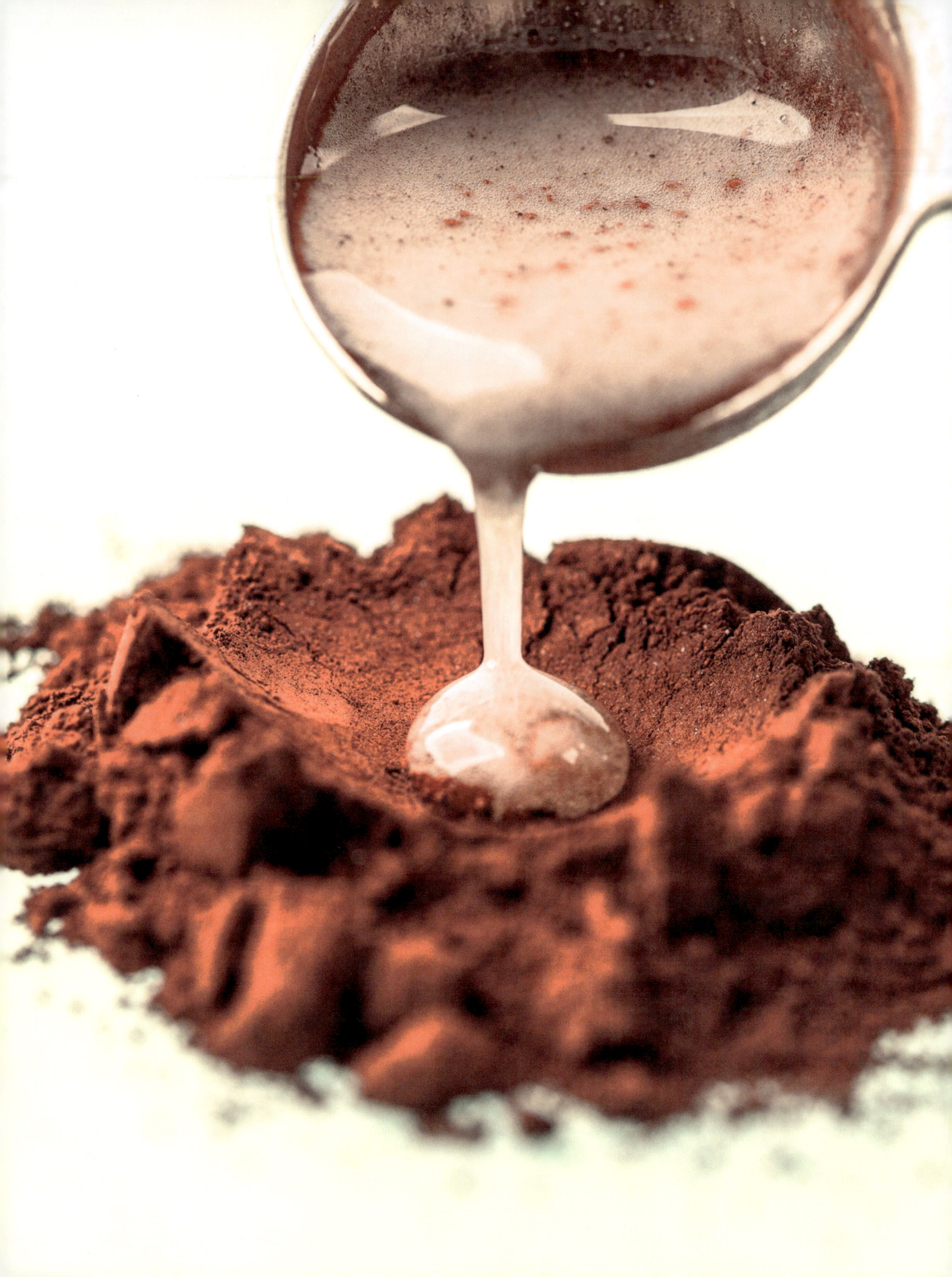

MAKING USE OF YOUR FINDS

In this chapter you'll learn how to make use of your finds and turn what you've foraged into pigments, one of the vital ingredients for paint. Step by step we will transform your finds, which might be lumpy, hard, gritty or raw, into the fine powder that we need. We'll start by smashing, then move on to grinding, sieving, and more.

All your senses will be involved, and you might become as addicted to making pigments as you are to making art. Pigment-making is a sensory delight: tactile, owing to its many textures; aural, the sounds change dramatically as we smash and grind; visual, as the colours brighten or deepen; even olfactory, when we work with earthy clays or charred wood.

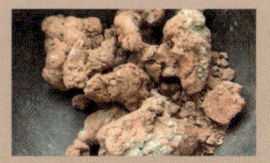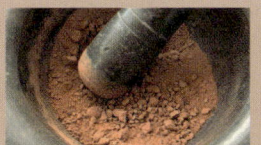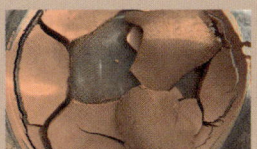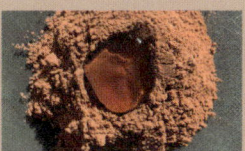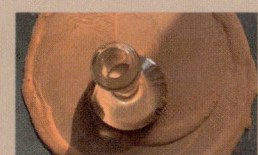

REFINING

The chapter is arranged and numbered in the order we will use to transform the materials, from breaking up the large stones to storing the resulting powder. Sometimes there will be a simple or ancient method as well as a more refined technique – and we'll look at both. Not all materials will need to be refined in the same way. You won't always need to use every stage: washing isn't always necessary, for example, if sieving results in a sufficiently clean, bright pigment.

Finding your way to making pigment from what you have found should be intuitive, as our ancestors have been doing this for tens of thousands of years. I've taught experienced fine artists, children as young as five, and adults who were previously convinced they didn't have an artistic or practical bone in their bodies how to make pigments and paints using these tried and tested methods. So, go and get your old clothes on: we're going to smash things up!

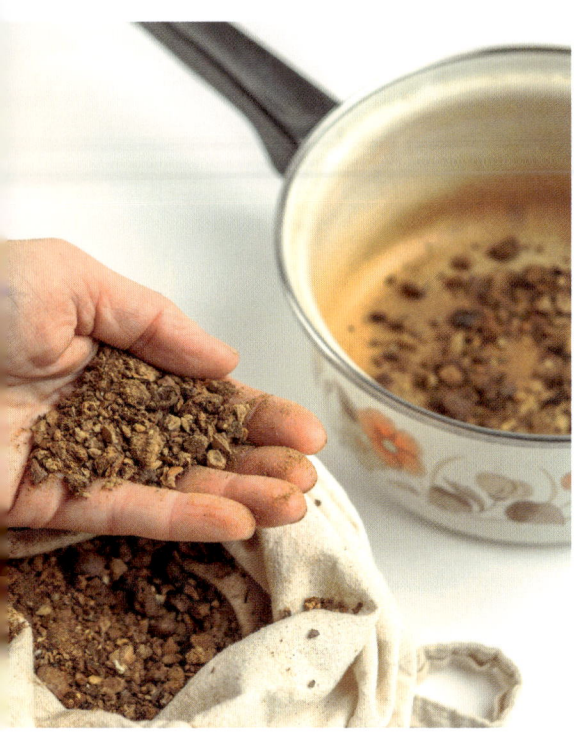

Refining tools

To refine raw materials into pigment, we need nothing more than ordinary kitchen or household items. These lists are not exhaustive; if you have something to hand that seems suitable, then give it a try. Once you have used kitchen equipment for pigment-making, don't use it for cookery. Store your paint tools in a different place from your culinary ones, to prevent mix-ups. I have included one or two art studio tools which will make your work more enjoyable and effective if you catch the pigment bug.

Tools for smashing A big rock and a concrete slab outdoors, brass pestle and mortar, wooden rolling pin and cloth bags or old pillow cases, lump hammer, mallet.

Tools for grinding Large and small stone pestles and mortars, pebbles with one flat side, slates and flat stone slabs, ridged grinding or milling stones, such as those once used for turning corn, acorns or chestnuts into flour.

Tools for sieving Stainless steel kitchen sieves and strainers, cotton muslin cloth. Advanced tools would be second-hand geologist's screens, which are very practical flat sieves with accurately graded steel mesh, to grade finer pigment particle sizes.

Tools for washing Washable jugs, cleaned repurposed plastic food packaging containers of a variety of sizes, lidded glass jars with shoulders (i.e. not straight-sided), spoons.

Tools for drying Funnels, recycled paper coffee filters, fine cotton cloths such as old handkerchiefs or tea towels, trays, newspaper or scrap paper, turkey baster, stiff, bristled clean brush (round stencil brushes or pastry brushes are ideal).

Tools for mixing Steel bowl, flexible spatula, spoons, a clean stick, pipette or dropper.

Tools for mulling Toughened glass kitchen worktop saver or chopping board, stone or marble slab (these can often be found in thrift stores and are sometimes sold for serving cheese), pickle weights or flat-bottomed jar/glass/small vase/paperweight/flat-bottomed stone. My friend Catalina Christensen uses an old vintage metal iron, of the cast-iron kind, which used to be warmed in the fire. If you get into making paint, then an artists' quality ground glass muller and slab are ideal.

Tools for storing Repurposed lidded jars, phials and glass containers of different sizes, stackable lidded clear plastic pots, sticky labels and a permanent marker.

Protective wear: PPE

Make sure you have access to a well ventilated and easily cleaned space: outdoors is ideal. Whenever you are working with dry or dusty materials, wear a mask. A well-fitting cloth or surgical style mask is usually adequate, but a good mask with a filter is better. Latex or close-fitting gloves of the kind you might use when painting or changing oil in a car are perfect. Simple goggles or large clear glasses can be worn while smashing materials, to avoid eye damage by any flying particles. Protect your clothes with an apron or overalls, or designate some old items as painting clothes. Whatever you choose, it needs to be easily washable, as we don't want to bring dust and fine powder into our homes.

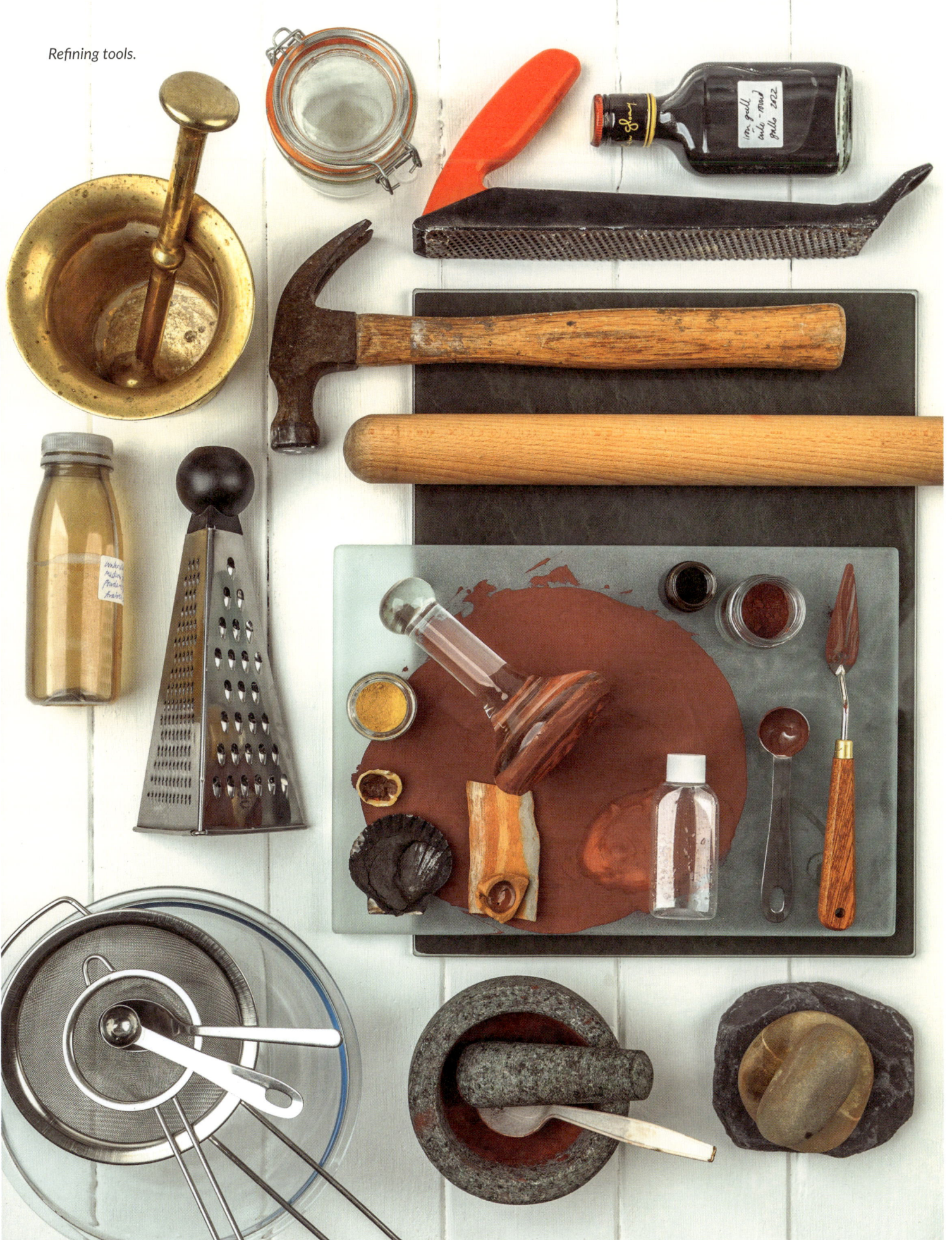

Refining tools.

1 Smashing

Wear a mask and goggles or glasses, and put on your work clothes. Work outside or in a very well ventilated area which is easy to clean up afterwards, to avoid spreading or breathing in fine particles.

Smashing with stones

A stone is suitable for simple, impromptu or outdoor processing of rocks, brick bits and other larger pieces. You'll need a clean stone or concrete slab on which to work.

Smashing with a hammer

Slightly more controllable than a stone, a hammer is ideal for working smaller samples.

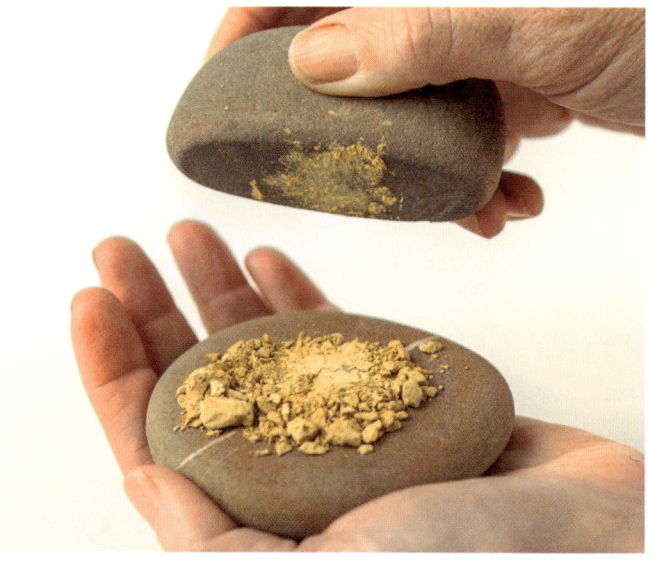

Place the material on one flat stone and firmly bring the other down – think of them as hammer and anvil.

It's a good idea to place the stones on a large piece of smooth paper to more easily collect the powder after grinding.

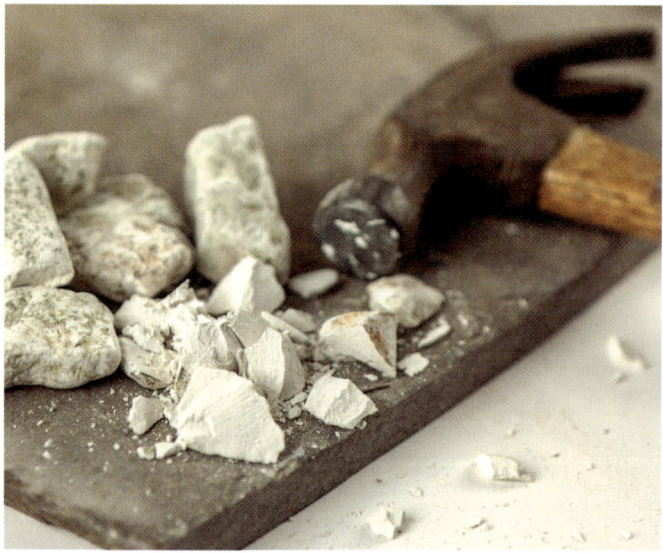

Smashing with a hammer is as simple as placing your material on a hard surface and hitting it! Start gently, and be aware of splinters or shards as you work.

Smashing with a pestle and mortar

A stone mortar (the dished receptacle) is fine for clays, soft crumbly rocks and charcoal, but can break if used with harder stones. A brass mortar, being metal, is less brittle and better able to handle hard stones.

Smashing with a rolling pin and cloth bag

Ideal for smashing up oak galls into the smaller-sized bits we'll need later for ink. Warning – it's extremely enjoyable and therapeutic!

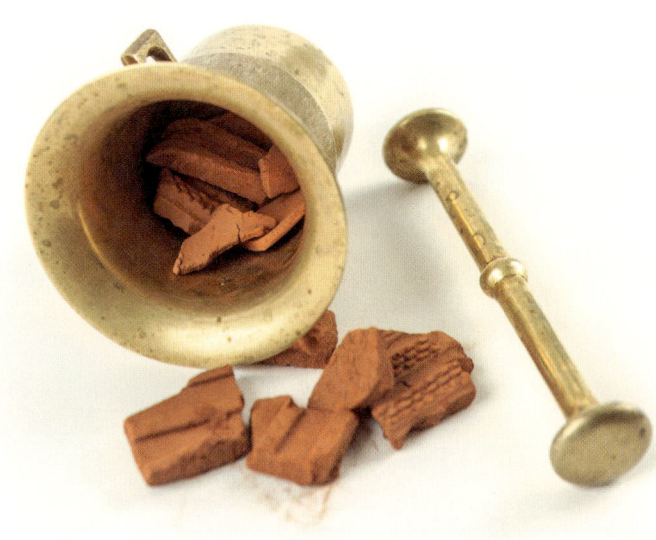

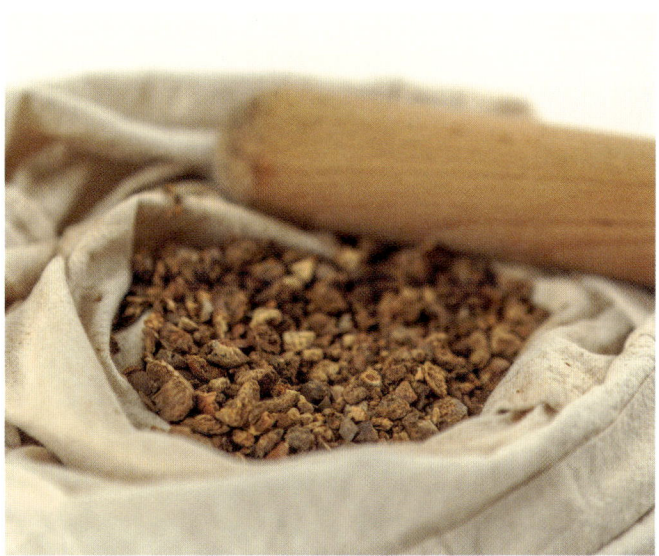

1 Fit your cloth mask and wear an apron or washable work clothes. Take one of your softer rocks and place them in the bowl of your brass pestle and mortar.

2 Place this, and your hand, inside a spacious net or cloth bag, and tie it loosely around your wrist.

3 Supporting the pestle from outside with the other hand, smash downwards with the mortar until the lump breaks up into smaller pieces. Continue until it is as fine as you can get it.

4 Let the dust settle for a minute, then carefully decant the smashed rock powder into a jar if washing it immediately, or into a sieve, if sieving it first.

1 Place all of the materials you want to smash into a cloth bag and seal the opening by gathering it or folding it over – this will stop any small parts or debris coming out.

2 Place the bag on a flat, solid surface, and repeatedly hit the bag. The more you work, the finer the resulting material – so check on it every so often. Just remember to seal the opening again before you begin.

3 Carefully pour out the results into a container.

Grinding

Most pigments need grinding down to a finer powder after smashing reduces the large mass to a manageable size. Wear a mask if you are going to use dry pigments. Pigments are best ground after smashing them, or you'll spend ages with the pestle and mortar, using more effort than needed.

We can grind most things with a little water and avoid dust altogether; though you can keep them dry (or leave them to dry after grinding) if you sieve them afterwards. Whether you work dry or with a little water added, keep working until you get all the lumps ground down. You may find little stones or sand particles, which will come out at the next stage.

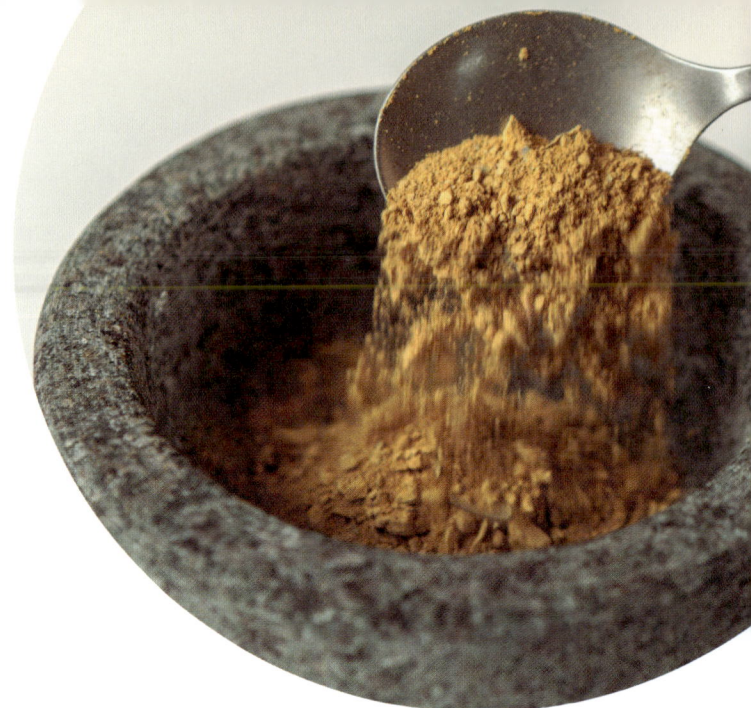

Grinding with a pestle and mortar

Once smashed small enough, we can continue the grinding process with large or small stone pestles and mortars. These ancient tools, unchanged for thousands of years, are found the world over. To avoid dust rising, I recommended placing the whole pestle and mortar inside a cloth bag so that it and your hand are enclosed while you work. One friend uses an old ski sock!

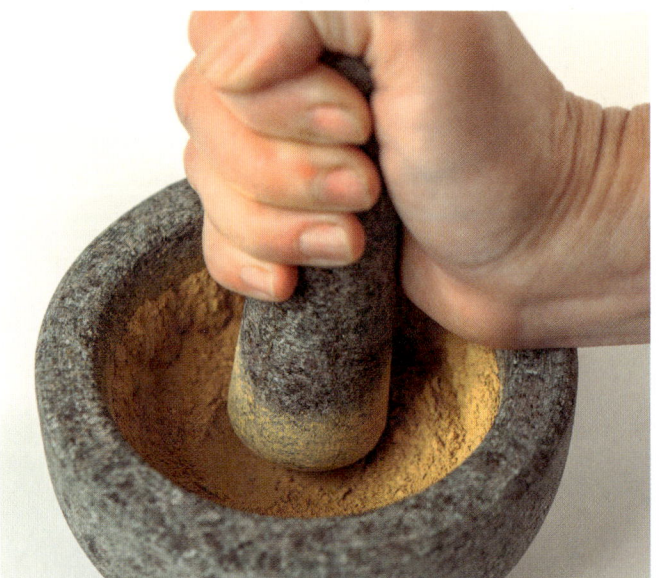

1 Place the smashed earth into the mortar. Use the pestle to grind the lumps down into a finer consistency.

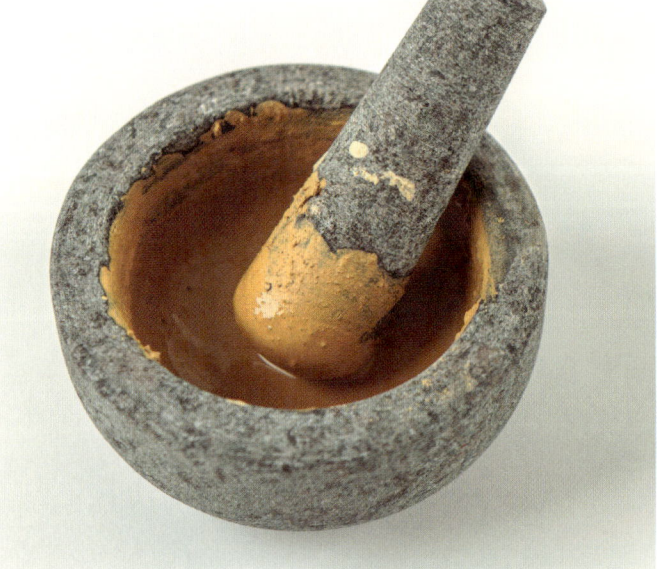

2 Add just enough water to turn the pigment into a paste to prevent dust or if you know that you will wash (levigate) the pigment – see page 67 for more on washing.

Grinding with stones

Pebbles with one flat side, slates and flat stone slabs, ridged grinding or milling stones... using simple stone on stone tools is great fun, and a sure way to feel admiration and respect for our ancestors. Work wet by adding a little water, as without the enclosed sides of a pestle and mortar, this can be somewhat dusty.

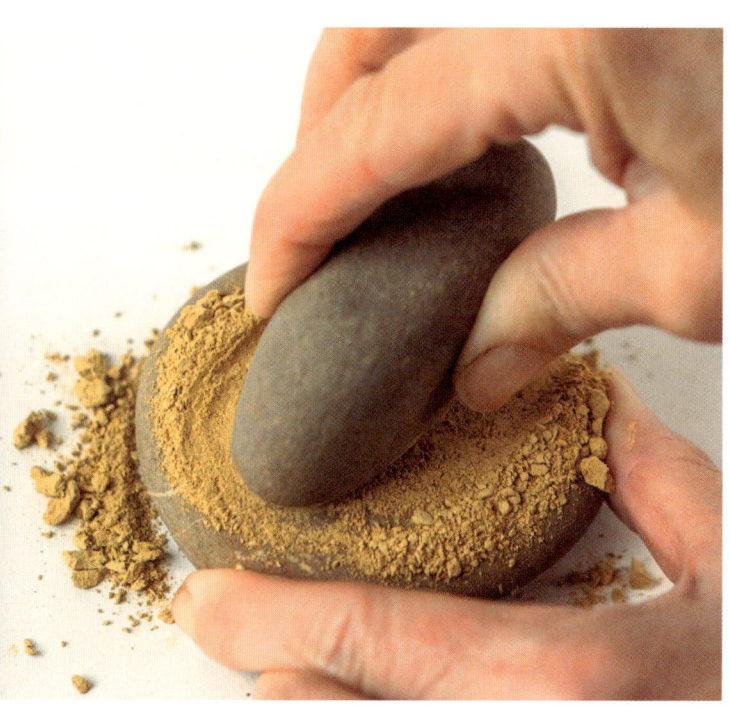 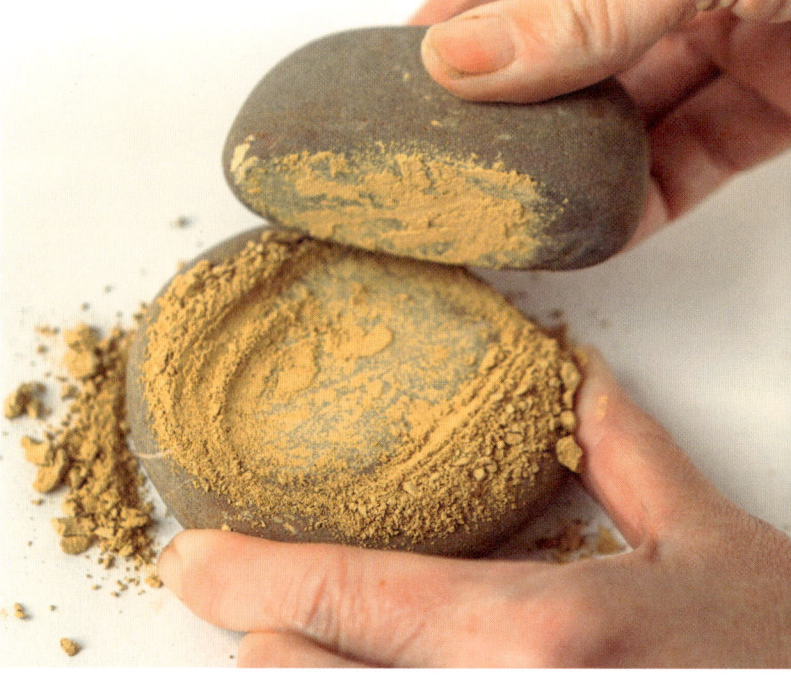

3 Sieving

Sieving will help to remove the little stones, vegetable matter or other inclusions from your ground materials, to give a purer pigment before you wash them. As when grinding, it's important to wear a mask when sieving dry pigments.

When working with chalk, charcoal, and similar fine soft rocks, sieving will often refine the pigment enough that you can skip the washing process (see page 67), as it's unnecessary.

Using a sieve

Stainless steel kitchen-type sieves and strainers: Place your sieve or screen over a container big enough to collect all the pigment. Gently tap or rub the powder through the mesh, as you would with flour when baking. This can also be done inside a fine cloth bag to prevent dust. Stones and grit remaining from this process can be safely added to your garden or gravel path.

Using a geologist's screen

These flat metal sieves can be bought online new or second-hand. I use a selection between 250-micron and 100-micron sizes. This will allow only very fine particles through and can be used to make fine pigment quickly in small quantities without the need for washing. Good pigment will still remain after this process, so you can move on to the washing stage with what remains.

As an alternative to a screen, you can use cotton muslin cloth for a finer improvised sieve, by adding a layer of muslin over a strainer.

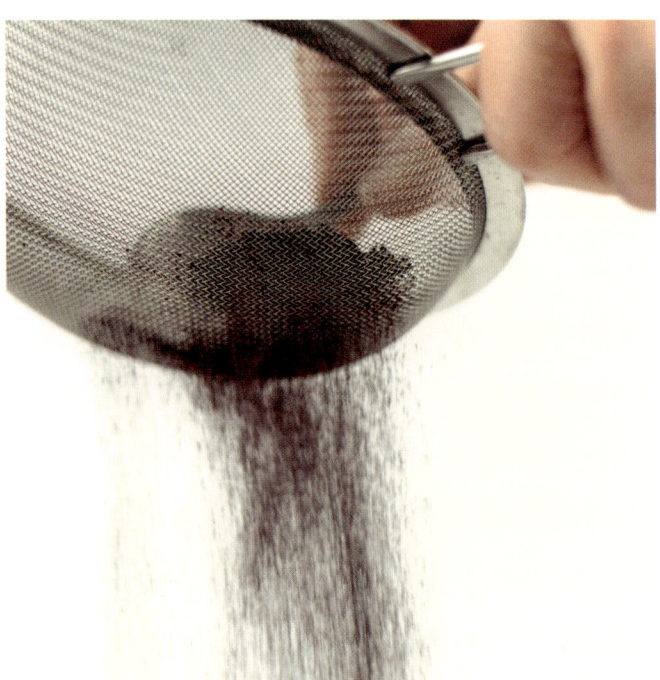

Add ground earth to sieve and use the back of a spoon to gently encourage it through the mesh, leaving larger particles and organic elements behind.

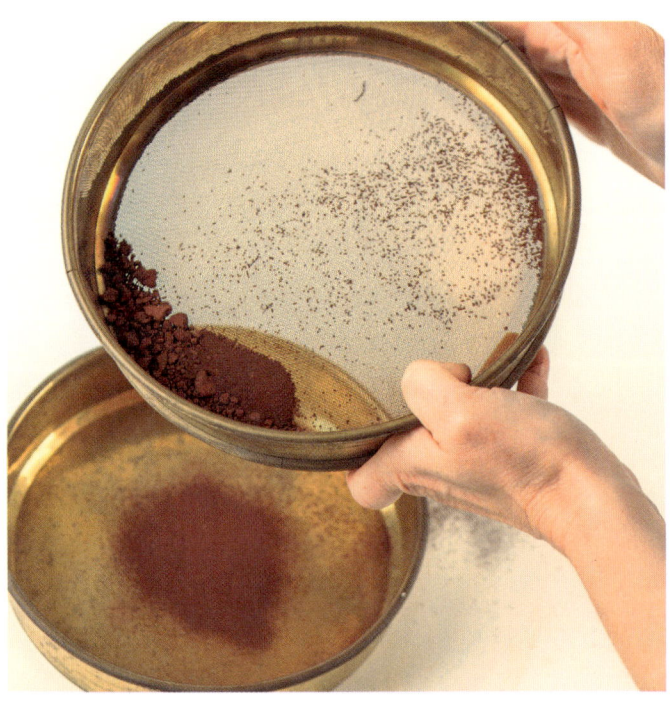

Add the ground earth into the screen and gently tap the side like a tambourine.

Washing

If you have obtained a clean, bright pigment from sieving, you can skip this step. If, however, you find there is still soil, vegetable matter or dull coloured rock in your colour, washing can help. For this stage, you'll need to gather at least four large glass jars, with lids, of the kind with a 'shoulder' – that is, not straight-sided.

Once you have ground your material to at least as fine as sand, and have either sieved it when dry, or have it as a paste in a little water already, you are ready to wash the pigment to separate the various sizes of particles. The fine sediments remaining at the bottom of the jars after washing are your pigments. These can then be dried, combined and stored for use.

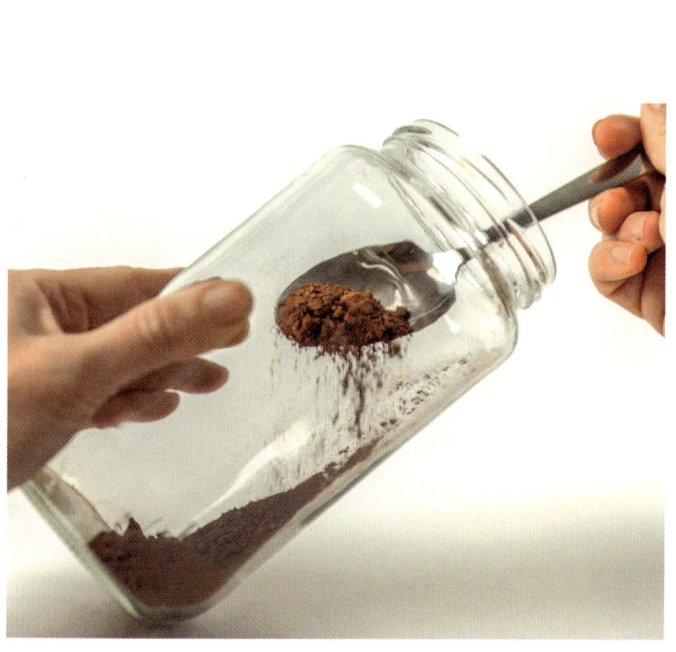

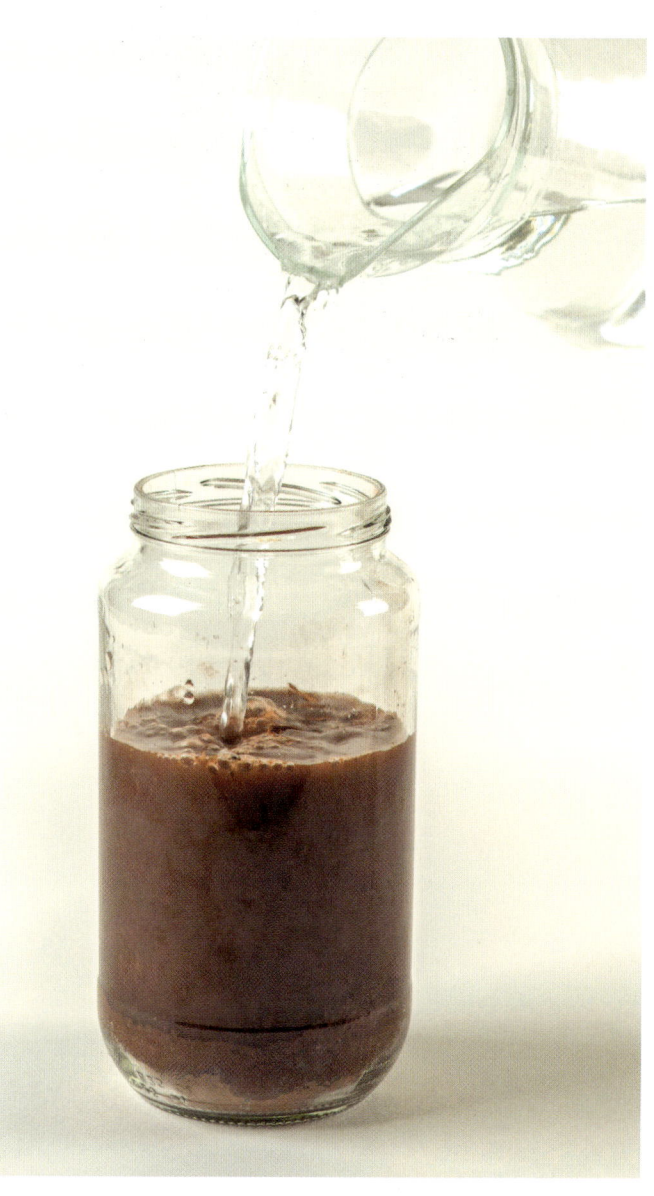

1 In the largest jar with a lid, place all the pigment from your bowl. It doesn't matter whether it is wet or dry.

2 Add enough water to fill the jar to about three-quarters full.

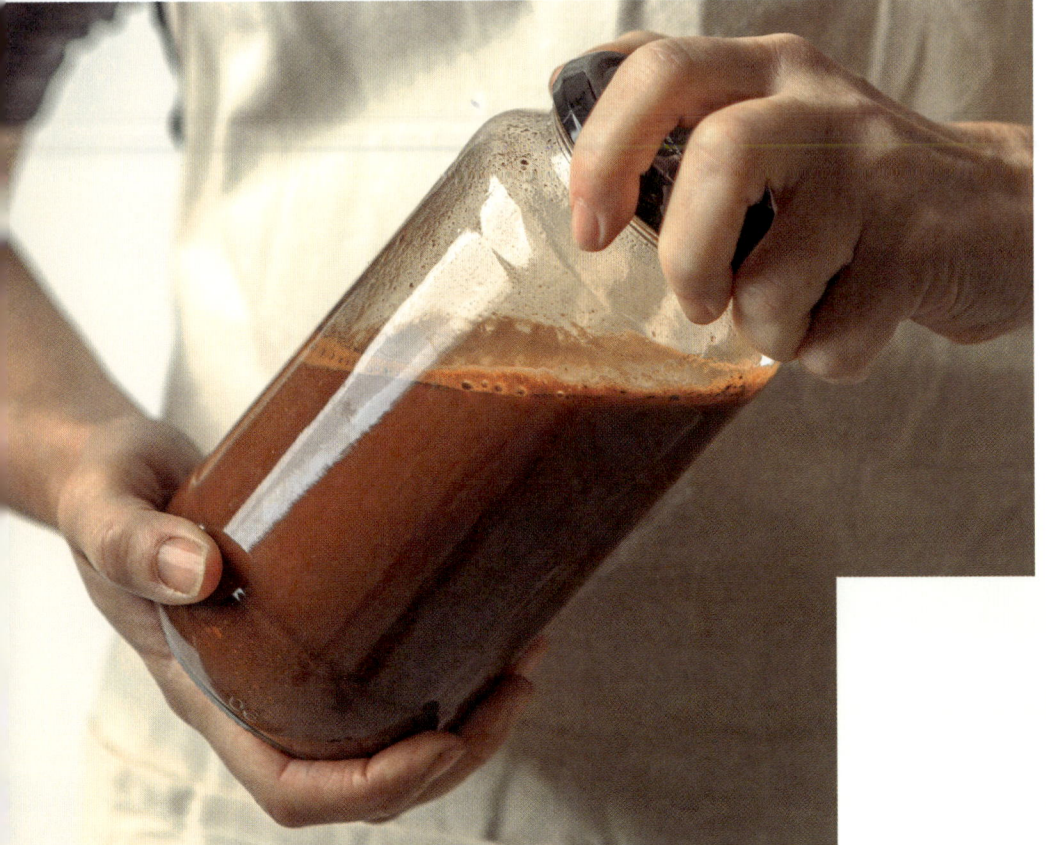

3 Tightly seal the lid and shake the jar vigorously for a count of ten.

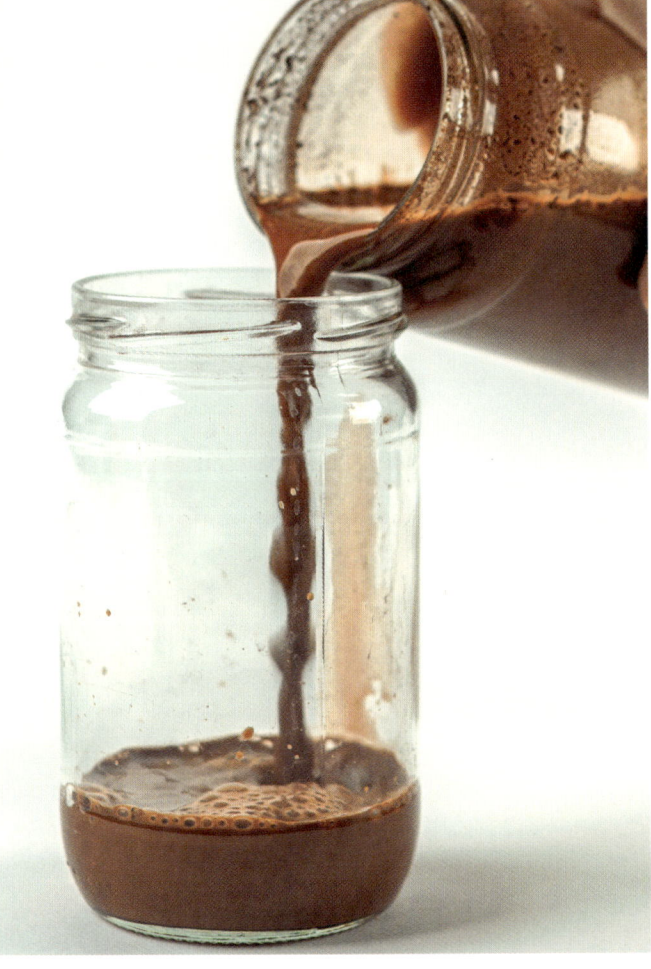

4 Wait for a count of five, then start to pour the coloured water, full of pigment, into another jar.

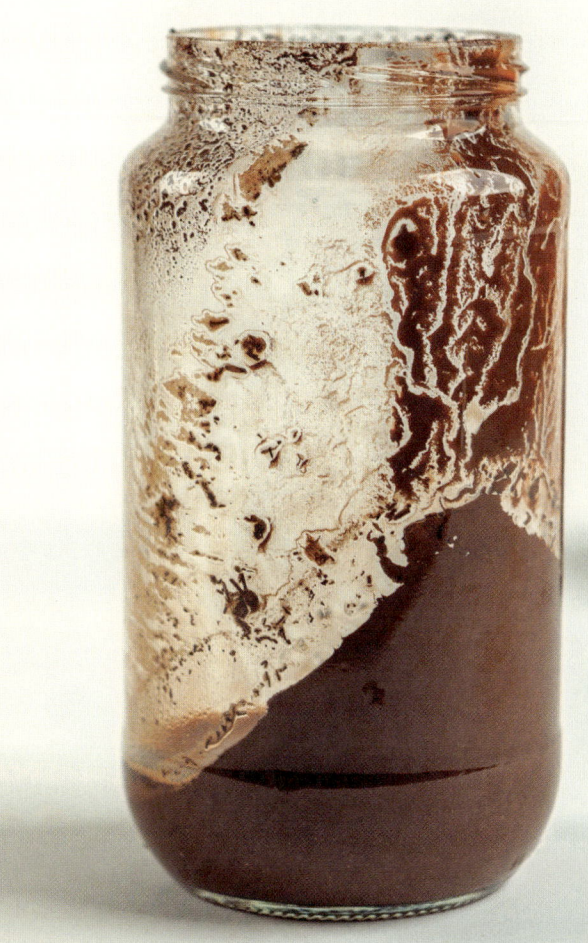
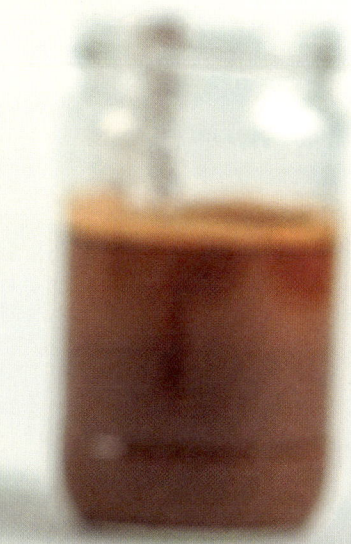

5 Leave the sediment in the bottom of the first jar (left of picture): don't pour any of this in. The shoulder of the jar will help you manage this. Put the new jar somewhere where it won't be knocked or disturbed, to allow the pigment to settle.

Grades of pigment

The first pour decants the smallest-sized floating particles, which results in the finest pigment grade. Each subsequent pour gives slightly larger particle sizes, and sometimes the colour varies; so each pour results in a gradually lower quality grade of pigment. The original jar should end up containing grit without any pigment left in it.

After drying each resulting grade of pigment, you may wish to regrind or sieve it again, to get it to the fine quality you require. Some pigments need lots of processing, others are almost pure as soon as they are first ground up. You'll get to know your local earths by experimentation.

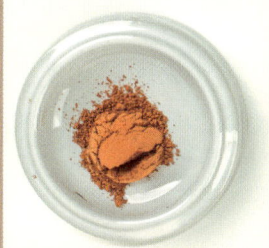

First pour – finest pigment

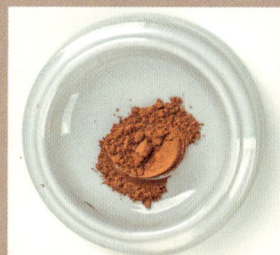

Second pour

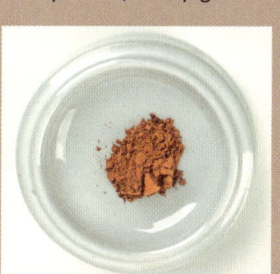

Third pour

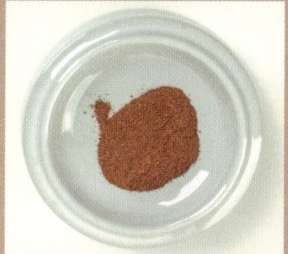

Last pour – coarsest pigment

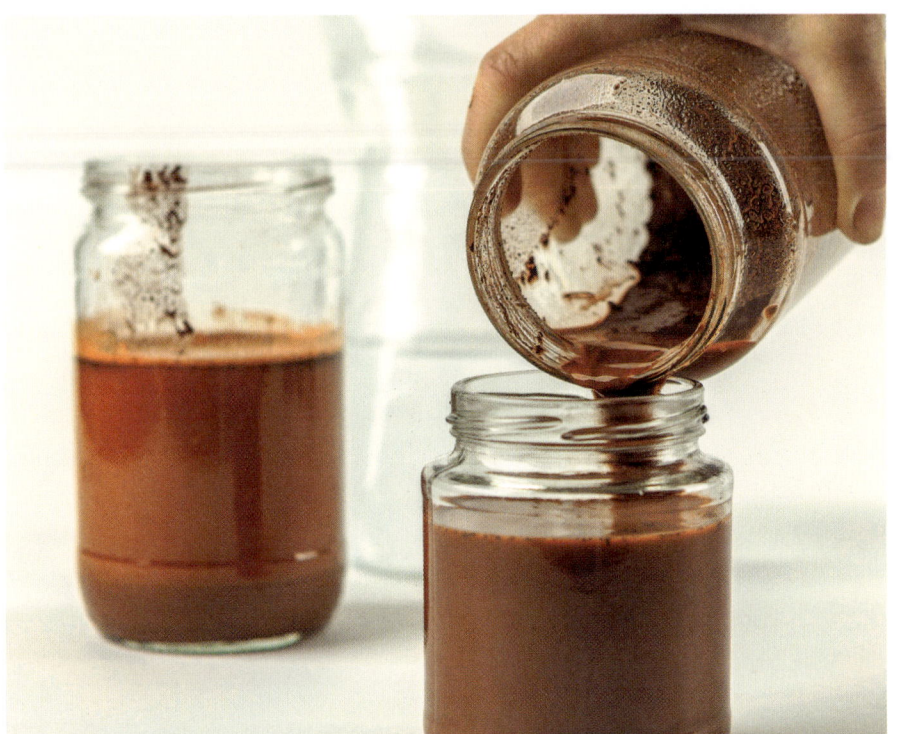

6 The first pour will produce the best quality pigment, as it has the most finely-ground, brightest particles. Repeating the process will let you use more of your earth. Fill the first jar (the one with just sediment remaining) with water once again. Work through steps 3–5 as before, and pour the next suspension into a new jar. Repeat the process another two to four times, or until the original sediment yields barely any more pigment.

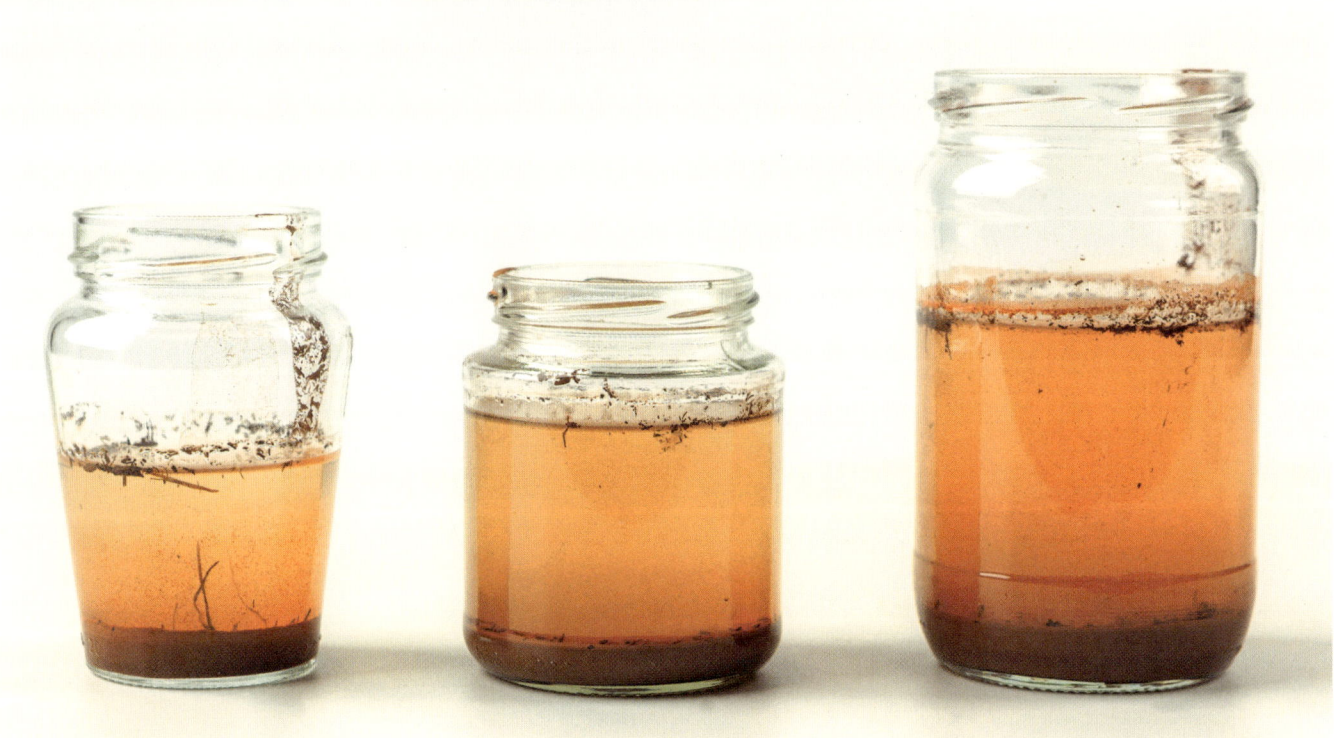

7 You will have a row of jars lined up in order of pouring. Let them settle for a few hours. The mixture will be ready to pour off once you can see clear water. The time will vary depending on the pigment you're using. The smaller the particles, the more time it will take to settle. Note that lower quality pigments will clear faster, as they have larger, heavier particles that sink more quickly. I prefer to leave them all overnight, wherever possible.

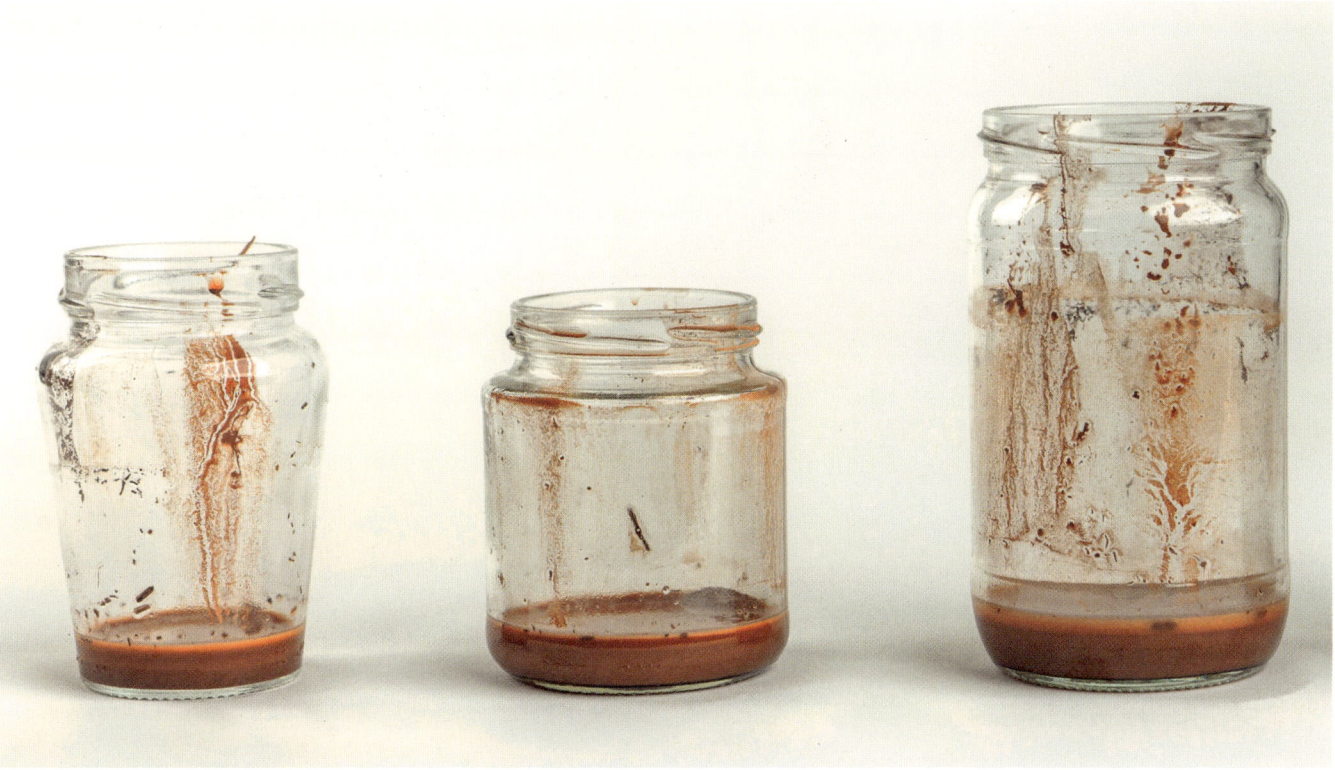

8 In the morning, carefully pour off as much of the clear water from each jar as you can. Some people use a turkey-baster or pipette for this, but I find a steady hand and a shouldered jar does just fine. Repeat this as soon as the pigment settles again until you have poured away as much clear water as you can. I usually make no more than four grades of pigment, and combine the products of the final pours rather than having endless jars lined up.

5 Drying

Once the pigments are completely dry, they will often look like cracked earth or peeling paint. There are two simple ways to dry your pigment ready for use or storage and the main difference is the time they take.

Evaporating

If you are lucky enough to have a sunny window sill, just leave the glass jars of damp pigment to dry by evaporation in the warm sunshine. These mineral pigments are not affected by ultraviolet light, so they will not fade. If you feel that dust might be a problem, you can lay a tissue or muslin over the jar mouths. Drying could be complete in a day or a week, depending on the temperature of your room. Some people dry their pigment jars on a shelf over a radiator or heater. Use what's practical for you. A greenhouse is also ideal.

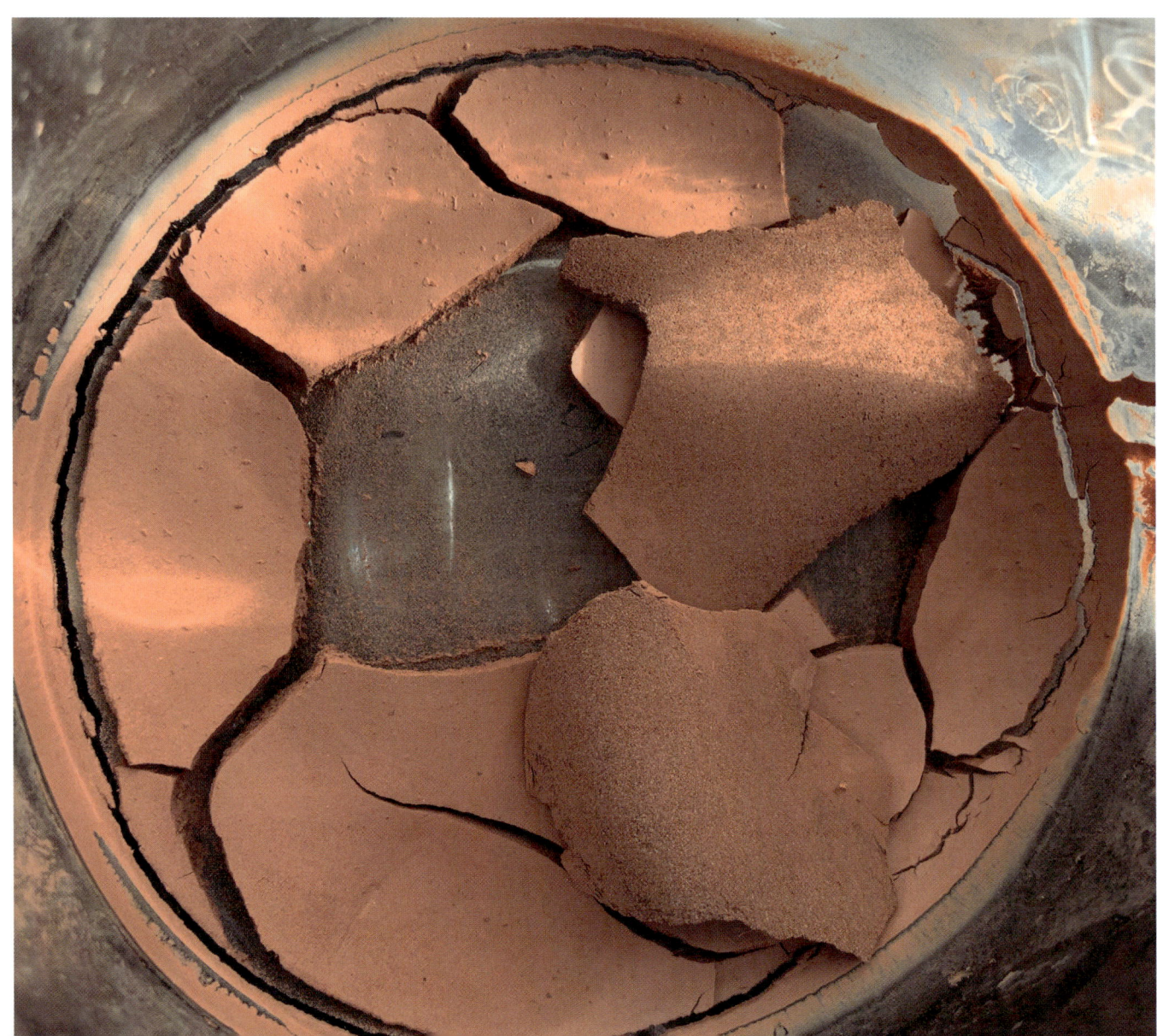

Scooping out

If you need to speed things up, you can scrape or pour the damp pigment from the jars onto coffee filter papers sitting in a funnel or sieve. Once the water has dripped through, the pigment can be spread in a thin layer, then you can dry them on a mesh rack in a warm place.

Some pigment artists use washable muslin, cotton cloths or silicone sheets for this stage. I like to use large unbleached recycled paper coffee filters, as I then use the delicately coloured papers as a source for paper cordage and yarn.

You will find the pigment colour gets paler as it dries. Don't be alarmed, the richness will return when we make it into paint.

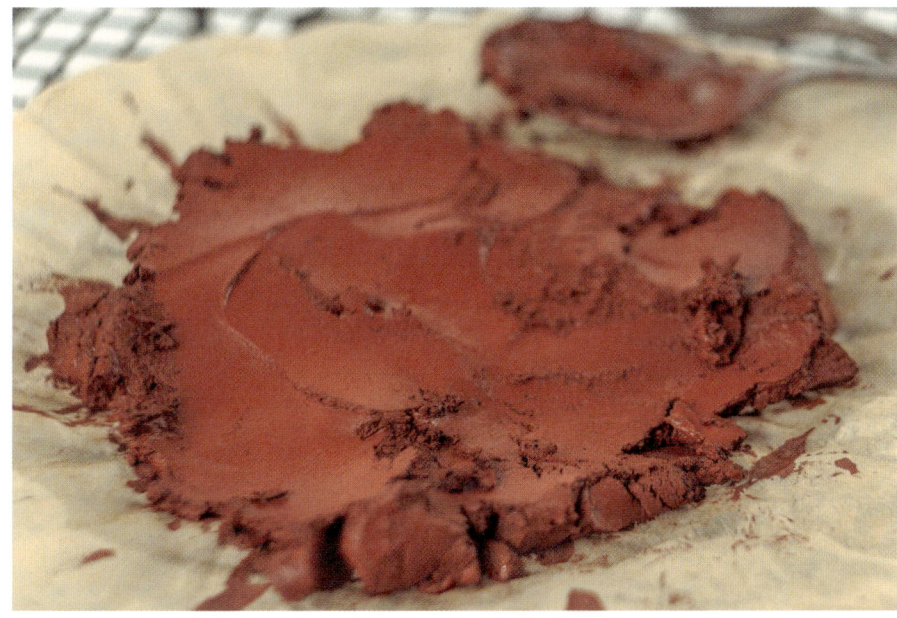

1 Scoop out the material from the bottom of the jar, and spread it out on a coffee filter. The coffee filter helps to draw out the remaining water, speeding up the process.

2 Once dry, you have a 'cake' of refined pigment. Don't worry if it cracks – we need to refine and break it up later anyway.

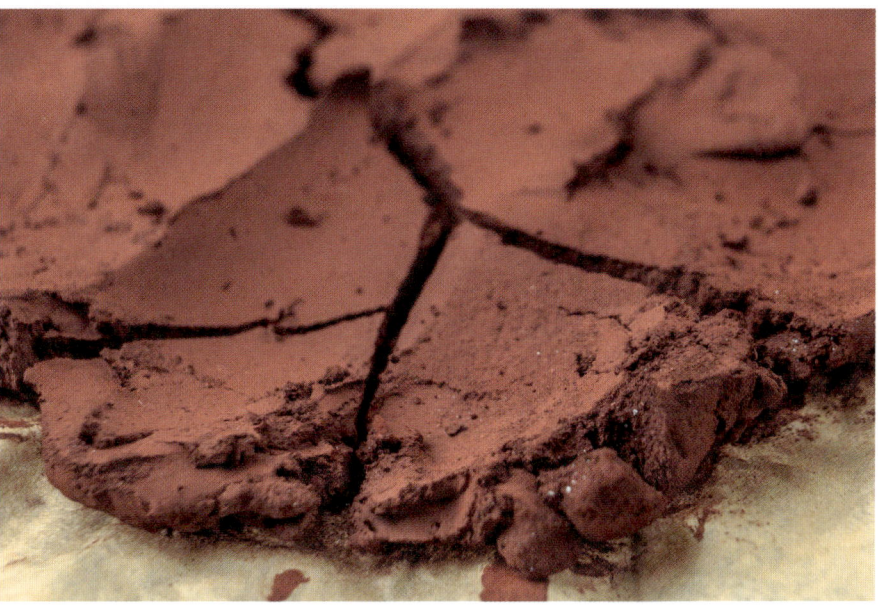

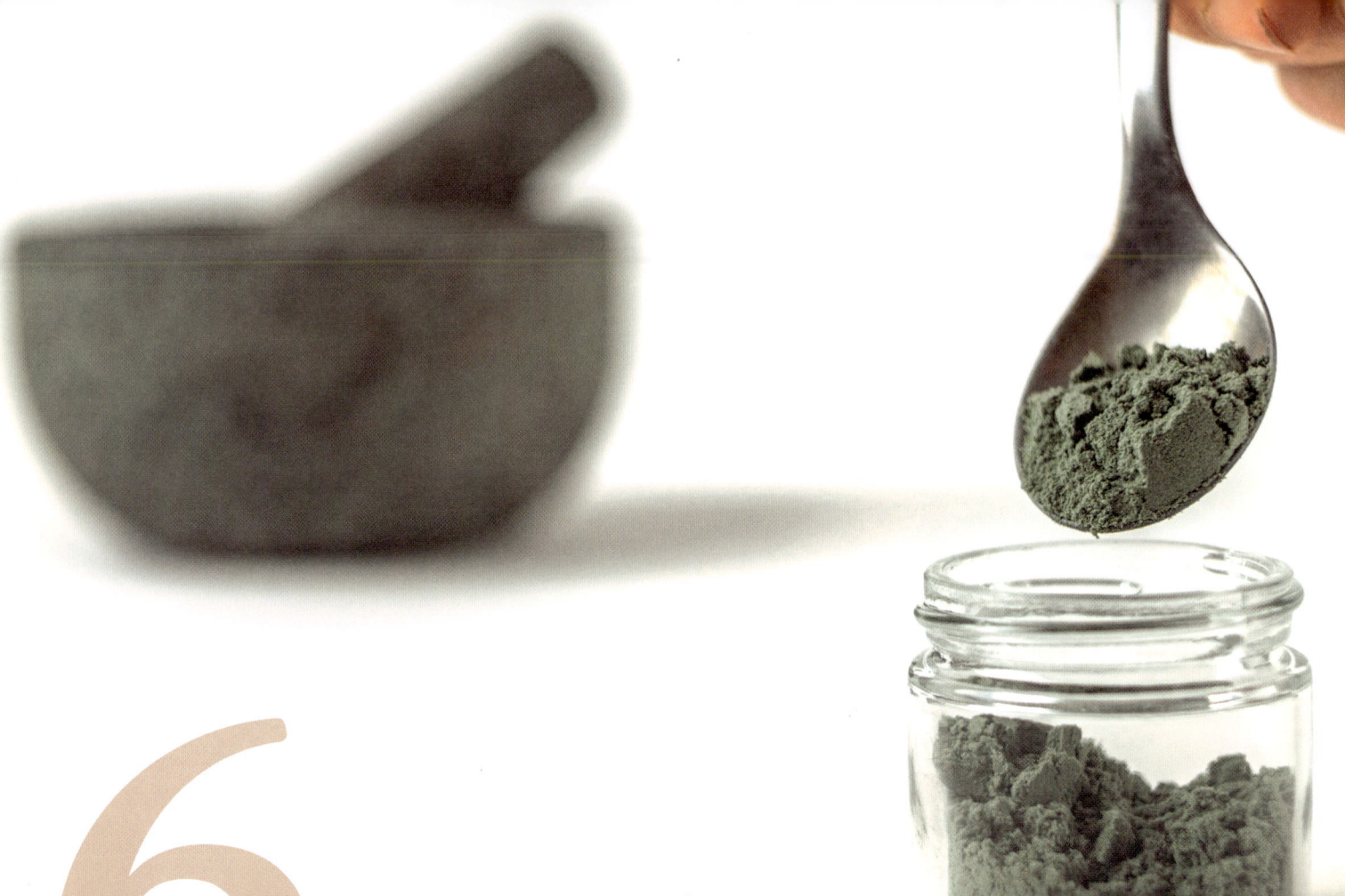

6 Storage

Whichever method of drying you use, you'll need to look at the resulting dry cakes of paint closely and decide whether you are going to combine any of the grades if they look very similar.

I always keep the first pouring grade (see page 69) separate, as this is the finest particle size, but often mix pourings 2 and 3 together. Break up the flakes with a palette knife or spoon and, using a firm brush, scrape them into little storage jars, ideally labelling each clearly with what the pigment is, the grade and the date. Wash the jars and brushes straight away ready for the next use.

At first you will probably store your pigments in any clean little jars you have available; single-portion jam jars are ideal for this. But after a while you may want to use glass vials, standardized jars or stacking tubs for your pigments. This is a matter of personal aesthetic preference and, as glass jars are endlessly reusable, there's no harm in indulging your tastes.

Briefly grind or sieve the cake to break it up back into powder, then spoon it into your storage (in this case a small glass jar).

Labelling

What is ephemeral information for one artist is essential for another. I always try to describe what the pigment is on my labels, which usually includes the place where I gathered it – so my labels usually read something like 'Red ochre from Totnes, 20/08/21, grade 1' or 'Clay from below St Anthony's Well, Imbolc 2022, washed'.

Other artist friends keep their pigments in jam jars along with a card with what amounts to a whole story about where and how the pigment was found, who they were with, the date, the weather, and more.

You could use a simpler number scheme, which is especially useful if your jars and labels are small. Using a notebook or swatch sketchbook, you can then wax lyrical and write to your heart's content beside the number for your pigment. There is more about swatching on page 92.

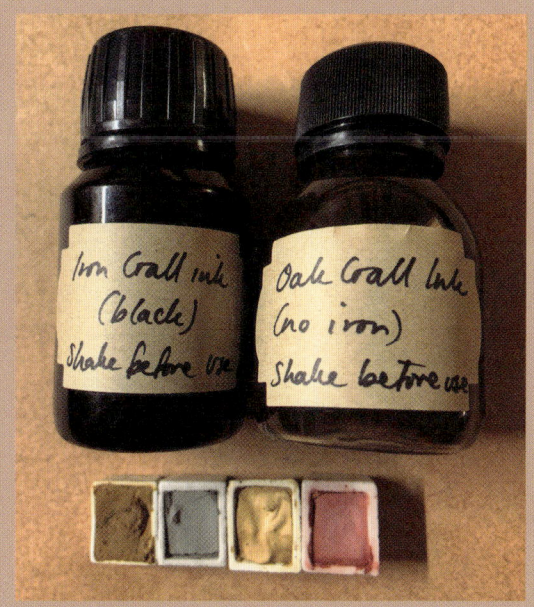

Hand-written labels suit these inks and handmade watercolours.

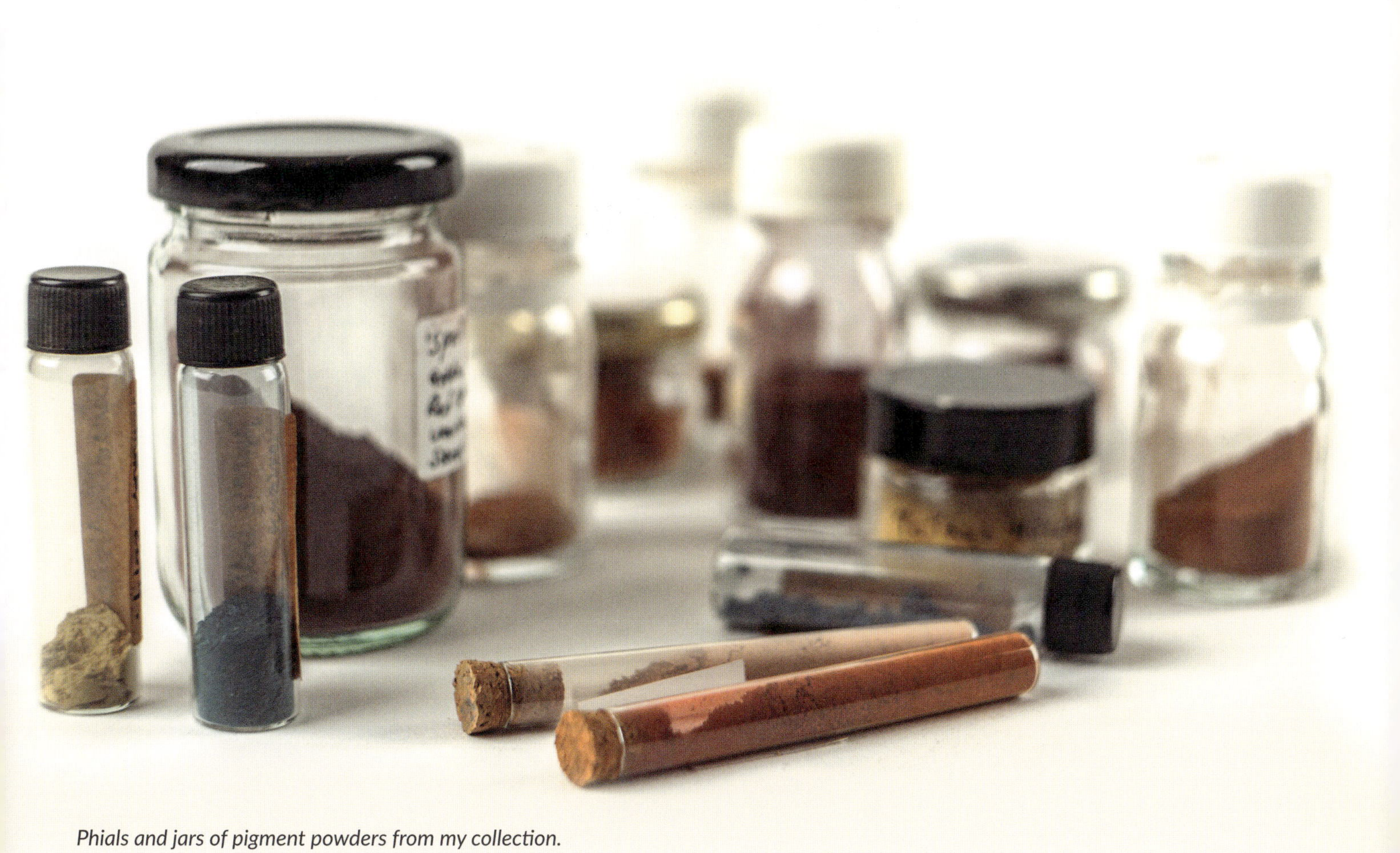

Phials and jars of pigment powders from my collection.

Creating your first paint

After years of my own ad hoc experimentation, I first learned to make traditional watercolour paints in person from Daniel Chatto at the Royal Drawing School, and later from a short studio-based course with David Cranswick. All the recipes in this book are from my own study notebooks from those times and from refinements from my experimentation at home over time with natural and foraged pigments and later, foraged gums. There are traditional sources in books that the avid reader can refer to, and I have added them as further reading at the back of this book. What is important to me is that you can pick up this book and make paint, with no specialist knowledge, so I've kept everything here based on the simple tried and tested recipes I use in my studio practice and when teaching in person.

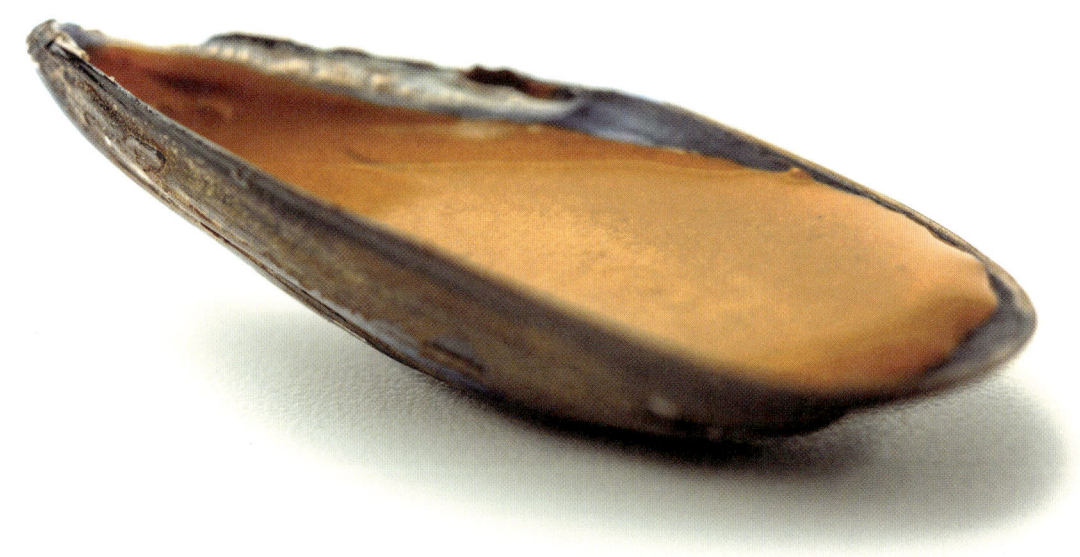

You will need

/ Measuring spoon and teaspoon

/ Pipette or dropper

/ Bowl or pestle and mortar

/ Your powdered pigment

/ Water

/ Liquid watercolour medium

/ Paintbrush

/ Paper for testing

/ Shell or small reused container for storing the paint

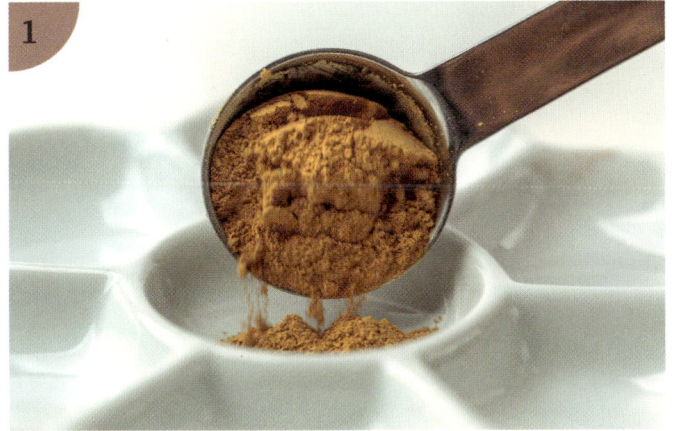

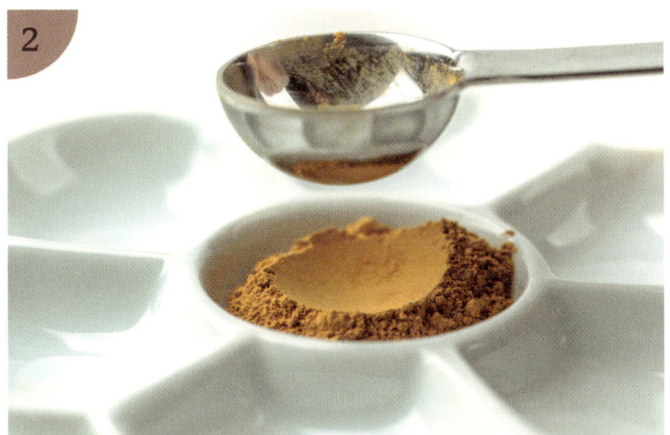

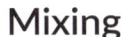

Mixing

You can mix your first paint using a bowl and spoon, or a pestle and mortar. Either way, use roughly 1 part volume of dry pigment to 1 part watercolour medium. It is easiest to work with about a teaspoonful of each, at first.

1 Measure a teaspoon of refined pigment into a palette well (or other suitable receptacle).

2 Use the back of your measuring spoon to tamp it down to form a small divot.

3 Use a spoon to add an equal amount of watercolour medium into the divot. You could, alternatively, use a pipette.

4 Use a teaspoon to stir and mix the ingredients together. You can use a brush, if you prefer. Next, add a couple of drops of water to the mix to wet it a little more. You're aiming for the paint to be easy to mix but not too sloppy. Mix thoroughly with your spoon. When it seems mixed, mix it some more with a clean damp paintbrush until it looks and feels even.

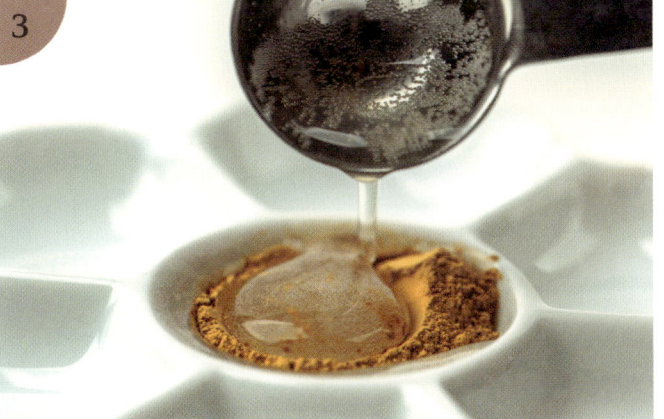

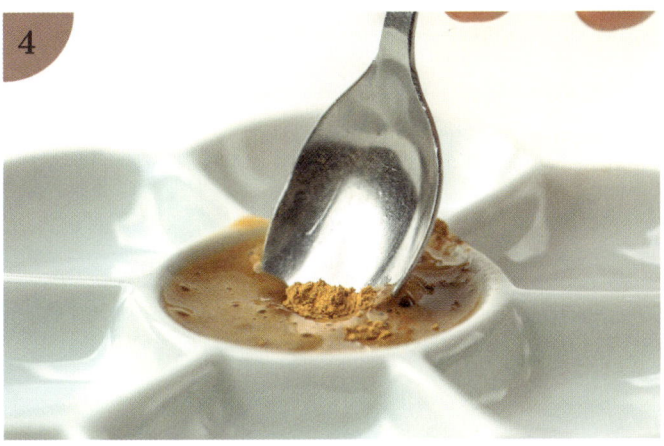

Braying

Instead of mixing in a bowl with a spoon, you can mix paint in the mortar by using the pestle: this is called braying. I have Joumana Medlej to thank for introducing me to this excellent term in her books.

Medium

You can buy watercolour medium made from gum Arabic from all good art suppliers, but if you'd like to make your own, go to page 86 where you can learn how to make it from bought or foraged gum.

Testing

Using your brush, test your paint on some paper. If it dries flaky or dull, you need more medium in the mix. If it is too glossy, transparent, or won't dry swiftly, it needs more pigment in the mix. Adjust until you are happy with it for your own purposes. Have a go at painting something with it right away. Make notes and swatch your colour in a notebook or test sheet for reference. Different pigments may require more or less medium, so experimentation is key, as there is no exact set recipe for watercolour.

That's it! You now have perfectly good watercolour paint to go. It won't yet be as smooth as bought tube or pan colours, but it is a great instant paint, and can be made in situ with rocks in the great outdoors, if you bring a little bottle of medium with you...

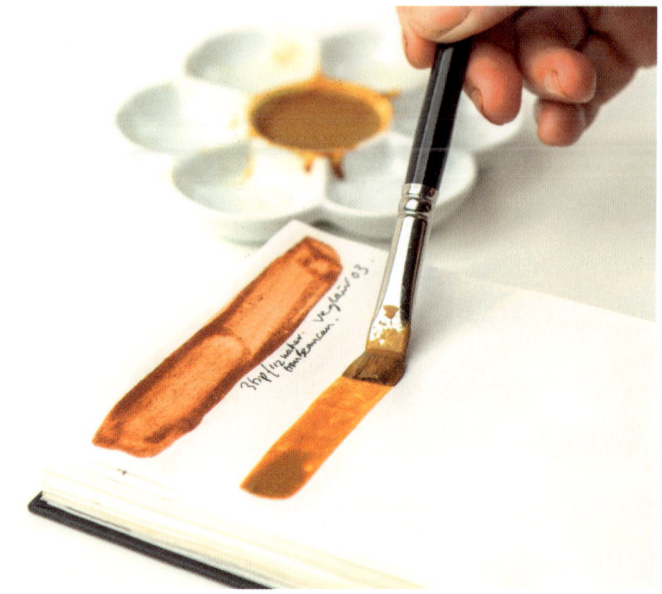

As you make each paint, create a swatch to test and record it.

Storage

If you are not going to use all the paint right now, gather the paint together using the brush and spoon and scrape it into a suitable container to dry for later use. I use: sea shells, nut shells, reused and vintage ceramic and plastic watercolour 'half pans', cleaned out old makeup sets, old blister packs from big pills, washed contact lens packages and cases, bottle tops, beer caps, small jar lids, food packaging... The list is endless and you do not need to buy anything new, just make sure the container is unreactive and spotlessly clean. Dry thoroughly in a shaded warm place rather than in full sun, to avoid cracking, and always store ventilated: a sealed box will encourage mould.

No waste

Lastly, so as not to waste your precious paint, add a small amount of water to your bowl. Mix the dregs of the paint and water with a stiff paintbrush and transfer all your colour as washes or textures to waiting scrap paper, sketchbook pages or watercolour paper. These make superb coloured grounds for artwork, materials for collage, and instant sources of beautiful gift wrap or craft supplies. I cannot recommend this practice highly enough as a way to show gratitude to the earth, plants and water that we use to make our art materials. An invitingly teetering pile of richly coloured hand-tinted papers is also an effective cure for the winter blues, I find. Now you can wash up your already almost-clean tools and put them away dry.

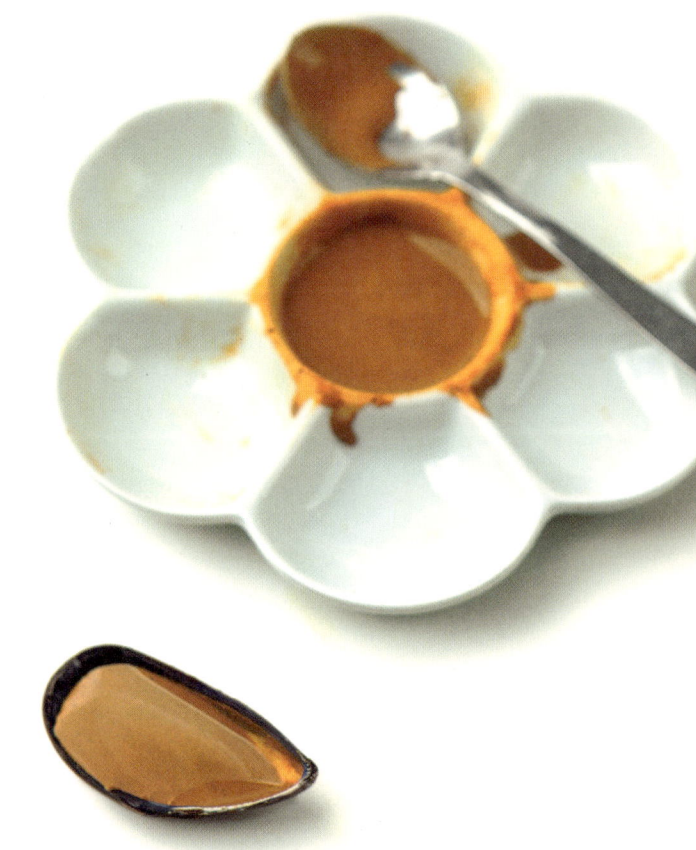

Spoon each paint into a shell for no-cost storage. On the facing page, you can see five freshly-made paints in their shells.

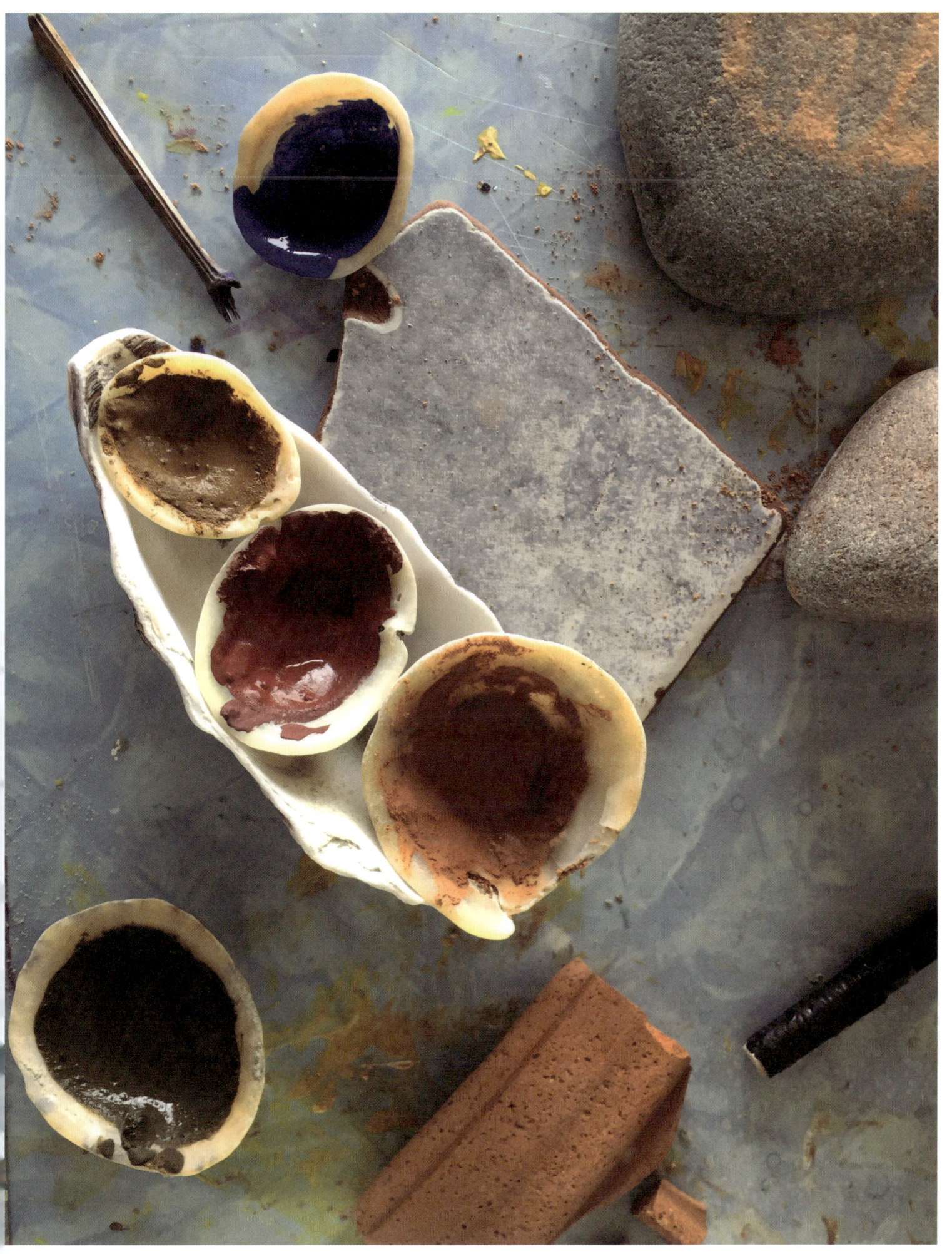

Creating artists' quality paint

You might be surprised to learn that there is no substantial difference in the ingredients between the first simple recipe and one for high quality artists' watercolours. The difference is how we work with the materials, especially the time and attention we pay to them.

Have you ever mulled something over? Thought your way round a gritty issue for a while until it felt a bit easier? This wonderful metaphor describes a real sensation. In paint making, mulling (from the German for milling) is the action of working paint on a glass or stone slab with a muller – usually a flat-bottomed piece of glass, stone or other resistant material.

A traditional part of refining pigment for oil paints, mulling is just as useful for water-based paints. We are not grinding the pigment any more finely at this point – that was accomplished in the pestle and mortar, or by grinding between stones. Instead we are coating every particle of the pigment in the medium until we have slick paint. This used to be called 'glib'.

Both 'slick' and 'glib', meaning smooth and slippery, found their way into general usage in English centuries ago – usually in the pejorative, indicating that someone's smooth ease in speech or writing was insincere or deceitful. However, we make no such judgements here: slick and glib are precisely how we want our paint to feel on the slab!

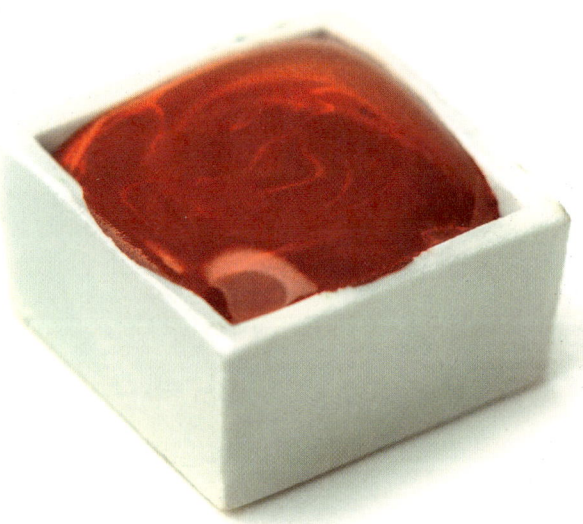

You will need

/ Spoons

/ Pipette or dropper

/ Palette knife

/ Your powdered pigment

/ Water

/ Liquid watercolour medium

/ Paintbrush

/ Paper for testing

/ Shell

/ Half-pan container, or small reused container for storing the paint

/ Muller and slab, toughened glass chopping board, or polished marble or stone surface

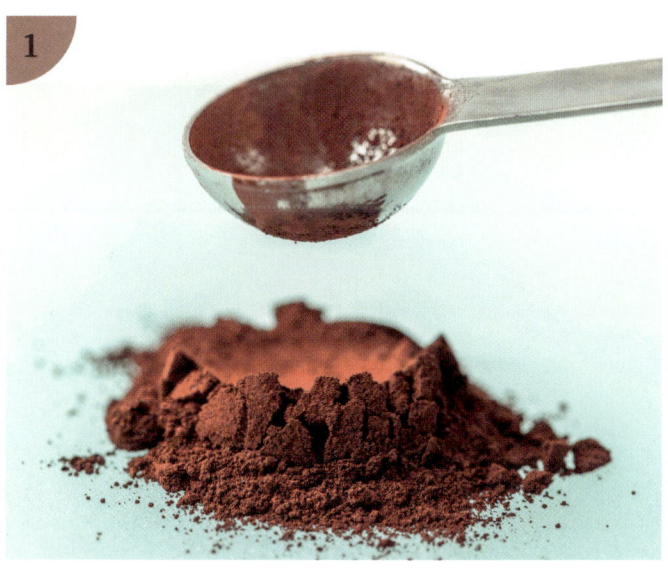

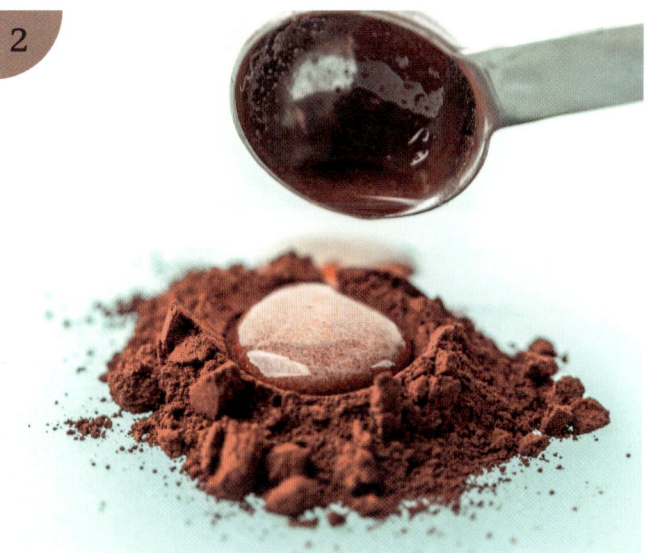

Mixing

This stage is very similar to mixing your first paint (see page 76); the main difference is the surface you work upon. Having said that, it is best to use the finest grade of pigment you made – i.e. that from the first pouring.

1 On a glass kitchen worktop saver, or an artists' ground glass or marble slab, place 1 part dry pigment. (A teaspoonful of each ingredient works well.)

2 Make a well in the pigment with the back of your spoon, then add 1 part watercolour medium.

3 Use a palette knife to combine the pigment and medium.

4 Add as many drops of water as you need to get the mixture to come together into a soft paste. I use a pipette, to ensure that I don't accidentally add too much at once.

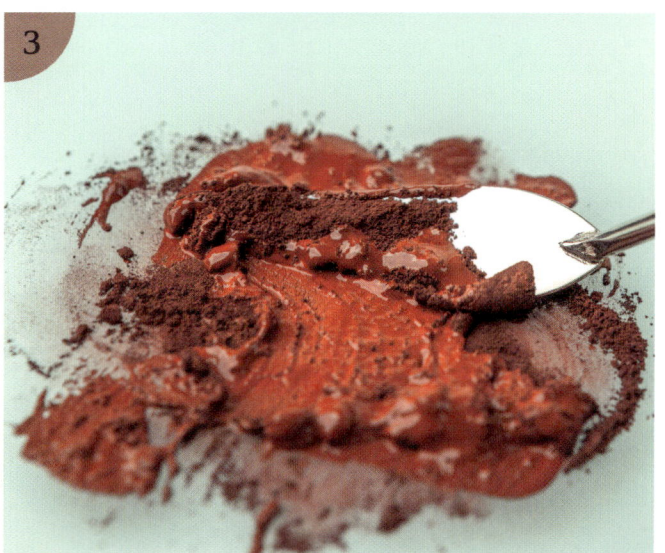

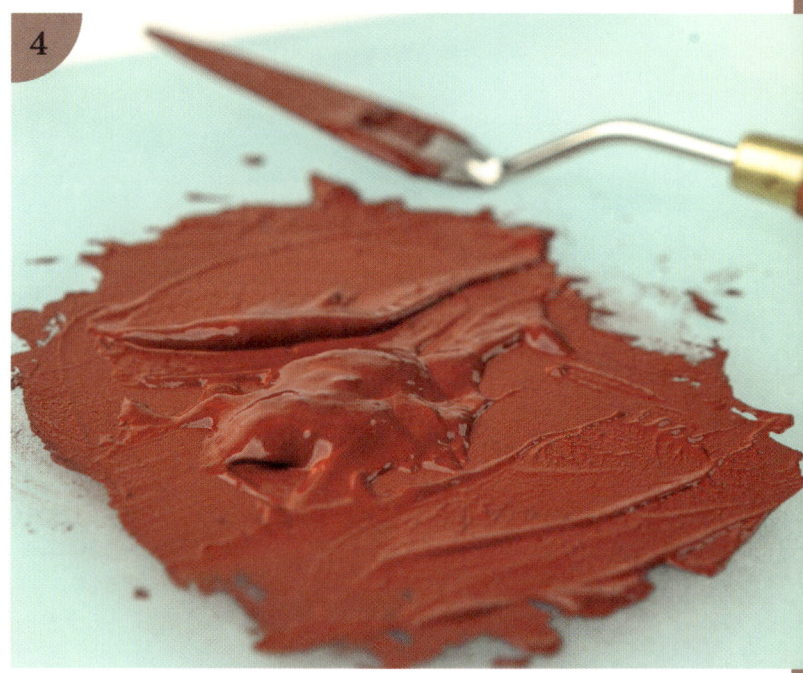

The texture should feel like toothpaste under your knife; if it feels a little gritty, add a drop or two of water with a pipette, then continue.

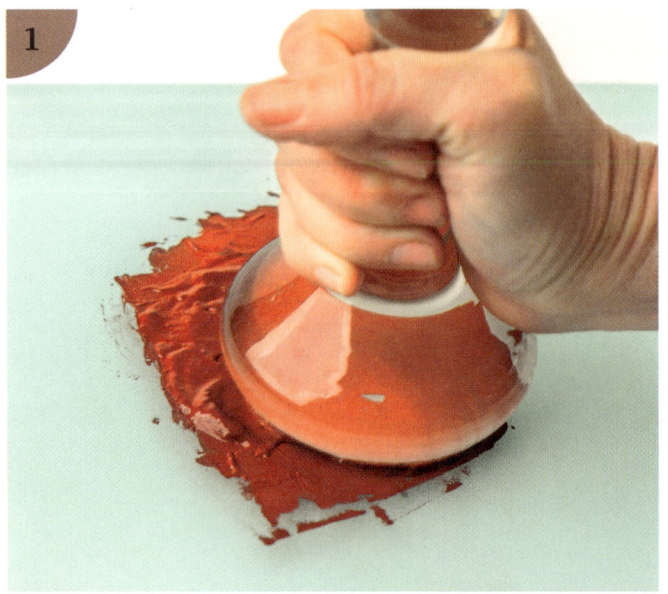

Mulling

Mulling your paint on the slab involves moving it round and round in circles with your muller (you can also use a pickle weight, old-fashioned glass paperweight or a jar – anything flat-bottomed and glass). The aim is to coat every particle of pigment evenly with medium and produce a fine paint. Mulling might take as little as 5 minutes, or over 20 minutes – but every minute spent on this stage will show in the quality of your final paint. If your room is warm, you may need to add a few extra drops of water as you work as the paint will begin to dry as you spread it finely.

1 Place the muller on the paint. Without pressing down hard, but with an even pressure of your arm's natural weight, begin moving the paint around by circling or making figure-of-eight movements.

2 Continue the gently circular motions. Listen for the change in sound as you move the muller. Early on, it will likely sound slightly noisy.

3 Lift the muller away and use your palette knife to scrape the paint back onto the surface.

4 Use your palette knife to gather the paint back to the centre of the slab.

5 Keep the paint moist and gather the paint into the centre with your palette knife often, then keep mulling it over until it all feels easy and smooth.

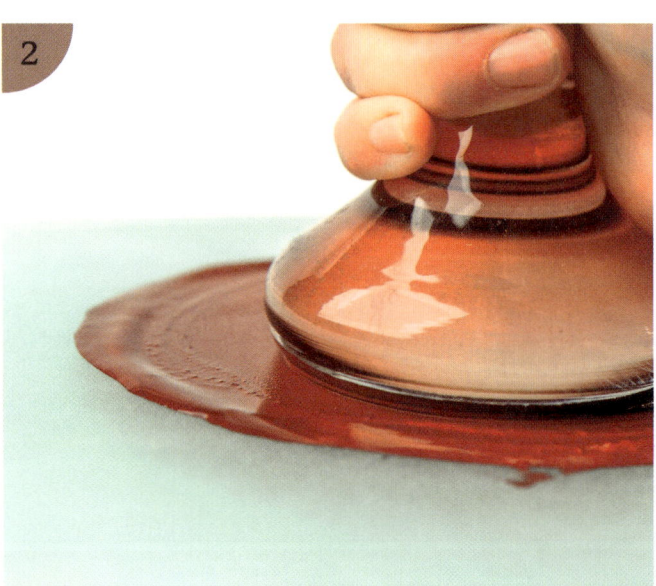

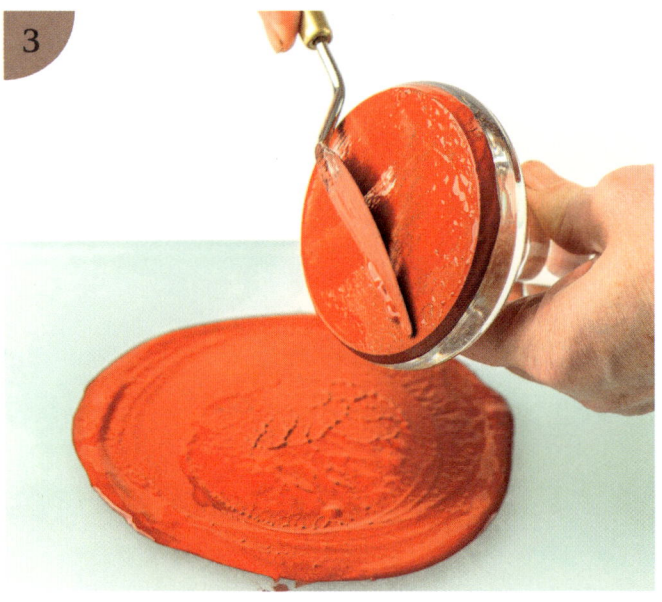

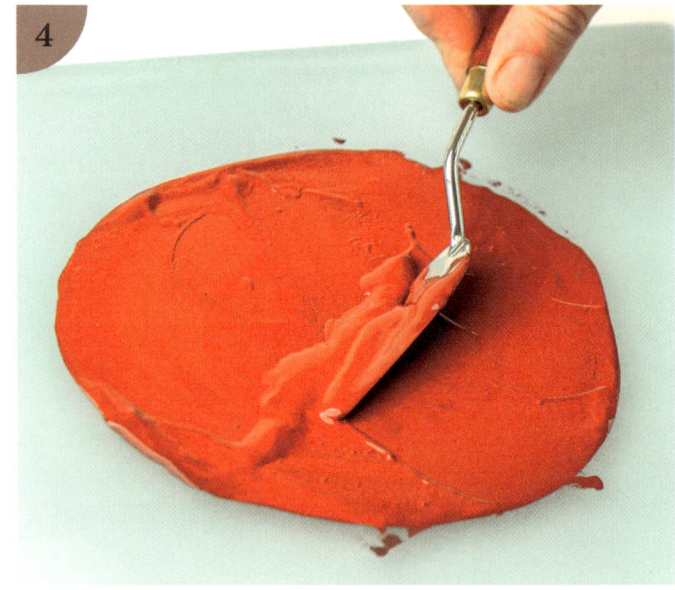

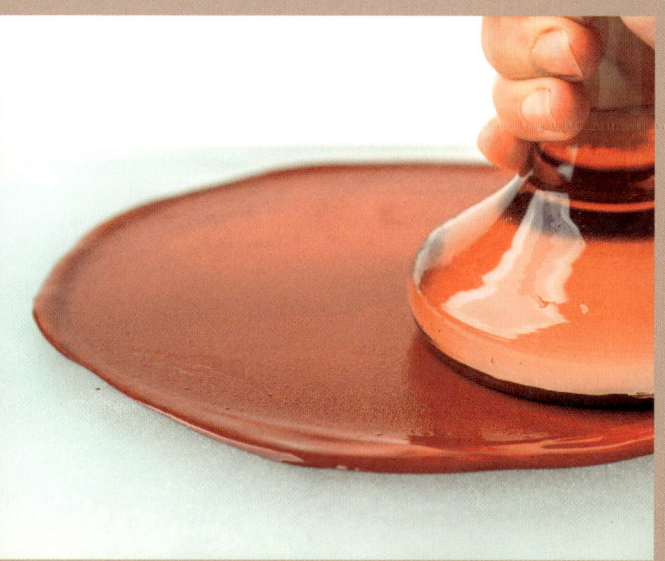

Sound and vision

When the paint is getting closer to being ready, you'll notice it becomes quieter and has a smooth sound, rather than making a raspy and uneven noise. Simultaneously, the feel of the paint under the muller will change from gritty and lumpy, with changes in the speed your muller can move, to something much more fluid with no sticky interruptions to the circling movement of your hand and arm. It is fascinating that making something as visual as paint, when we get better feedback at this stage in the process from our hands and ears than from our eyes.

Storage

When you feel the paint is ready, test your paint on some paper, and adjust as described on page 78. After mixing the paint with the palette knife, gather, scoop and scrape it all into your chosen container before leaving it to dry thoroughly – ideally for three days to a week – in a warm, dry place out of direct sunlight. You can store it as described on page 74.

The paint you have made can be used alongside your conventional bought watercolours as the basic ingredients are just the same.

For picture-perfect filled half pans, the paint can instead be added using a syringe. After filling halfway, the pan is left to dry, then refilled to the top a day or two later. This gives the full cushion shape found with commercial paints.

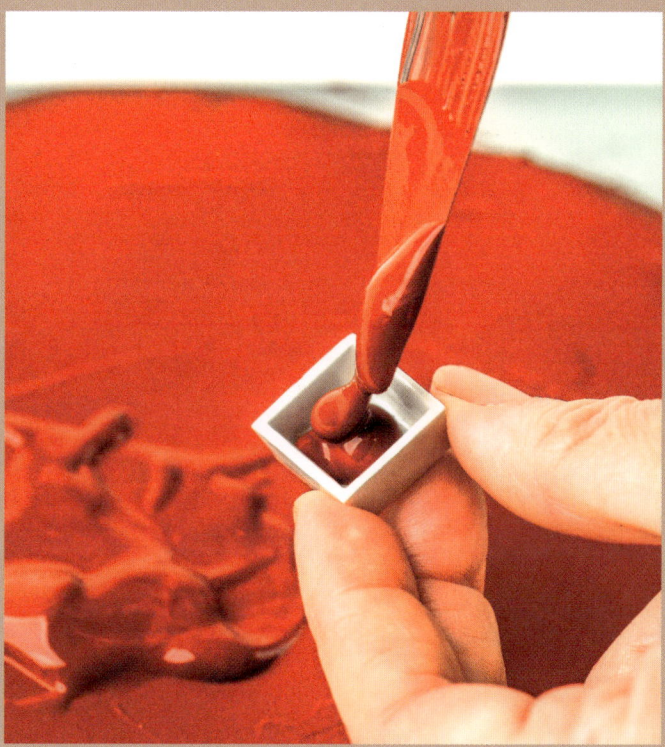

Creating your watercolour palette

Now you've created simple and refined watercolours, it's time to make a palette from all the rocks, clays, chalk, charcoal, slate and brick bits you have found. Before you begin, take stock. Lay out all your finds and have a good look at them, making a mental note of which one you'd like to start with. This is a good stage to take a few pictures, too. Many natural pigment artists and collectors keep a small amount of the raw pigment chunk in a little container, even if they process the rest into pigment and paint. As more of an artist than a collector, I am happy to use up all of a pigment, as my swatch book, photographs, and location notes help me remember specific details.

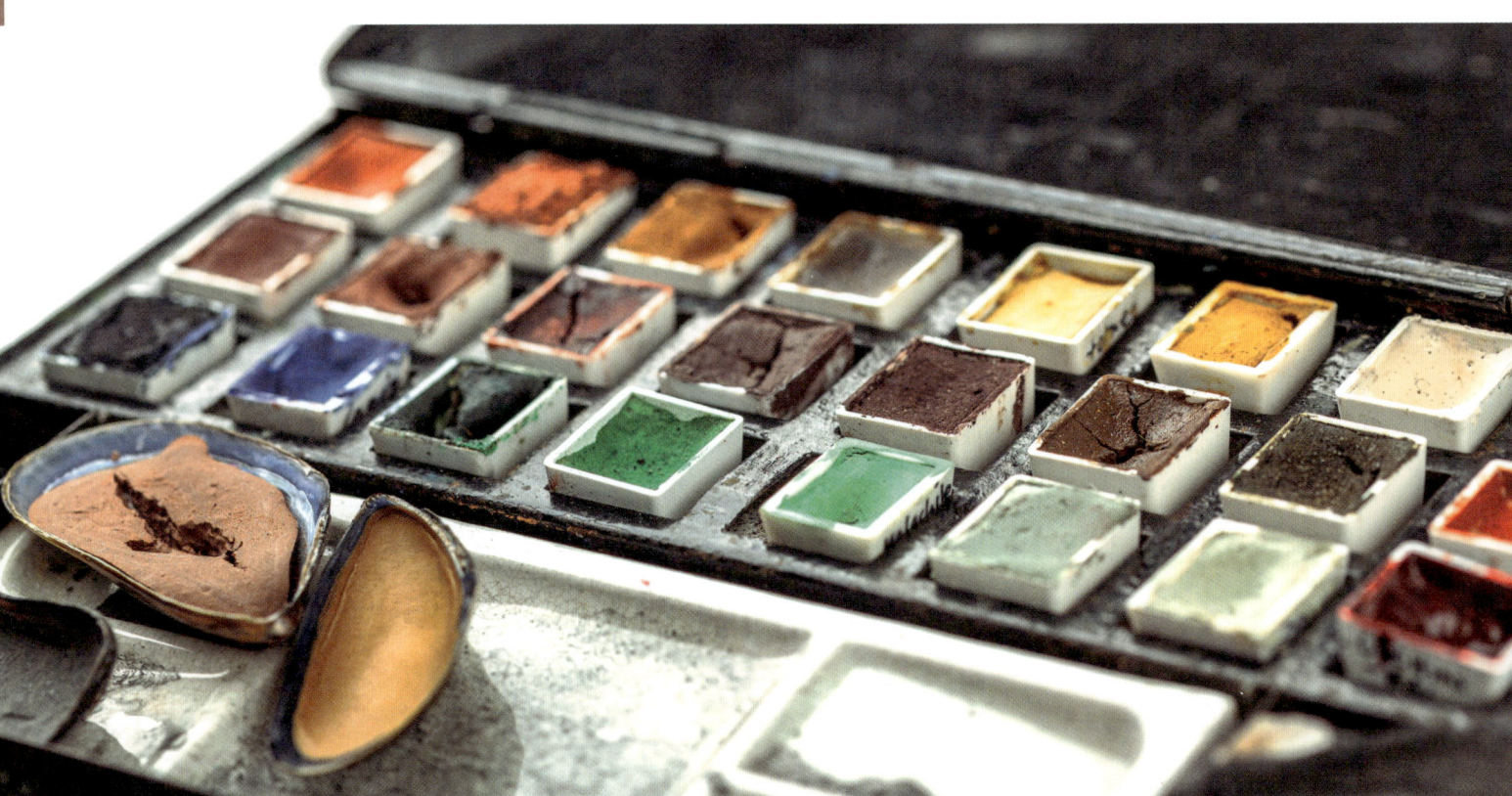

You will need

/ Tools for refining pigments (see page 60); and for making simple or artists' quality watercolours (see page 76/80)

Containers

Choose what containers you'll use for your paints. I particularly like mussel shells which are traditional for use as palettes in Britain, and are still used by miniaturists and illuminators to this day. The bright pearly white curve of the inside surface is an excellent receptacle for paint. Some of my shells are from the beach, some from the tow path of rivers and canals, where the birds drop them, and some come from meals I have had at home or at restaurants. I always wash the shells thoroughly and air dry them, checking each one over for strength and making sure they have no tiny holes or cracks. You might like to use bottle tops, 'disposable' contact lens packaging, walnut shells or half pan cases for your paints. Make sure they match, as for your first palette, it will be nice if they all go together.

Make a plan

Some people like to prepare one pigment at a time and take it all the way through to paint in one session: smashing, grinding, sieving, mixing, mulling and filling their containers. However, if you plan on washing a pigment, this won't be possible, as that stage takes a day to settle and another day to dry at least. So have a look at your finds, and if there is chalk or charcoal, which only need sieving, not washing, you can make these into paints while other pigments levigate or dry. You will now truly understand why traditional painters had studio assistants, before the days of ready to use paints! Lists are a friend here, and with a little forethought, you can process all your foraged goods without too much fuss.

Tools

Once your pigments are washed and ground ready for use, make sure you have time and space to make a few paints in a row, washing the tools and surfaces between each colour. This way, your method will be consistent, and you'll be able to compare the colours, qualities and handling between the pigments, and adjust your ratios and technique based on your own experience. There is no rush; we are not trying to replicate the efficiency of machines. Take your time, rest in the tactile richness of the tasks at hand, allow yourself to slow down and work at maximum enjoyment speed, whatever that is for you.

Your local palette

It might take up to a week for your paints to be dry enough to store, but they are usable as soon as you have made them, somewhat like the texture of bought tube watercolours, rather than pans.

Once you have assembled all your colours, you might like to place them together on a plate or tray, in a box or bowl and just enjoy the colours and textures of the paints you have made. You now have the wonderful task ahead of you, of swatching and testing your unique local palette – hopefully the first of many highly personal colour schemes you will create. Congratulations on making your first set of paints.

Naming your paints

From Payne's gray to Naples yellow, traditional paints have some interesting names with unique histories behind them – well worth researching.

You can name your own foraged pigments as you see fit. Some of mine are named after the places I found them, such as 'Dart yellow', and 'St Anthony's Well ochre'; others take their name from the history of the foraging site, such as 'spoils red' or 'ironstone orange'; and others still are named after the qualities of the pigment – such as 'sparkling malachite (coarse)' and 'pale malachite (fine)'. Be as poetic or as descriptive as you like with your naming scheme.

Creating your own watercolour medium

Years ago, while studying traditional art materials with Daniel Chatto on his course 'The Stuff of Painting and Drawing', I heard him mention in passing that cherry tree gum had been used historically as a paint binder in place of gum Arabic. This piqued my interest as a forager and an artist as I searched for natural art materials and media to replace synthetic products in my art practice.

The techniques used to make watercolour medium are simple, and will be familiar from making your paints. Once you've gathered even a teaspoonful of gum, you've got enough to make some medium. Unless you are going to use all your medium while it is fresh (within a day or two), you need to add a few drops of anti-fungal essential oil to the mix or store it in the fridge.

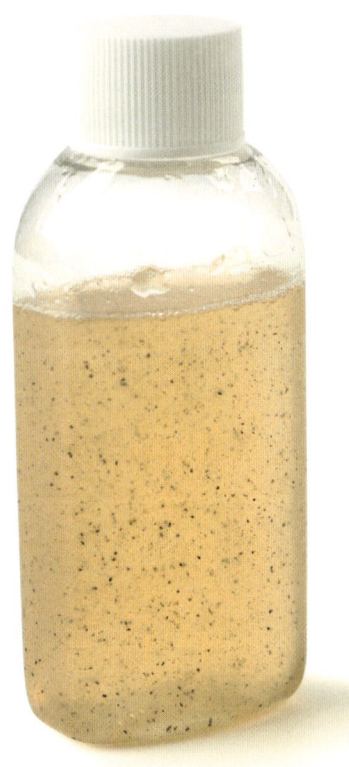

Cherry tree gum watercolour medium

You will need

/ Solid dry tree gum – either bought lump gum Arabic; foraged cherry tree gum; acacia or eucalyptus tree gum; or other non-coniferous tree gum

/ Water

/ Pestle and mortar

/ Glass jar

/ Spoon

/ Mesh bag

/ Saucepan

/ Tea strainer

/ Container

/ Honey

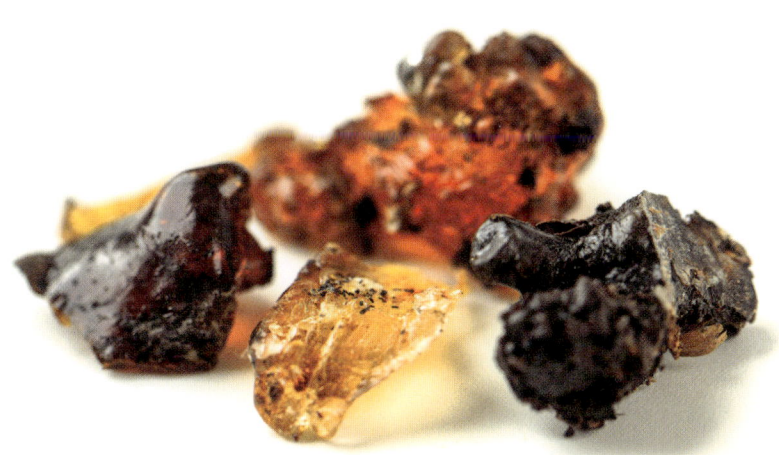

Foraged cherry tree gum. Tree gum was historically used in the Baltic as part of recipes to make imitation amber for jewellery and ornaments and some large lumps I find look good enough to set in silver. Most, however, are destined to be used for my watercolur medium.

Foraged tree gums

Authentic gum Arabic comes from Senegal, where it is harvested from acacia trees. Some other acacias, as well as fruit trees of the *Prunus* and *Eucalyptus* genera, sometimes exude a sticky gum from fissures in their bark. This gum can be collected without harming the tree at all if you follow some simple guidelines: gather where it is abundant, and take only what is on the surface of the bark, never cutting into or picking at the bark itself.

Suitable trees include cherries, plums, gages, damsons and various acacias. Cherry tree gum produces a light, gel-like medium with a matt finish, whereas the more traditional gum Arabic from acacia gives a honey-like consistency that binds pigment well and gives a little sheen to the paint finish.

The gum is softer after rain, when it can be scooped off with fingers or a spoon. In dry weather it will dry solid, and you'll need a knife to remove it. Carry it home in a tub or plastic bag, then allow it to dry thoroughly before storing it. It lasts indefinitely if kept in a paper bag or cardboard box.

In the spring, as the sap rises, the gum can be a clear, pale yellow or even colourless. This a real find, as the absence of a yellow tinge means the gum can be used to make white, mauve and blue paints, where a yellower or amber-coloured binder would muddy the tones with the complementary colour. You may also find clear droplets of gum like little teardrops exuding from fruits in the summer, caused by wasps piercing their skin. These too can be gathered to make binder for the very finest pale blues.

In late summer and autumn, the gum can become darker in tone – amber, deep brown or even almost black. It picks up specks of bark and tannins from the wood as it passes through, and these give the gum its colour.

All colours of gum are useful, and once dry, it's worth grading them into separate shades for different uses. It is possible to use the paler second and third flushes of gel from the cherry tree gum to make watercolour medium, however dark your lumps of fruit tree treasure.

Method

I'm using cherry tree gum here, but you can use whatever bought or foraged gum you have. The medium produced from cherry tree gum will not be as sticky or as glossy as gum Arabic, so be prepared to add up to a quarter more medium to your paints, to adjust the honey/sugar ratio until you get it just right for your needs. Alternatively, paint a top layer of the medium over your work to add shine, if needed.

1 Start with half a teaspoon or so of dried gum.

2 Using a brass pestle and mortar within a mesh bag (this prevents fragments flying out), break up the pieces until they are like sand.

3 Put the smashed gum into a jar and half fill it with water. Stir and leave overnight.

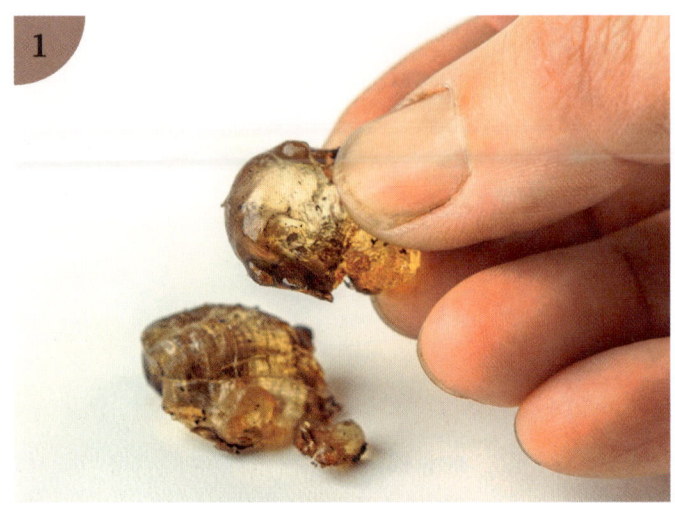

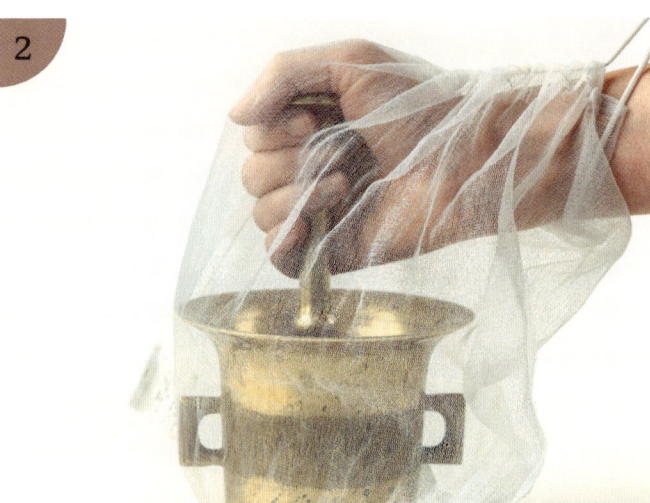

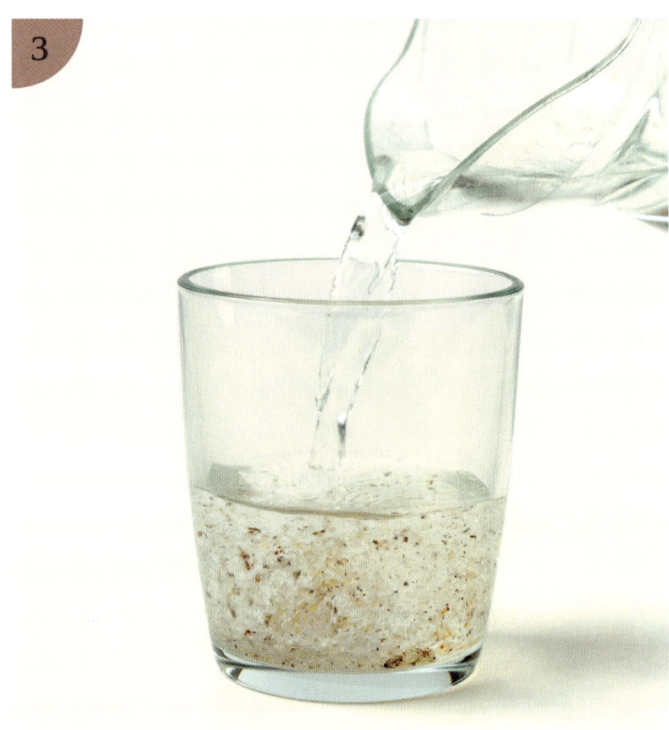

Keeping things clean

Some artists add a drop of anti-fungal essential oil to the medium, which also has the benefit of smelling lovely. I leave out this step and instead use spotless bottles and jars which I store in the fridge, with equally good results.

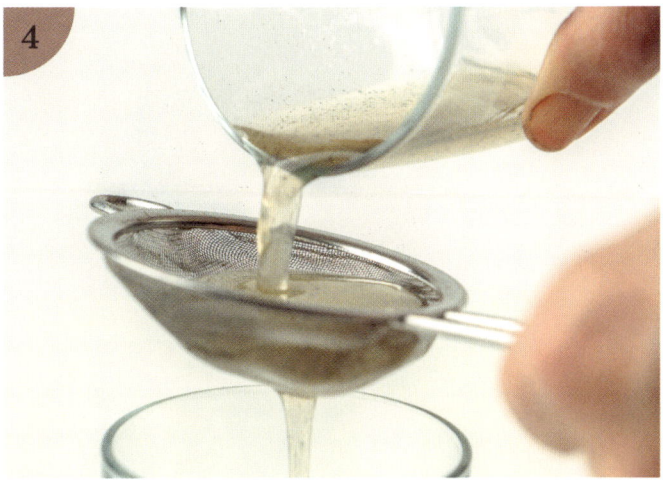

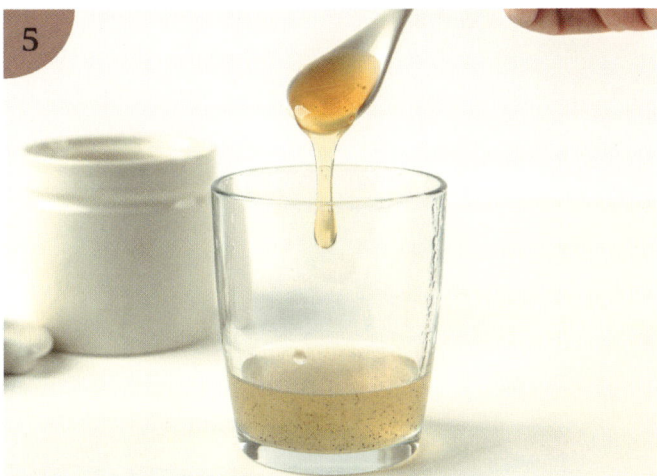

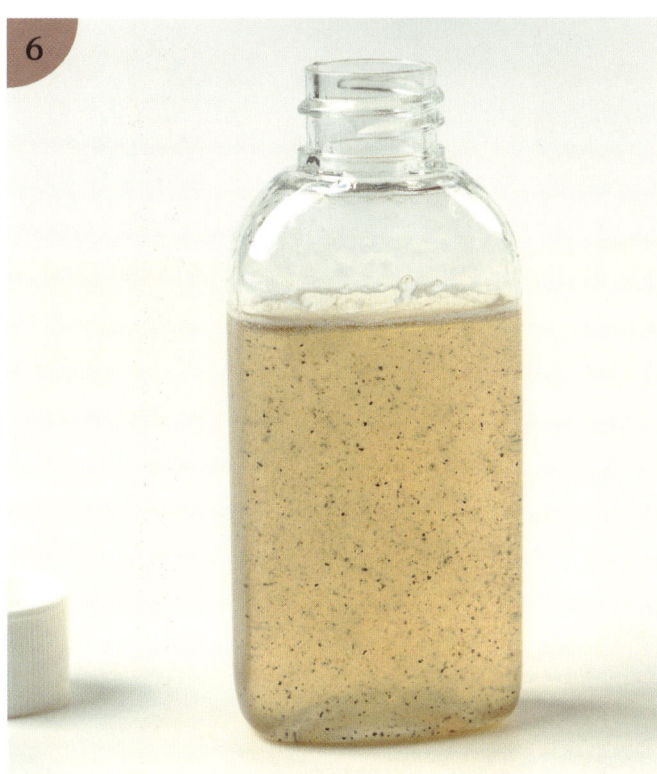

Additional batches with *Prunus* gum

When processing foraged gum, there will probably be some lumpy gum gel left in the strainer after step 4. This can be reused. Just return it to the saucepan, add a cupful of hot or just-boiled water, and repeat the cooking, cooling and straining processes. You can do this up to two times. Each batch will be a little paler. You can either add them all together or keep them graded for different colour paint making. They are not as adhesive as the first medium but produce a very matt binder.

4 In the morning, you'll find the gum has turned into a gel or has begun to dissolve. Pour this into a saucepan and warm it on a low heat for half an hour or so, until the gel is the consistency of runny honey (you can add more water if there is not enough for it to be stirred easily). When it has cooled a little, place a tea strainer over a container and pour the gel through. The little flecks of bark and other detritus should be left behind in the strainer, you can just wash these away.

5 Add a rewetting agent such as honey (vegans can use glycerine or powdered sugar dissolved in a little warm water). You need approximately one-part runny honey to nine parts gel. Stir the mixture well.

6 Decant the mixture into a spotlessly clean jar. I like to sieve it again through a finer mesh strainer into the jar at this point. This is your homemade watercolour medium, which you can use in the same way as you would shop-bought medium, or one you have made yourself with liquid or powdered gum Arabic.

THE FINISHED WATERCOLOUR MEDIUM
Once you've filled your vessel, label it well with the ingredients you used and the date you made it. It will look and smell delicious, so I always suggest adding a 'Do Not Eat!' label before putting it in the fridge.

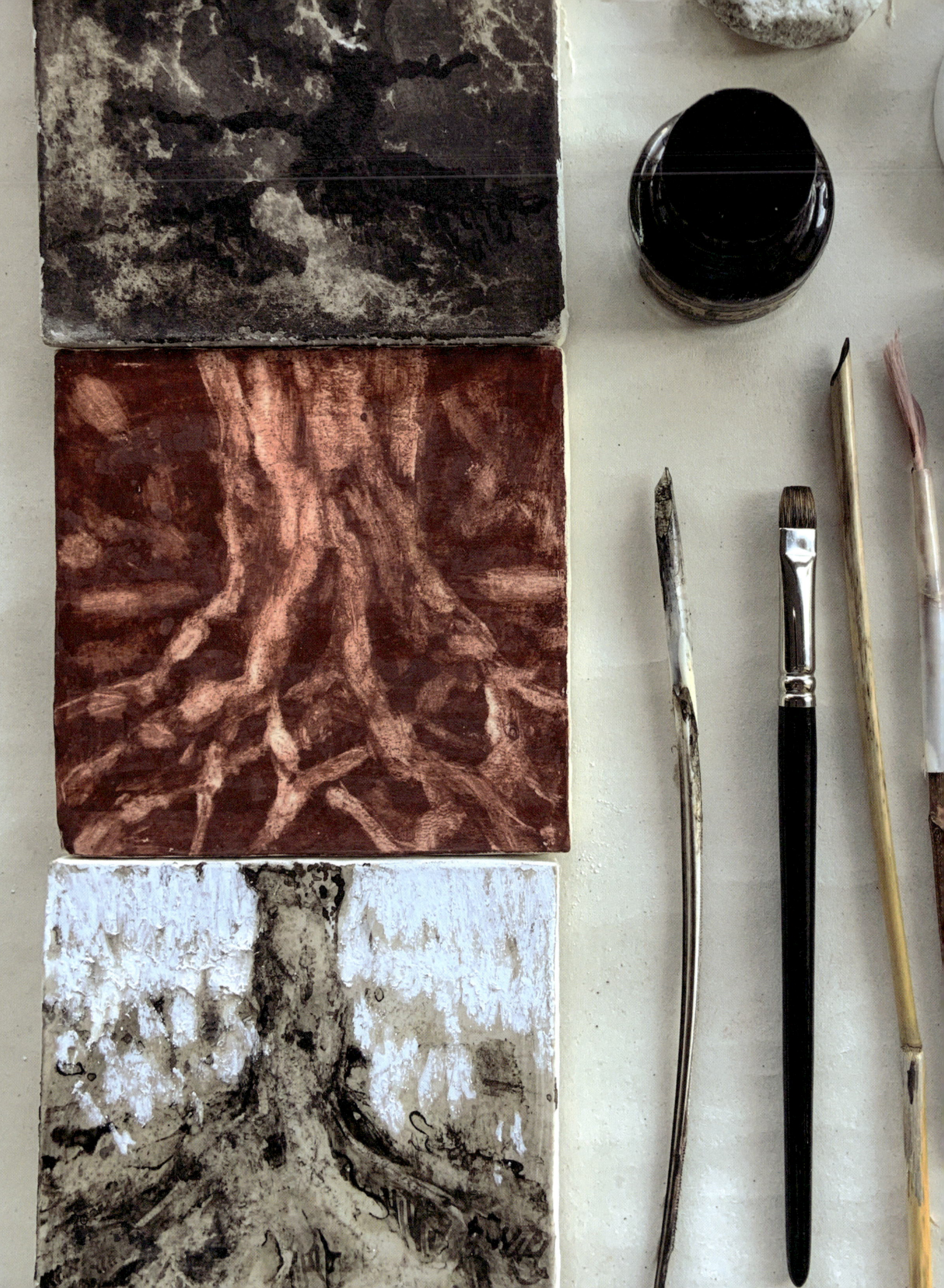

COLOUR YOUR WORLD

EXPLORING YOUR PAINTS

Last winter I remembered an assembly from when I was at junior school. The headmaster told a story of a young child who had only red, black, and brown coloured pencils left in the pencil case, but dearly wanted to make a card for their family, as it was Christmas Eve. A robin came to sit on the snowy window sill as the child gazed sadly out, and they immediately they knew what to draw with just three colours...

Occasionally, looking in the art shop window at all the bright acrylic paints and fluorescent markers, we all feel a little like this child. What if our first palette is, well, a bit heavy on the brown? Firstly, don't worry. As we get a more experienced forager's eye, we'll find more and more tones in nature. More importantly, we'll learn how to make paint well, so that when we find new foraging places we'll do them justice.

Restrictions are some of the best stimuli for making good art. If you have your selection of five or so local pigments to hand, and you don't allow yourself to add anything else to them yet, what can you make? Making a colour mixing chart can be a great first experiment. Tonal studies of a still life or from nature are also great ways to get used to handling our own paints – particularly if we are used to factory-made consistency.

Spend a few hours – or a few days – exploring what can be painted with just what you have made. Rub up against the boundaries, take your shells of paint out and work outside. Sketch family, friends or your surroundings with brush and one colour only. Experiment.

Recording your palette

Making swatches is a great way to record your finds, refine your technique and take a snapshot of your pigment's time and place. A book or file of swatches is helpful when trying to remember where you found a pigment stone, long after the shell of paint is all gone.

There are as many methods of swatching paints as there are natural pigment artists, but here's a few my colour colleagues and I use.

A dedicated sketchbook My first port of call is the style used for the examples earlier in this book. I paint a long line the width of the page, adding more water to the final inch to test for granulation. I add simple notes and the date.

Card file Neat boxes of cards are ideal for longer written notes and bigger swatches.

Large sheets of quality paper These allow you to see many swatches at once, and to compare subtle variations easily.

Test strips If you are a natural dyer or ink maker, you may already use strips of quality acid-free paper to test or record your dyebaths. They're also perfect for swatching. Store them stapled together in a scrapbook or box.

Specialist swatch papers Some fine art suppliers stock sheets of watercolour paper already divided into squares or circles for a neat, consistent look.

One-off paintings or designs Paint a one-off card or sheet in your sketchbook with the new colours you've made, placing the date and any pigment notes on the back.

Linocut or stamped cards Making swatches is an ideal opportunity to express yourself in line drawing to create personalized records – as shown below. You could, of course, use a large ready-made stamp instead. Whichever you use, be sure to print with permanent (non-water-soluble) ink, so your paints don't mix with the black outline.

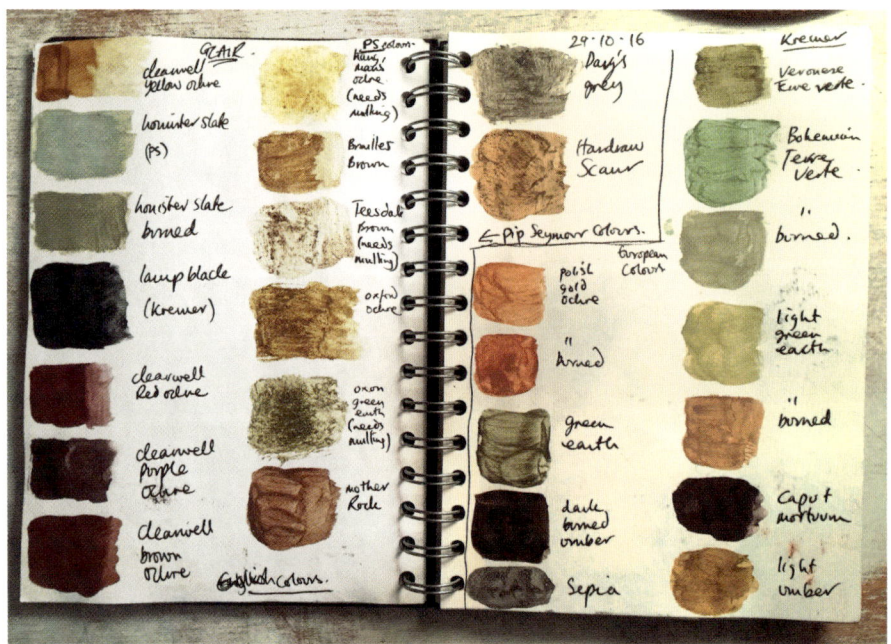

EXAMPLE SPREAD FROM MY SKETCHBOOK

A swatch page made of all the pigments I had in store on one particular day.

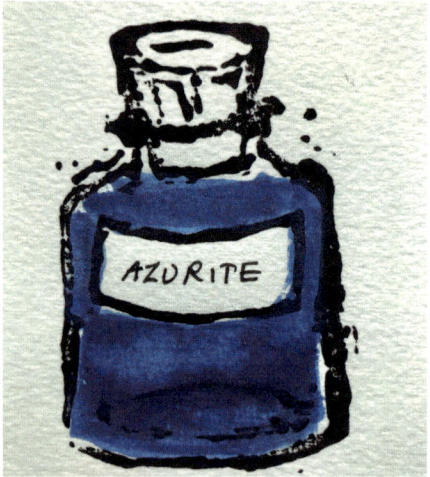

LINOCUT STAMP SWATCH

Ruth Siddall, a geologist at UCL, created a little ink pot stamp, which she uses to make blank spaces for her signature swatch file cards. The shape is then filled in with the colour, and the name written on the 'label'.

The stamp was linocut, and the print made with a homemade oil-based ink made from Frankfurt black and Paris black pigments along with copper plate oil (thickened linseed oil).

Beyond shop-bought

There's no need to be purist about mixing handmade and shop-bought paints, as they complement each other well. By now you will have a selection of foraged watercolours sitting in shells, lids or half pan cases, and perhaps you've noticed the similarity between a few of your tones and those already in your bought watercolour sets. Substituting your handmade earth paints for similar ones in your bought sets will hone your colour-matching skills and is an easy way to start personalizing your palette.

Starting points

Some of the most common colours found all over the world are red and yellow ochres. You are likely to find some on your travels, if you haven't already. These iron oxide-rich colours are some of the most ancient pigments used, and are stable, widely found and beautiful. Test them to see how they handle compared with commercial versions: are yours grittier, more opaque or more transparent?

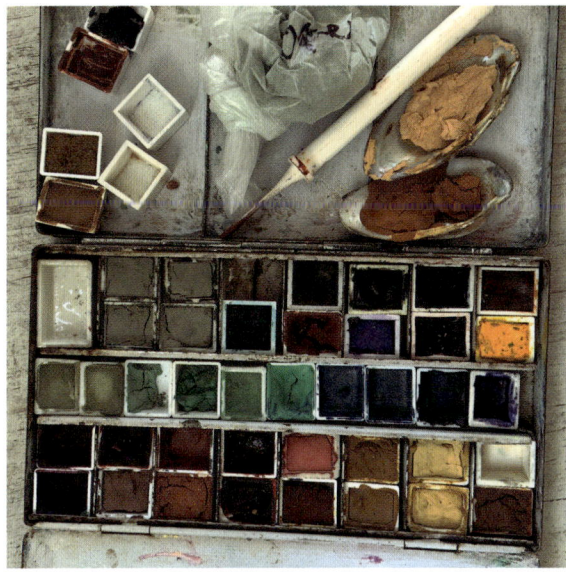

Paints and earths in the studio.

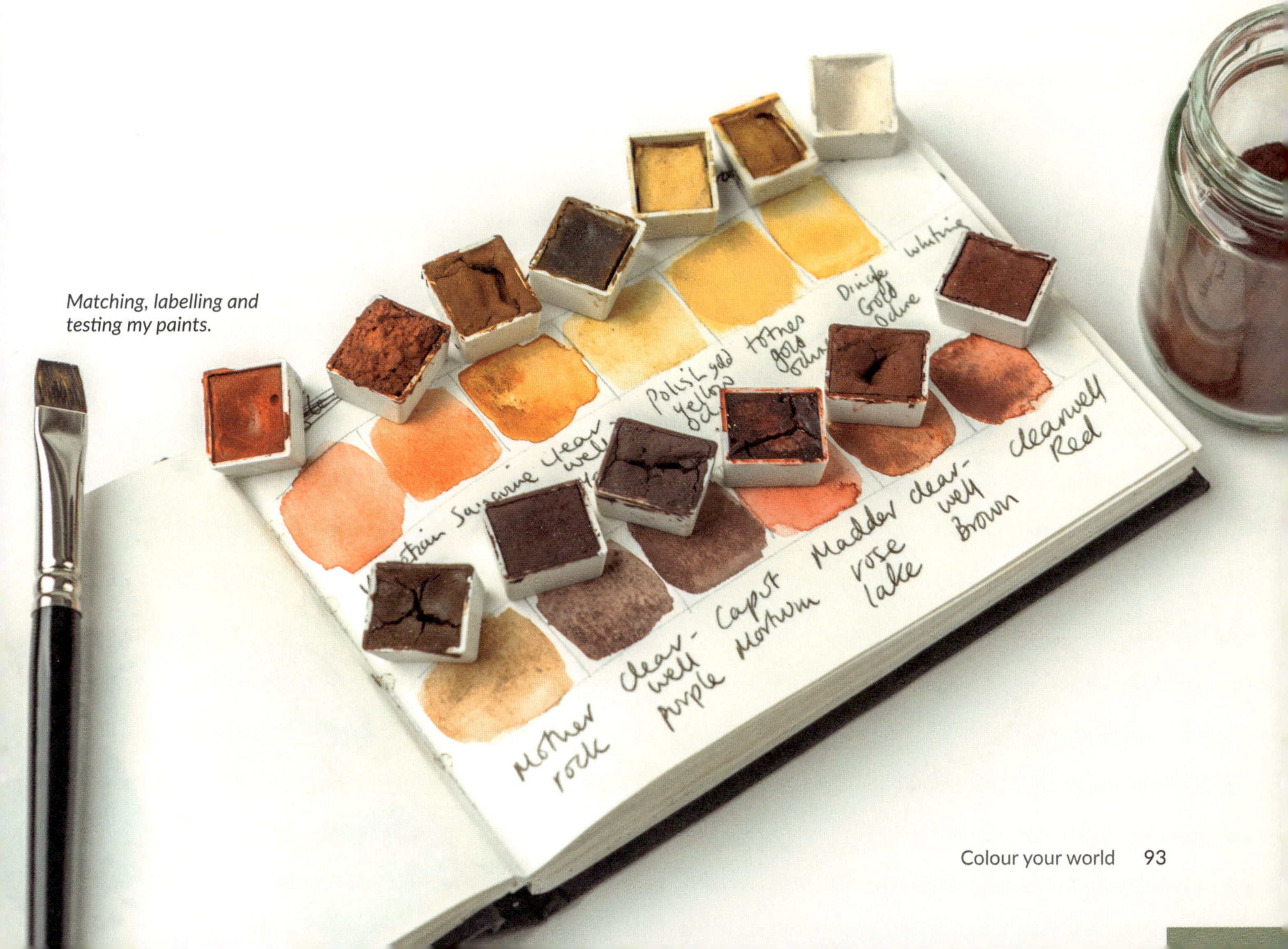

Matching, labelling and testing my paints.

'But what about blue?'

This is a very old question, perhaps as old as painting itself, and a source of great ingenuity, early worldwide trade, and fiercely guarded secrets. Blue pigments are quite rare. Lapis lazuli, literally 'stone of heaven', has been traded since neolithic times, as it is the source of ultramarine pigment – meaning as it does 'from beyond the sea'. The secrets for making other blue pigments, such as smalt, have been passed down in oral traditions and periodically lost for centuries on end.

Because of their rarity, you are unlikely to find strong, rich blues when foraging. Don't worry about buying a commercial blue to fill that gap, if you feel that you need one. You could buy blues from small local makers of paint (easily found online) who use natural binders and high-quality ingredients.

Alternatively, because you now possess the ability to make your own paints, you could buy a pure blue pigment, and create your own. Suppliers of pure pigments are listed online on Bookmarked (www.bookmarkedhub.com) – search for this book by title or ISBN: the files can be found under 'Book Extras'.

You can find bright colours containing non-toxic synthetic pigments that are available from all reputable suppliers. These will mix well with your finds. In my own palette I have two regular blues. Ultramarine is expensive, but you only need a little. Indigo, from plants such as woad, makes a good denim blue when combined with chalk, or can be baked with powdered shells to make the beautiful bright 'Mayan blue'. I sometimes add a third: vivianite, which comes from pine cones, anthropogenic sources, and mineral deposits on organic matter.

Although a purely earth palette is a rich and wonderful thing, varying from place to place reflecting the underlying geology, a contrasting 'zing' is sometimes required. Always feel free to mix things up. This doesn't just apply to blue – add any colours you feel would set off your finds, complement your emerging local colours, or which you feel you need to carry on making the paintings you want to make.

Vivianite

This blue mineral was once a staple of the indigenous cultures of the Pacific Northwest of North America before colonization and assimilation broke the chain of traditional knowledge. Blue paint on artefacts, once mis-ascribed as copper-based, was later found by Melonie Ancheta to be a form of a hydrated iron phosphate blue – vivianite.

Knowledge of this incredible pigment is finding its way back into Pacific North West indigenous art and wider use, thanks to her groundbreaking work. If you're not lucky enough to have foraged some vivianite, but you'd still like to bring blue into your palette, then there is a vast range available commercially.

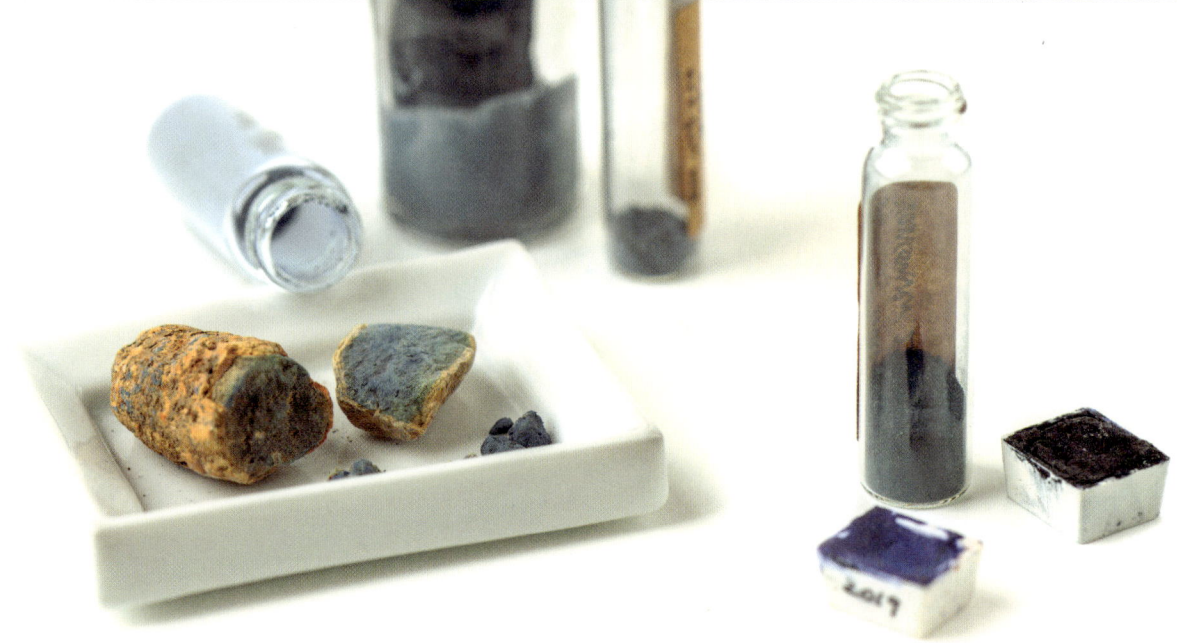

Enriching your palette

We artists have always traded colour, ideas, techniques and materials, and formed deep friendships along the way. Despite being an unapologetic 'sticks and stones' kind of person, one of the upsides of the internet for me is how much easier it is to connect with other natural pigment people. There is nothing stopping you swapping rocks with friends, near or far, to obtain other colours to enrich your palette. I encourage you to make trades! Do you have a glut of that beautiful cool greenish clay watercolour? Connect with someone online or in your locale who has just that warm orange ochre paint you need. Did you grind some local ironstone into a rich red, and now have a bagful? Swap a pot with someone for a lump of their English chalk, which might be as rare as hen's teeth where you live.

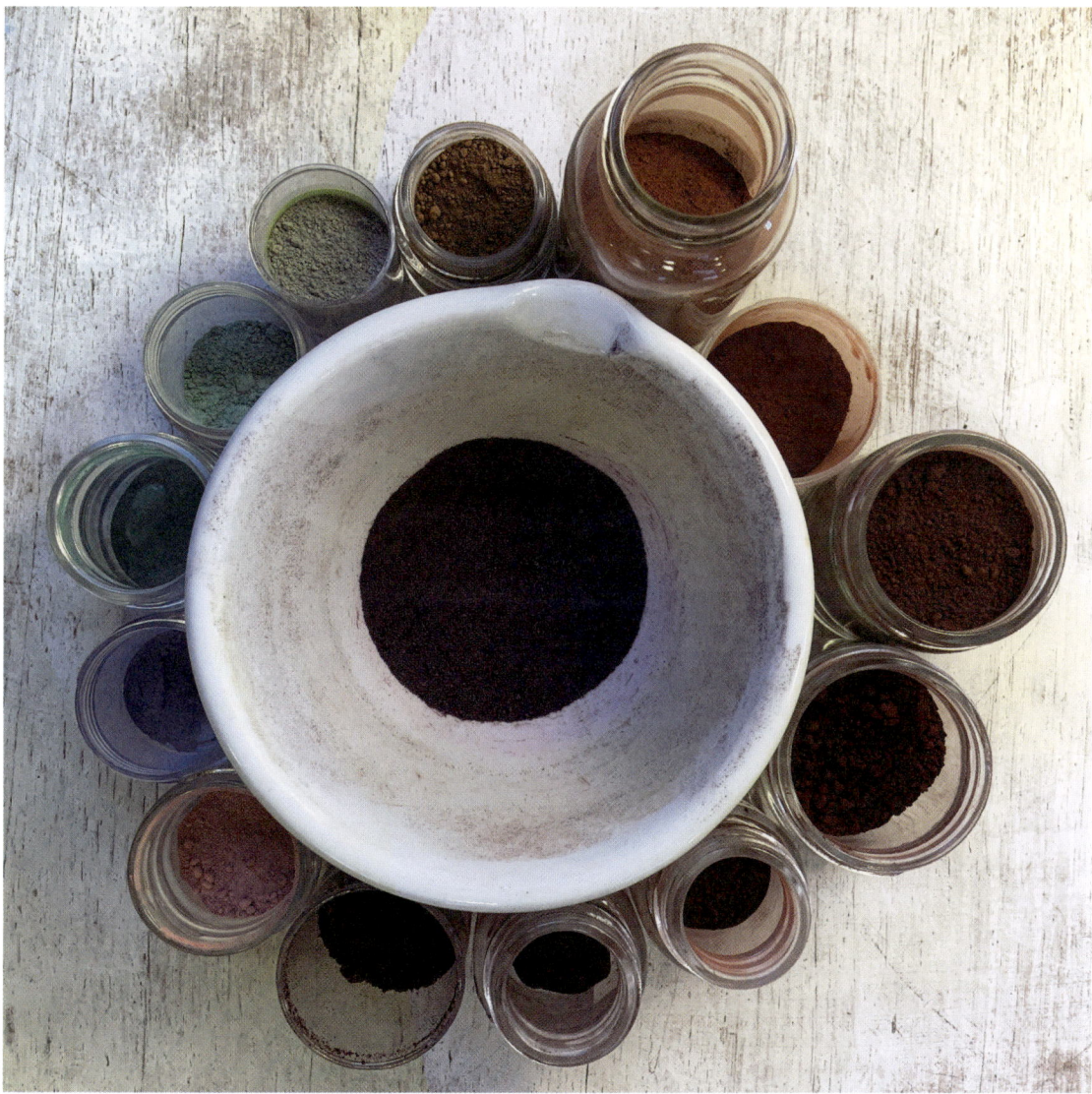

Handmade natural pigments. Shown here are a variety of colours foraged by me, by friends, and natural pigments bought from reputable suppliers or direct from source.

LOCAL COLOUR

The Bohemian green earth in my collection is bright and cool compared with the warmer, softer terre verte I've recently used from France. The brightest red ochres in the UK are found at Clearwell Caves in the Forest of Dean, while the astounding blues of vivianite are to be found mainly in the Pacific North West of America. All of these colours have been traded for centuries, but the traditional and historical art and artefacts from specific places reflect their local colours, whether in frescoes, easel paintings, shields, totem poles or even oil-based paint for iron bridges.

There is indeed such a thing as 'local colour'. For this reason, I can't tell you what you might find, nor what you might want to paint, but the following pages explore the local palettes of different artists from across the world to provide you with ideas and inspiration.

> ❝ **The ingenuity and perseverance of our ancestors the world over are an inspiration.** ❞

A hyper-local palette

At the end of my road is a sandstone clifftop, at the bottom of which is the beach. Many colourful stones wash up along the foreshore due to longshore drift and I occasionally bring a few home to make paint. Here are five from 2022, all from within a kilometre of my home.

I love the rich red ironstone which has a very high tinting strength, so a little goes a long way when mixing. The deep coal black granulates beautifully in watercolour medium. The terracotta, subtle green and off-white tones all blend well and balance the palette with high and mid notes. What's missing from this selection are yellows or blues, neither of which can be found on this stretch of beach.

Enriching this palette

If I want to supplement this palette, then my first port of call is to message one of my colour friends abroad I met online and suggest a swap. Ironstone deep red for some vivianite blue, perhaps? As for yellow, I could add a bit of bright ochre clay from Devon and stretch the palette's terrain west a bit. Alternatively, I could buy a special pigment from Cornelissen or Kremer, such as lapis lazuli or gold ochre, to add highlights.

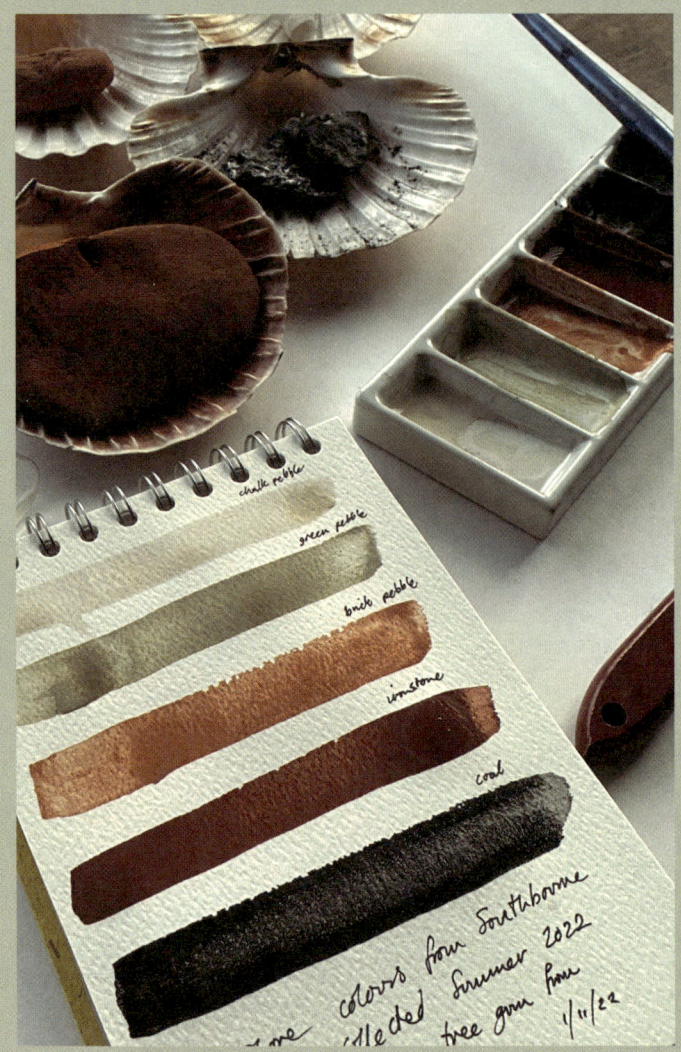

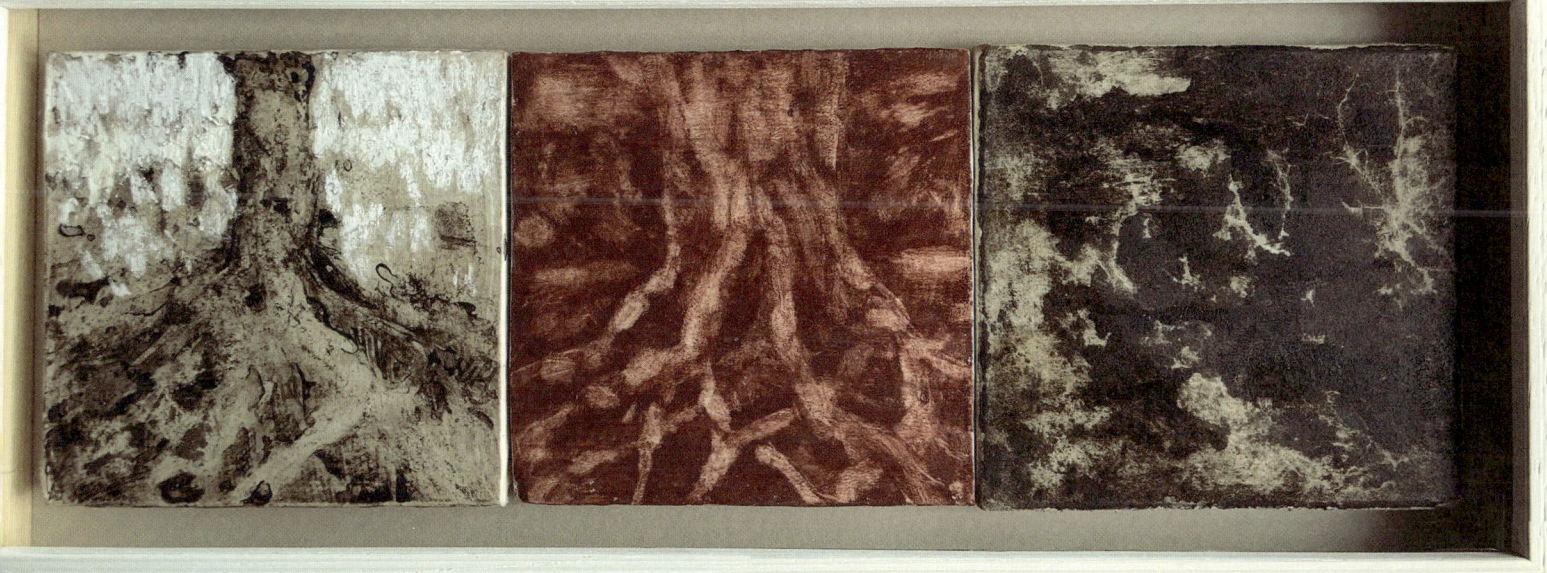

BENEATH THE LABYRINTH 41 x 18cm (16 x 7in)

Red ochre watercolour, iron gall ink and chalk on parchment. I relish a restricted palette, especially the alchemical colours of black, white and red. Made for a show with the Wild Pigment Project at Form and Concept Gallery, Santa Fe, only raw lump chalk from near Stonehenge, the red haematite paint shown on pages 80–83 and iron gall ink were used to paint three trees on deer skin parchment.

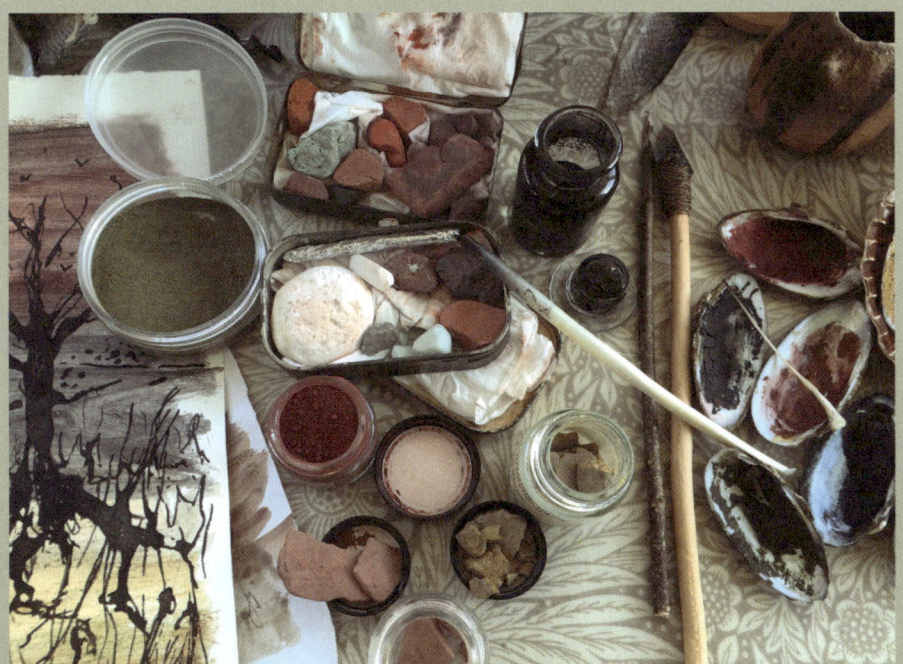

There are no rules. Keep our colours strictly geographical or mix them up? For me it always depends on the context and, even more importantly, what is needed by the piece I am painting at that moment.

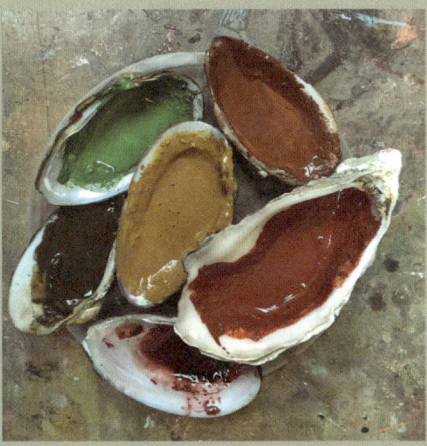

The first artists' quality watercolours that I ever made.

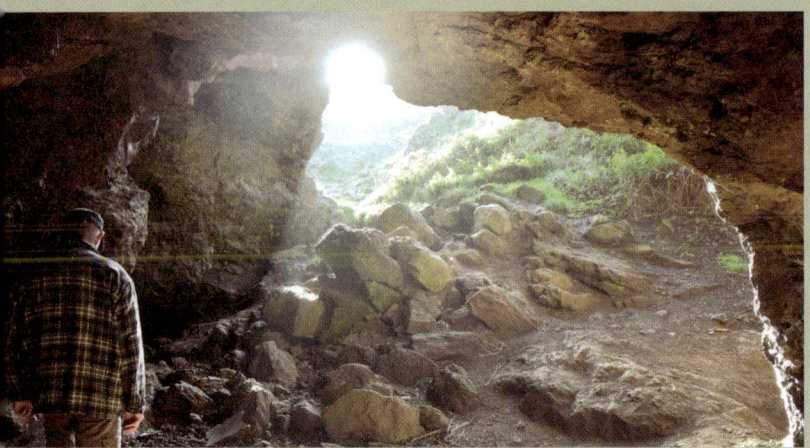

Peter Ward's palette

Artist Peter Ward's interdisciplinary creative research involves aspects of geology, ecology, social and art history around the materials he encounters and selects, and whose provenance forms the basis for the animated contemporary conversations that are expressed through his painting and workshops.

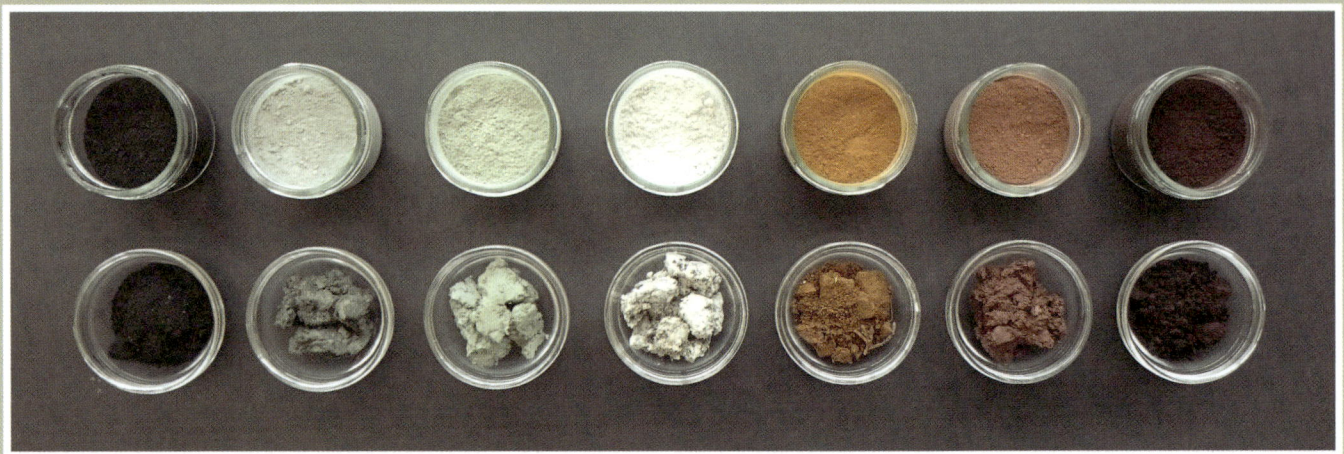

A Cornish landscape – raw and processed earth pigments from Peter's palette.

Colours from Cornwall

Peter works exclusively with pigments that he has sourced and gathered himself in Southwest England. Peter's artistic journey with earth pigments began in 2007 in North Devon, focusing on the historically renowned pigment Bideford black. He moved to West Cornwall in 2017, where his study highlighted pigments sourced from both natural geological landforms and historic mining waste.

He says: 'When painting, the limited colour range available in localized areas amply represents the spirit of place, while challenging Western preconceptions about the nature of painting itself. The limits offer a counterpoint to the indulgence of the overconsumption that underpins contemporary society, and asserts a sense of unity with earth cultures around the world.'

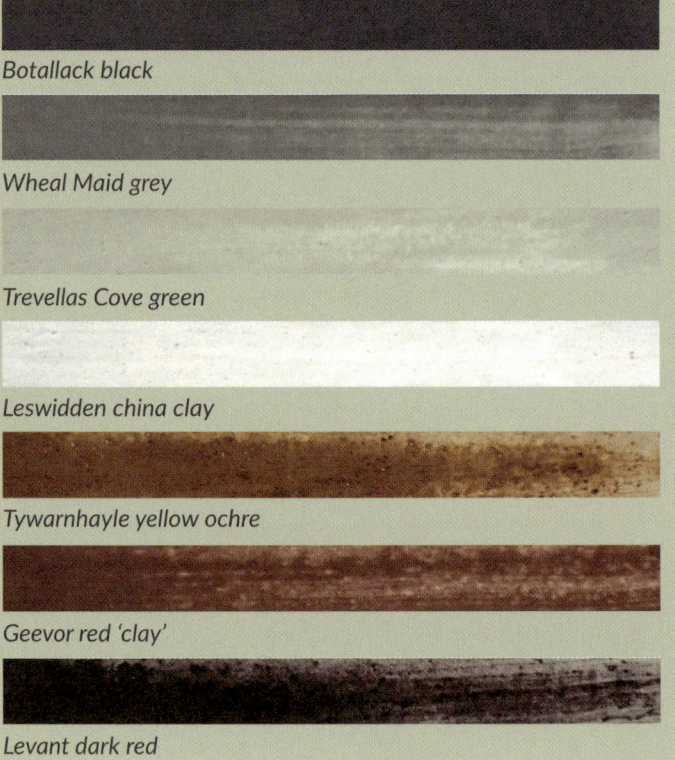

Botallack black

Wheal Maid grey

Trevellas Cove green

Leswidden china clay

Tywarnhayle yellow ochre

Geevor red 'clay'

Levant dark red

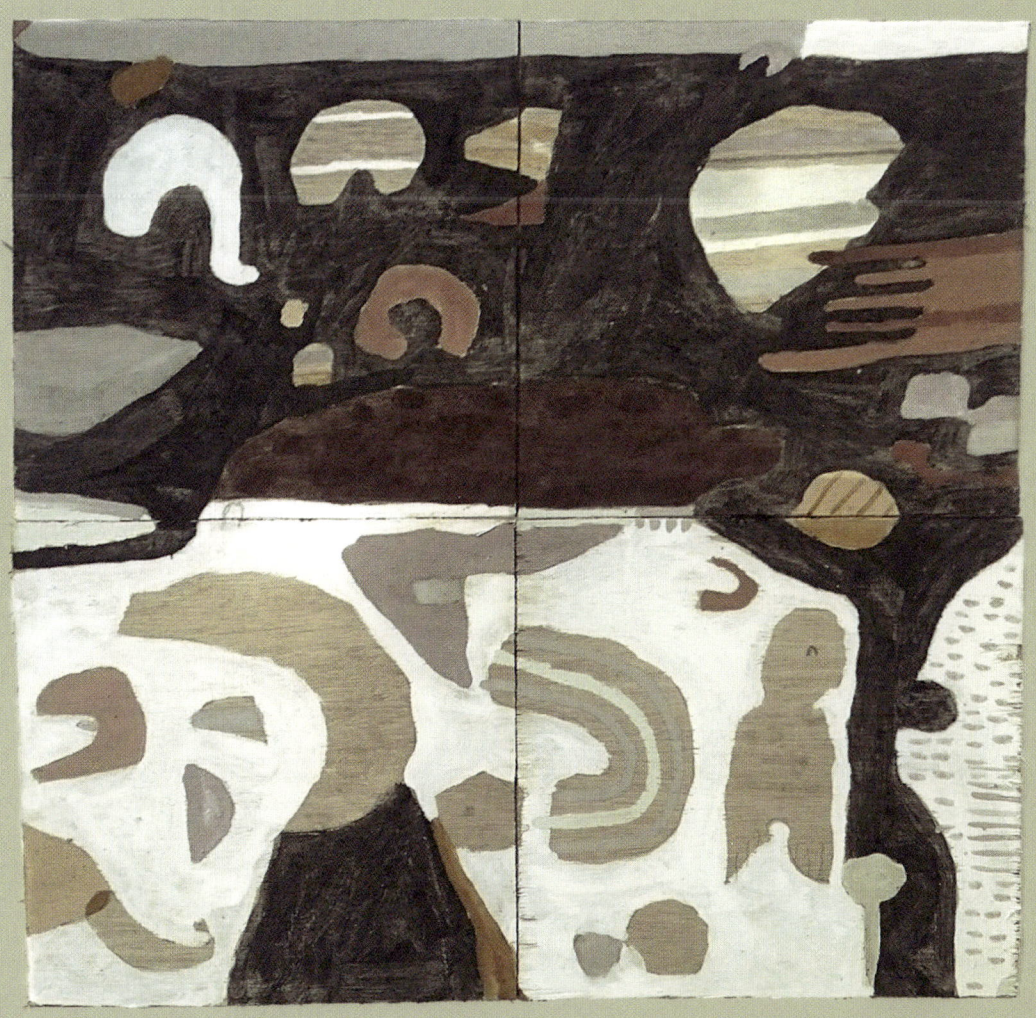

MEYN HIR DRE DEVEL YN GWELYOW, GANS ELERGH HA
BUGHES HA GODHOW – PENWITH
68 x 70cm (26¾ x 27½in)
*Cornish earth pigments on salvaged board, 2019. The title translates into English
as 'Stones that Stand in Fields with Swans and Cows and Geese – Penwith'.*

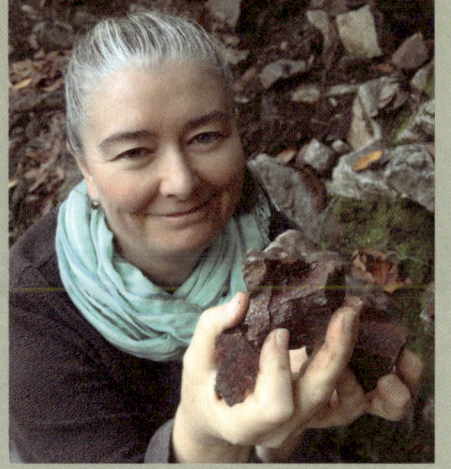

Shinehah Bigham's palette

Shinehah, from the USA, uses locally foraged earth pigments from stones, ochres, clays and botanicals to make abstract and representational paintings. When using the handmade mixtures, her aim is to let the expression of the paintings embody the nature of the pigments themselves, as what they are made of is a part of what they are about.

She says: 'The lands from which I respectfully gather these precious pigments is within the unceded indigenous homelands of both the Awaswas- and Mutsun-speaking peoples, from whom the modern Amah Mutsun Tribal Band is descended.'

Shinehah Bigham, holding some of her foraged raw materials.

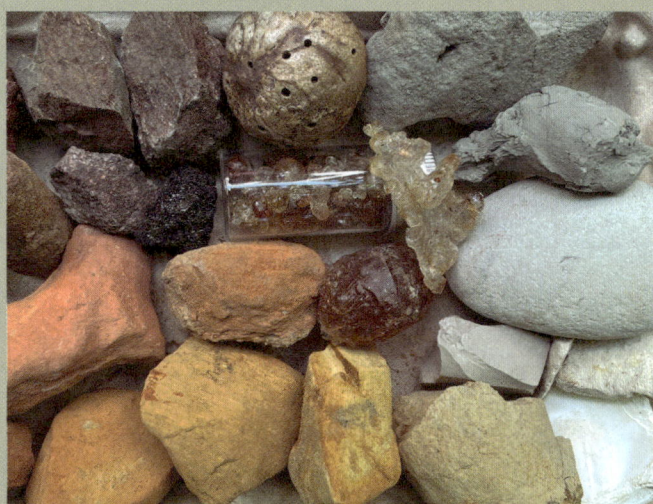

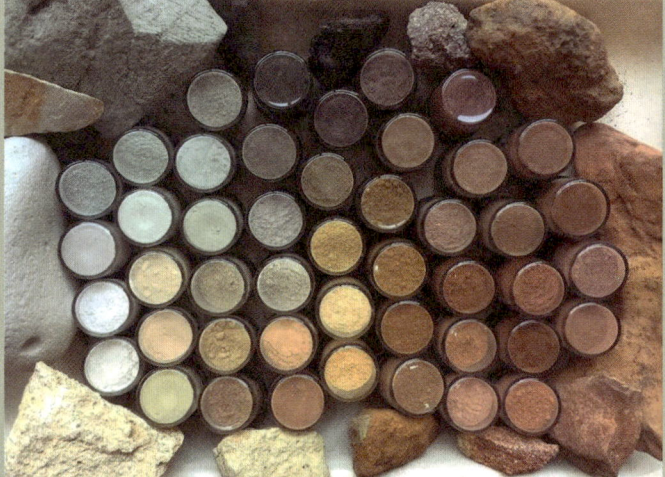

Shinehah's pigments and paints

Shinehah forages from lands known to the Amah Mutsun as *Popeloutchom*, within an area nowadays called Santa Cruz County, California. The pigments come from wild, windy cliffsides, serene creeksides deep in the forest, and 150m (500ft) deep under the ground, unearthed by the digging of water wells.

After the intimate process of foraging these pigments from her nearby environment, she grinds, levigates and mulls them into pigments (see above right), and then produces paint using the traditional tempera technique (see pages 108–109) with egg yolk as binder; or as handmade watercolours with foraged binder of acacia or plum tree gum. She finds stones with holes formed by the actions of clams boring into them on the beach. These make perfect containers, as you can see to the right.

The colour of earth pigments can change dramatically depending on the size of the particles of pigment. Shinehah sometimes leaves a pigment slightly grainy to keep the colour as it is at that stage. That can determine the type or thickness of the medium with which it can be painted.

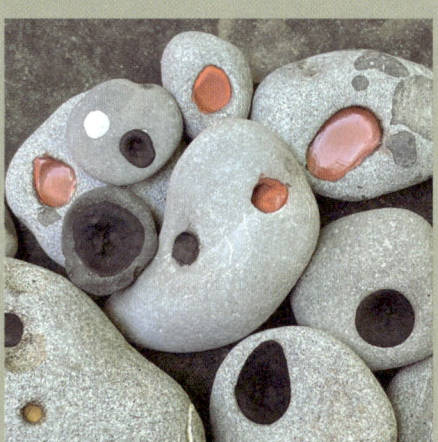

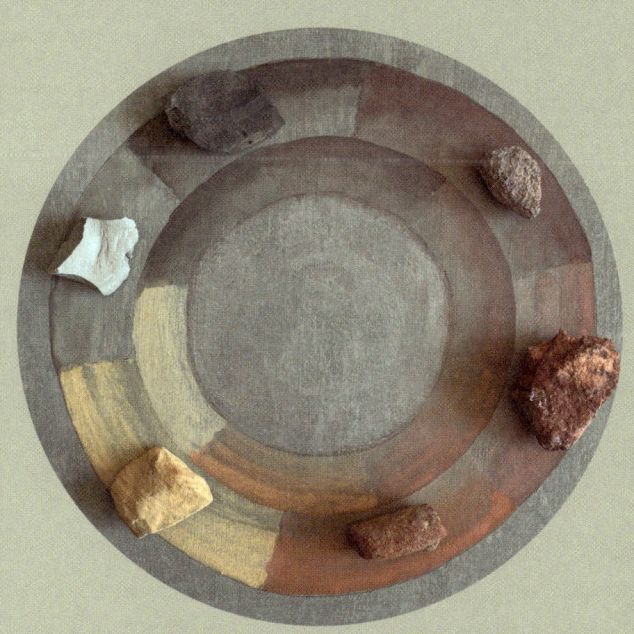

COLOUR WHEEL OF SHINEHAH'S PAINTS

My local region has differences in geography, geology, economy, race and culture. The outer circle of this colour wheel shows six pigments – three from the south of the county and three from the north – while the inner circle shows the colour combinations made by mixing together those next to each other.

This poses the question: 'Is this a map, a chart, or a piece of art in itself?'

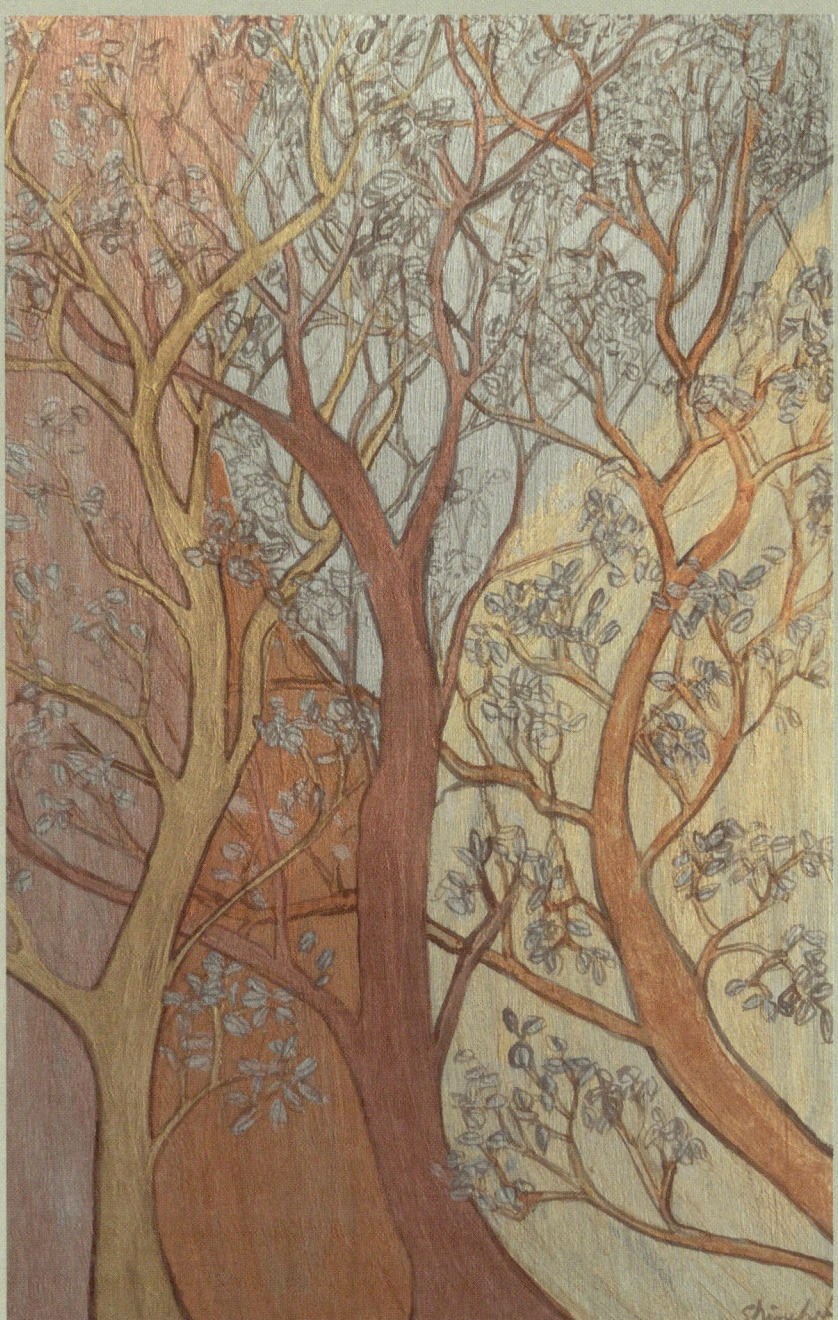

THREE OAKS   19 x 28cm (7¼ x 11in)
Ochres and clay pigments in egg yolk tempera on native clay-covered wood.

Ground yellow ochre from a sea cliff, ground shimmering micaceous pink from a redwood forest trail, orange ochre washed and levigated from an eroded bluff and blue clay from the digging of a water well. Painted using egg yolk as binder over rough homemade clayboard, this painting is an experiment of how each of these pigments show up overlapping and next to each other.

Nina Cadzow's palette

Nina enjoys the connection with nature that she experiences while collecting mud and rocks – reminding her, as she puts it, 'of the fact I am of the earth'. She uses minerals from her home in the south-west of England and Australia, where she was born.

She says: 'The process of pigment hunting is as important as the art I make. Both elements are on a continuum and can't readily be separated out. I predominantly use the earth on which I live to render my paintings, letting the colours determine the direction I can take, and being content with the fact that there are boundaries and limitations.'

Nina supplements her palette with exotic earths when her art demands (see right). These additions include Italian yellow earth, oriental red and a synthetic ultramarine – the latter because she hasn't found any blue in either of her usual locations.

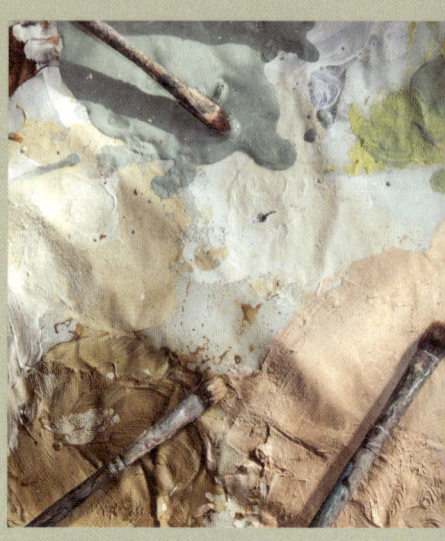

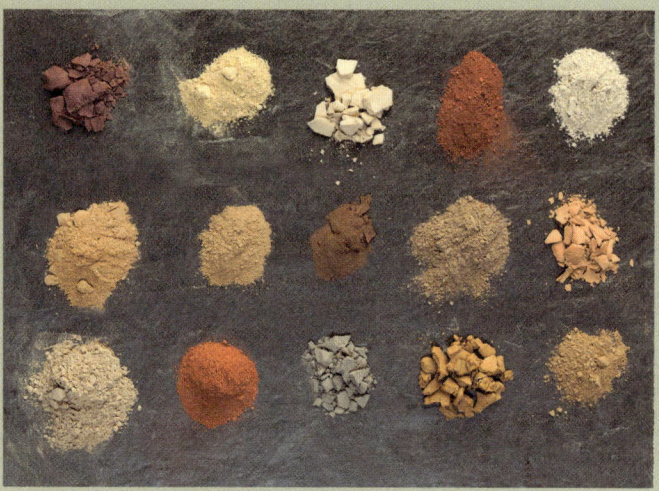

The gorgeous Australian pigments in their raw state. Foraging colours, Nina says, 'means that I get to wander in lovely places, hear fascinating stories and meet interesting people along the way – all acts of connectivity.'

Dual heritage foraging

Colour in minerals and earth is determined by oxidation and hydration, and since Australia is one of the older geological formations it stands to reason that the pigments are more vibrant than those from the comparatively young geology of the UK. The Australian continent is a vast and varied place with many climate zones, ranging from cool temperate, tropical, and arid desert.

Nina forages from Melbourne and the nearby Yarra valley, in the modern state of Victoria. Cold in winter and wet in good years, it is also baking hot in summer. The region is traditional Wurrundjeri and Boonawurrung country. She is careful to pay her respects to the traditional owners of the lands: she says 'taking the time to acknowledge the traditional owners of the land reminds us that we live, work and dream on native country.'

Nina refers to her UK-foraged colours as her 'TQ colours', referring to her home postcode in Devon. While not as vibrant as the Australian equivalents, her TQ colours show a huge variation in the hue of the ubiquitous red earth that covers the fields for miles around her UK home.

NINA'S 'TQ' COLOURS

The cherry sap is from the cemetery next door to Nina's house, the bright reds from rocks salvaged from an interior wall in her stone cottage, the pale clays and greens from the pathways leading out of town towards Harberton, and the postern yellow gathered from beneath a tree that blew over in a big storm.

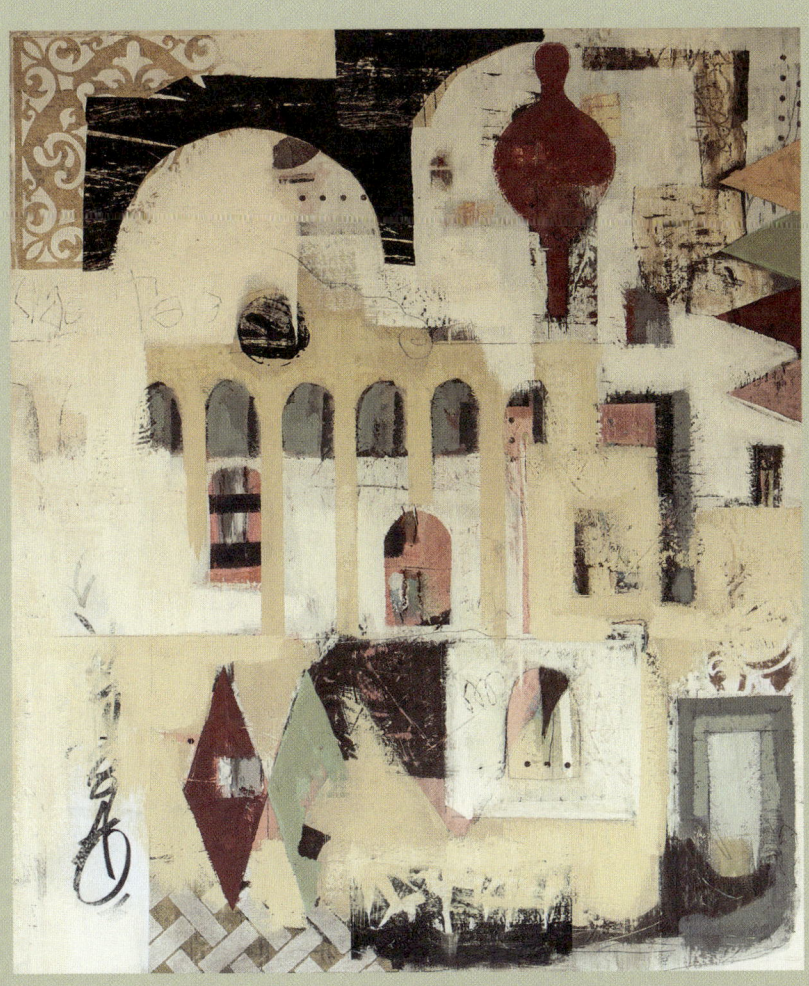

CARLTON NORTH 50 x 60cm (19½ x 23½in)

I want my work to convey a sense or feeling of a place. Postern yellow, toolangi red, oriental red and ultramarine paints are combined here with oil pastel and collage.

My exposure to indigenous Australian thinking fostered thoughts about my own – and others' – indigeneity. How many of us have lost our connection to the land, and therefore our concern for it?

In digging for pigments and foraging on my ancestral lands, I remind myself of our diminishing resources, and take only what I can reasonably process.

COLOUR WHEEL OF NINA'S AUSTRALIAN PIGMENTS

Both the English and traditional names of the locations of the pigments are recorded in this wheel. Clockwise from top, the text reads: Mt Riddell pale ochre – Wurundjeri; Sunnyside grey – Boonwurrung; Mt Riddell chocolate – Wurundjeri; Mt Riddell olive clay – Wurundjeri; Cape schanck chocolate earth – Boonwurrung; sunny side beach pink – Boonwurrung; Sunnyside beach red – Boonwurrung; Port Macquarie orange – Biripal; Toolangi orange – Taungarong; Mt Riddell orange – Wurundjeri; Kunyung beach yellow – Boonwurrung; Port Macquarie gold – Biripal

The outer band shows the pigment mixed with gum Arabic to show the colour at its most transluscent.

The second band shows the pigment mixed with egg tempera, to show the pigment in its most dense and saturated form.

The third and innermost bands show tonal variations of the pigment mixed with clay, which reveals whether the pigment is yellow-, red- or grey-based. In turn, this allows Nina to play with subtle variations of 'white'.

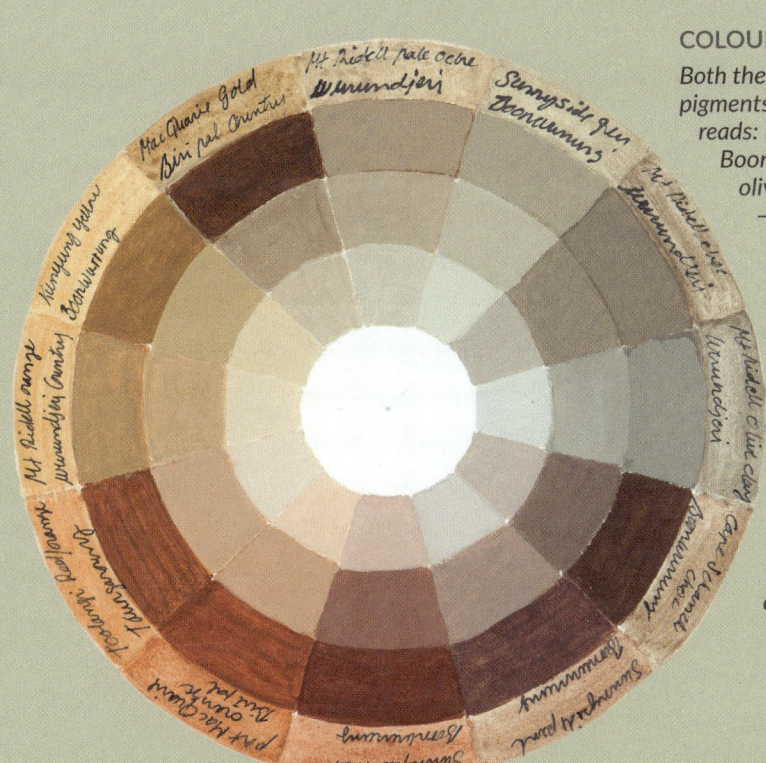

Scott Sutton's palette

Based in Taos, New Mexico in the USA, Scott Sutton's background lies in fine art, and making paints with mineral and plant pigments. Under the name, Pigment Hunter, he aims to create a space that celebrates the culture of colour in a world where we are witnessing a shift back to living in partnership with nature.

His vision is to create an educational environment for workshops, a gallery space for exhibiting art infused with the natural world, and an artist in residence programme for other artists who want to live and create art that embodies an intimate relationship and sensitivity to place.

The artwork opposite, part of a larger piece housed in the Taylor Ranch Community Center, is influenced by his degree in landscape architecture, and integrates his interests in mapping, 3D modelling, and fabrication using a CNC router.

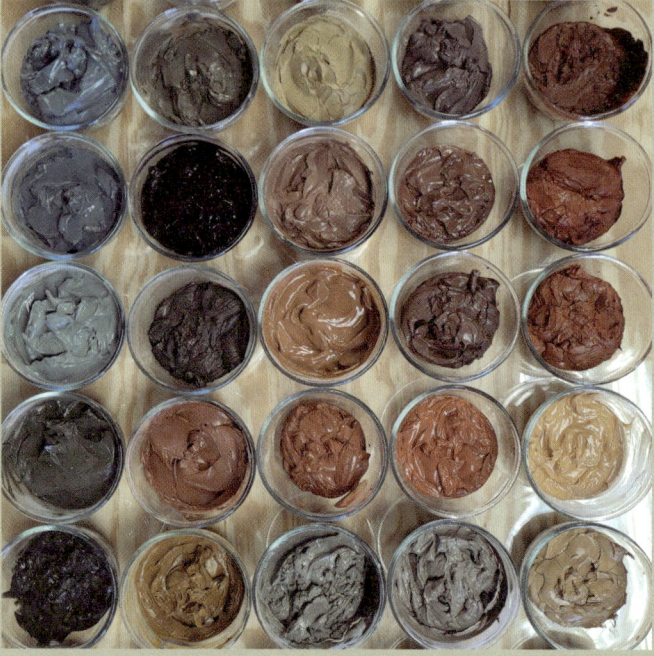

Scott's pigments and paints

The paints shown to the left are egg tempera (see page 108), made with stand oil binder mixed with mineral pigments collected from the Middle Rio Grande basin, and Japanese indigo, grown in the headwaters of the river basin. It is the latter that provides the shades of blue, while the mineral pigments provide the ranges of red, yellow, orange, browns, blacks, and whites.

Most of the minerals in the area are iron rich and vary in colour depending on their chemical composition. Anhydrous iron oxide, also known as haematite, provides various shades of reddish colour, while hydrous iron oxides – such as limonite or goethite – provide the various yellow hues. Other natural elements, such as manganese, combine with the iron oxides to make darker ruddy colours along with purples and browns.

Besides these pigments, Scott also uses coal for black, limestone for white or grey, and incorporates flakes of mica into some of his paints to give them their distinctive sparkle.

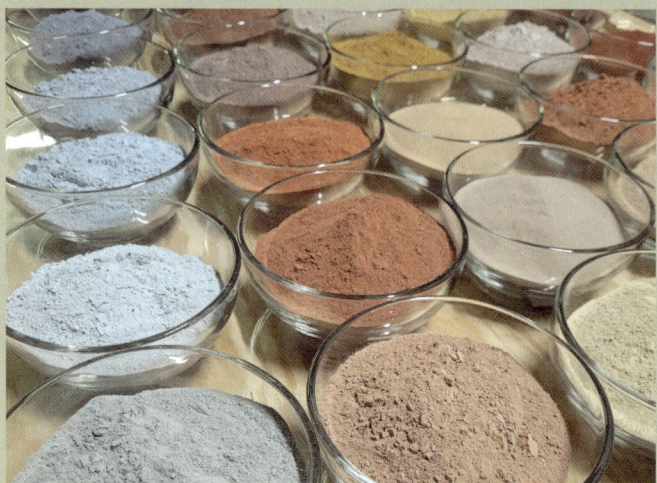

Hand-collected and processed mineral pigments from the Rio Grande basin.

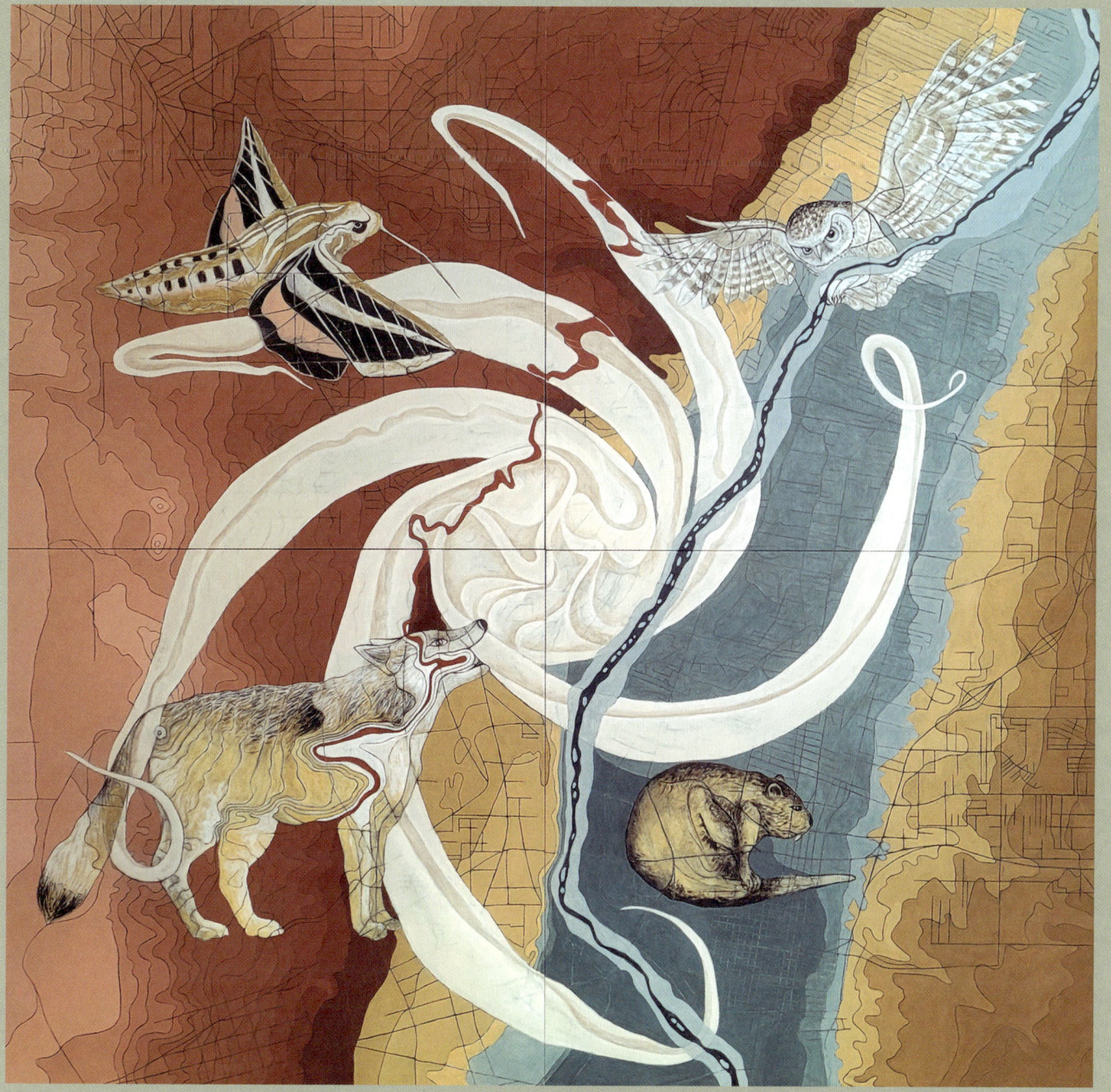

NOCTURNAL SUBTERRANEAN SPECIES OF THE RIO GRANDE BOSQUE
244 x 244cm (96 x 96in)

Part of a three-panel triptych, this geographical/topographical map is focused on the Taylor Ranch Community Center with the volcanoes of the Petroglyph National Monument and the Rio Grande bosque (forest environment). The map includes the roads that criss-cross the landscape, the contour lines, the flow of hydrological systems, and the diverse ecological habitat.

The species in this panel are all active at night, and include those whose territories range from burrowing beneath the ground to flying above it. Central to the piece is the night-blooming Datura flower, sacred to the Havasupai people of the region. It is depicted opening up as a spiral while providing nectar for the hawkmoth.

The other species – the owl, beaver and Mexican grey wolf – all historically dwell along the bosque or in the nearby mountains.

BEYOND WATERCOLOUR

By mixing your pigment with another carrier medium, you can create various other kinds of paint. Different materials will produce different types of paint, from opaque gouache to rich tempera. Art continues to develop, so you can likewise grow and experiment – as I show here with my creation, veglair.

Gouache

Gouache (or poster paint) is watercolour with added chalk or filler to give it body and opacity. It is completely intermixable with watercolours.

In a pestle and mortar, place one part of your chosen ready prepared foraged pigment, with anything up to one part powdered chalk, whiting or ground washed eggshells, and one part of your homemade watercolour medium. Mix it well and test a little of the paint on a piece of paper to see how it brushes out. We are looking for an opaque, fluid paint that covers well and doesn't streak. Add more water or pigment to adjust the flow or to lessen the gloss. When the paint test is dry, rub it a little and add more medium to your recipe if you find it too powdery.

Each pigment you use might need a different amount of chalk or binder to get the feel and coverage just right. Gouache is stored moist and ready to use. When you have a gouache mixed just right, make your final notes, then add a drop or two of antifungal essential oil to the mix, stir it in, and decant into a spotless little jar and label it well. If you are storing it in a refrigerated or in a cool place, you won't need the essential oil.

You will need

/ Teaspoon
/ Sieve
/ Bowl
/ Smooth surface
/ Palette knife
/ Prepared pigment
/ Finely-ground foraged chalk
/ Whiting (refined calcium carbonate powder)
/ Small clean jars with lids in which to store the paint
/ Watercolour medium
/ Paintbrush and paper

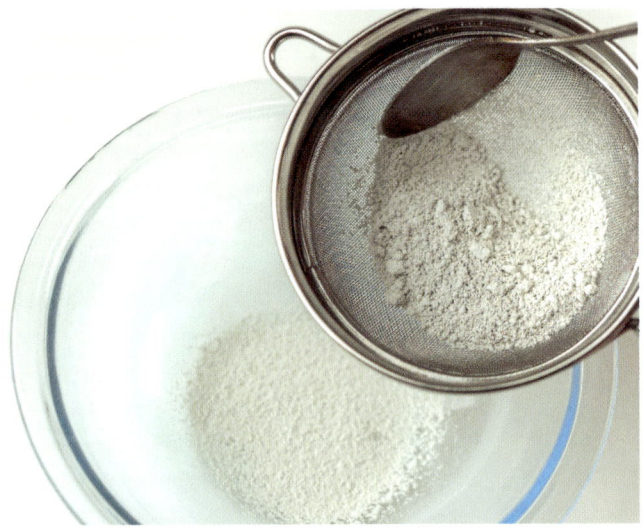

1 Sieve some smashed chalk, using the back of a teaspoon to encourage it through the mesh.

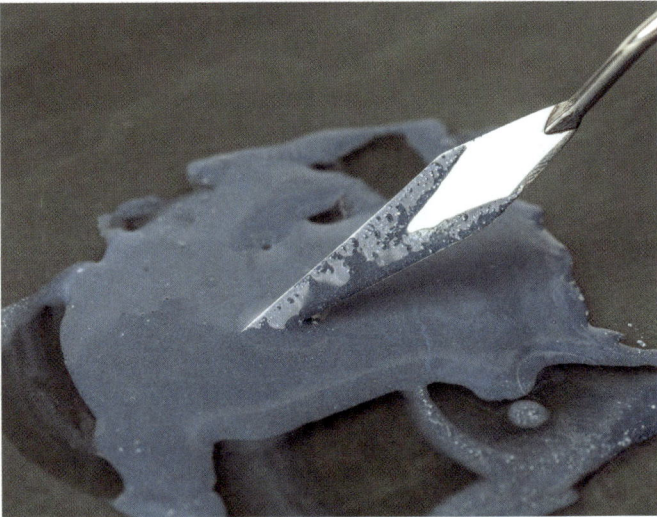

2 On a smooth surface, use a palette knife to combine one part refined pigment with one part sieved chalk.

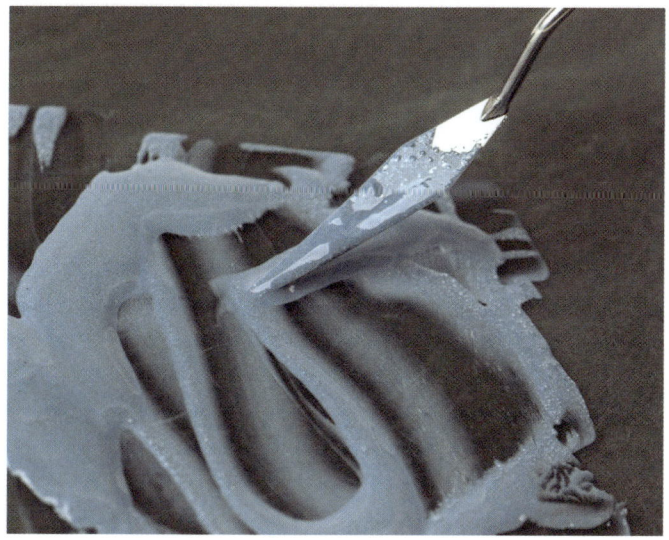

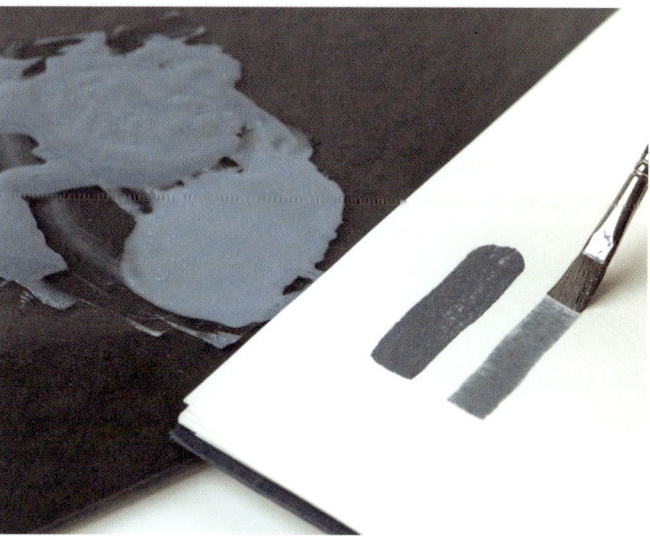

3 Add the same volume of watercolour medium as the powdered pigment and whiting mixture. To make your gouache paint opaque, you may find you need to add more filler. Add chalk or whiting gradually until it is the required consistency.

4 This is now ready to be used, usually slightly thicker than with watercolour paint.

How to use gouache

Gouache is an excellent all-round paint with good covering power, and can even take a little layering and overpainting, if used quite dry. As such it is a good replacement for acrylic, especially for children, where they are just painting on paper and won't be reworking it later.

Gouache prepared as described here should store indefinitely in a cool dark place. If it dries out, just add a little water and mix well to reinvigorate it. Gouache is ideal for use on heavier card and paper to make cards and craft items.

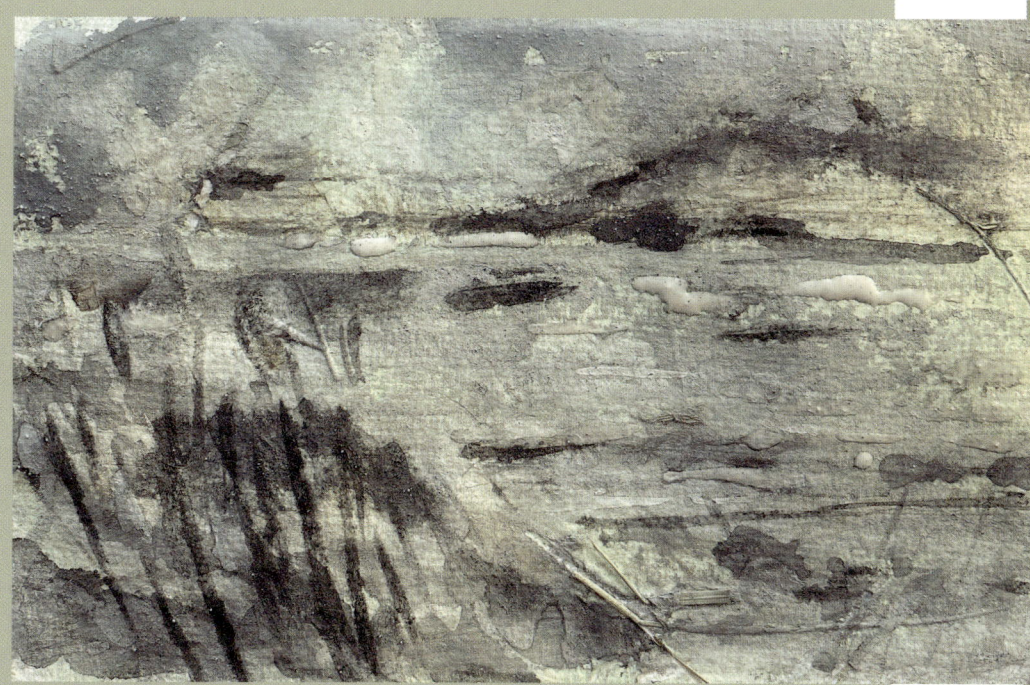

VIEW TOWARDS MULL SKETCH
Vivianite and chalk gouache with coal details on a malachite watercolour wash ground.

Egg tempera

You will need

/ Egg
/ Glass tumbler
/ White vinegar
/ Prepared pigment
/ Measuring spoons
/ Paintbrush and paper

Egg tempera is a versatile medium that can often replace acrylic. Made from egg yolk, it is beautiful, long-lasting and simple to use. Before oil painting, it was the mainstay of easel painting in Europe. Although water-soluble, the medium is an emulsion of tiny oil particles in liquid. Unlike gum watercolour, tempera is made fresh as we use it. There are countless recipes for making tempera from egg yolk, some involving wine or white wine vinegar. I have had great results creating glossy, smooth paints with just yolk and water, so see what works best for you.

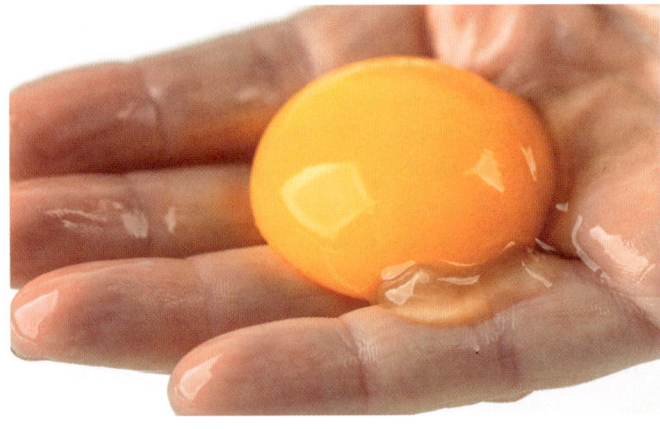

1 Separate an egg so that you have the yolk in your palm. (If you keep the white, you'll be able to use it for glair, overleaf.)

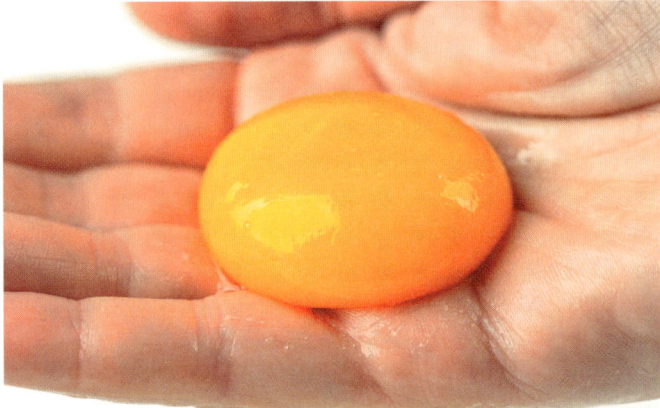

2 Roll it gently from hand to hand to dry the yolk sac. This will make it less slippery and easier to pick up.

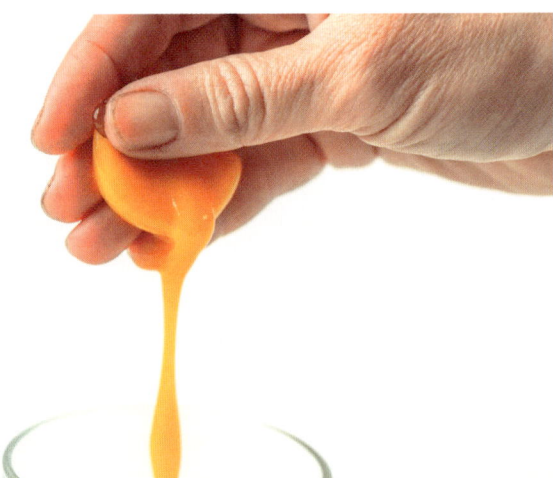

3 Hold the yolk over a glass, and gently pinch the yolk sac between two fingers to break it, releasing the yolk itself into the glass. Discard the empty sac.

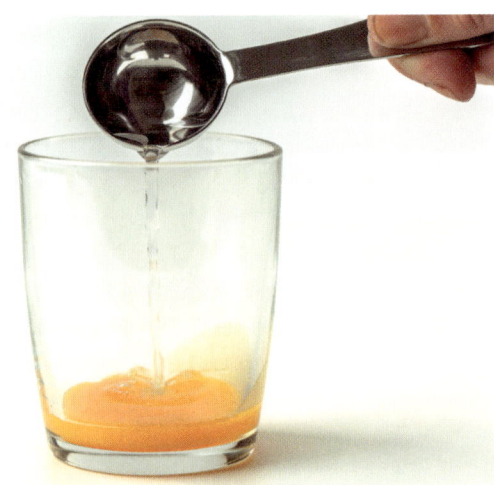

4 Add up to twice as much white vinegar as yolk to the glass, then cover securely and shake vigorously to mix and emulsify. This is the tempera medium.

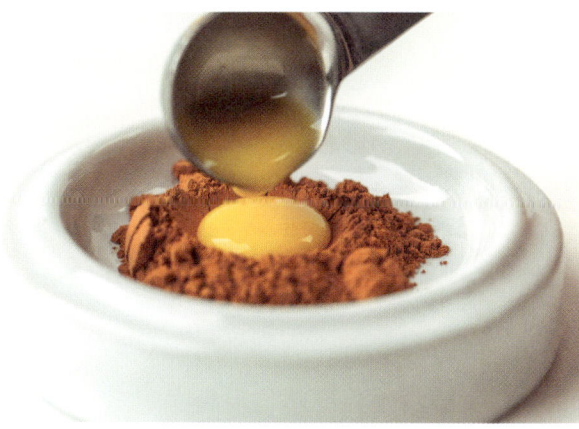

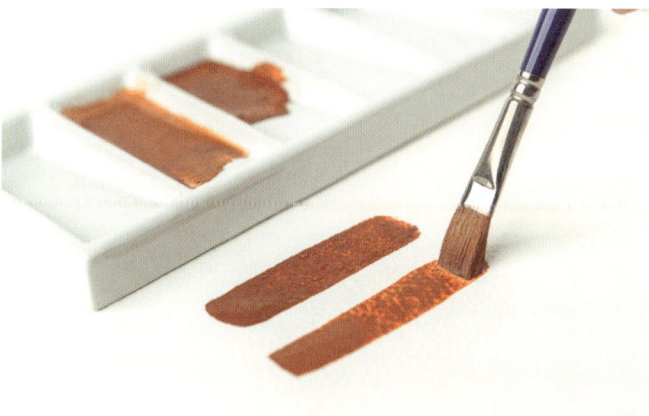

5 To make up into a paint, start with equal parts tempera and refined pigment, then mix as for watercolour (refer to step 4 on page 77 if you'd like a reminder).

6 Add water to the mix to dilute it, and you're ready to use your tempera. You can store it for weeks in a fridge: just smell it to check if it's still okay.

How to use tempera

The classical tempera technique is to apply tiny brushstrokes of separate colour onto finely prepared boards of gesso ground in order to build up tones by optical mixing. You can also use tempera as a broad painting medium on good quality paper in the same way as you might gouache, watercolour or fluid acrylic.

Once tempera is on the paper, you can't rewet or change the paint (although you can paint over it once it is fully dry), so preparation is key. When planning a tempera painting, gather little mixing pots for each colour you wish to use so that you can prepare each colour as you go. A glazed ceramic mixing palette, with round indents arranged like petals around a central well, is a good alternative.

Keep your jar of tempera medium close to hand, along with a couple of jars of clean water: one for cleaning brushes, and one with a dropper for adding water to mixes. It is also sensible to have a few brushes on hand to mix colours separately, and a sheet of paper nearby to test colour and consistency.

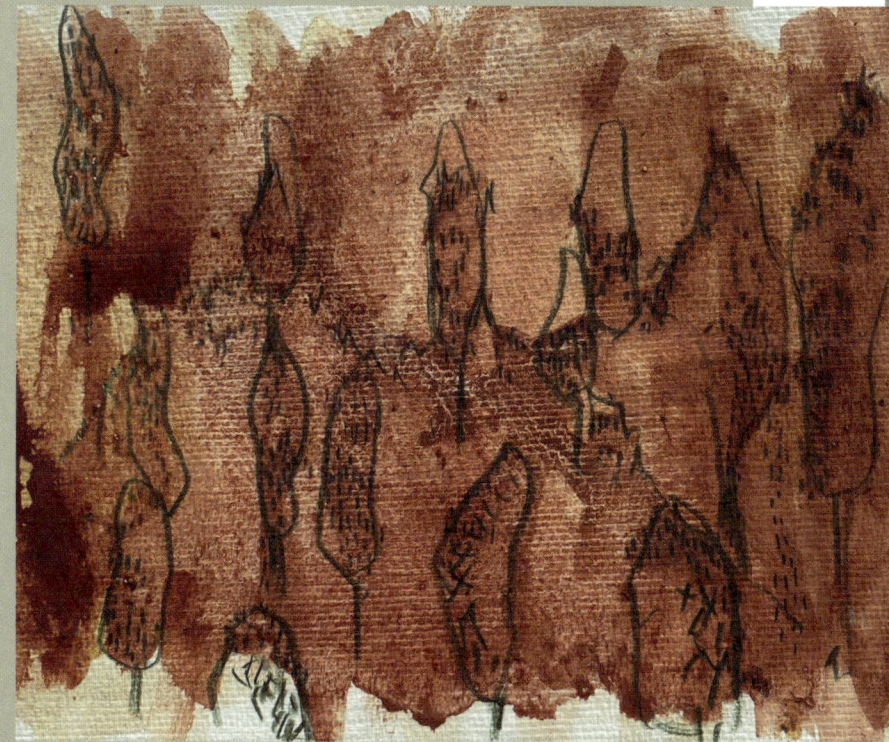

MEDITERRANEAN HILLSIDE SKETCH
Produced with ochres in tempera medium, with details in watercolour pencil.

Glair

Glair comes from the French word '*clair*' meaning clear. Made from egg whites, glair is a transparent medium with a slight gloss. It gives a similar effect and flow to watercolour but with a little more sheen once it has dried. A versatile medium, it has been used for over fourteen centuries in Europe as one of the binders for pigments for illuminated manuscripts on parchment (along with tempera, gum Arabic, cherry tree gum, hide glue and isinglass).

You will need

/ Large clean mixing bowl
/ Electric whisk (or a hand whisk if you have plenty of time and energy to spare)
/ Spatula
/ Eggs
/ Prepared pigment
/ White vinegar
/ Tumbler
/ Measuring spoons
/ A spotless storage jar with a lid
/ Paintbrush and paper

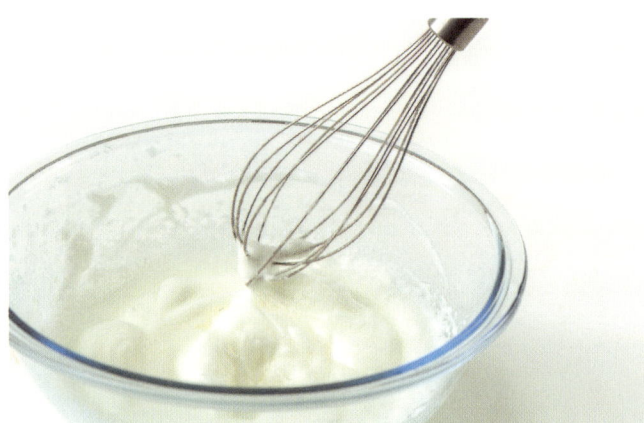

1 In the large bowl, whisk an egg white to stiff peaks, and set aside. Leave to settle until a clear liquid starts to form underneath the froth. This will take between half an hour and two hours.

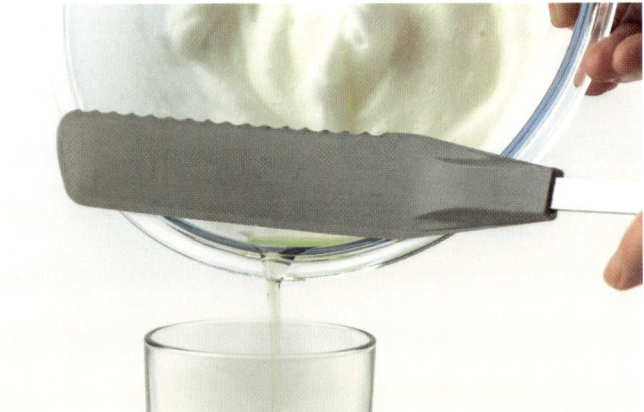

2 Using a spatula to hold back the froth, pour off the clear liquid every half an hour or so into a clean jar and keep it in the fridge. After a few hours, the peaks won't give any more liquid, and you can discard them. The liquid in the jar is glair.

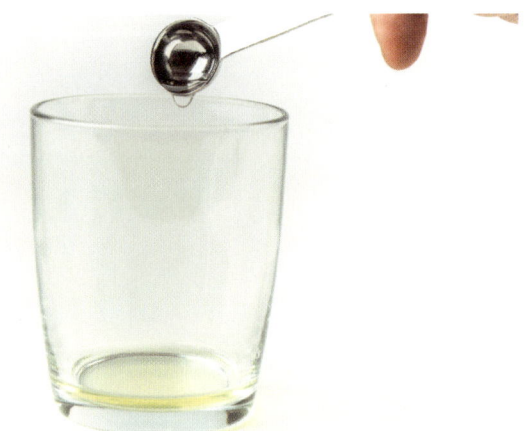

3 Add just a drop of vinegar to help preserve it, and the glair is ready.

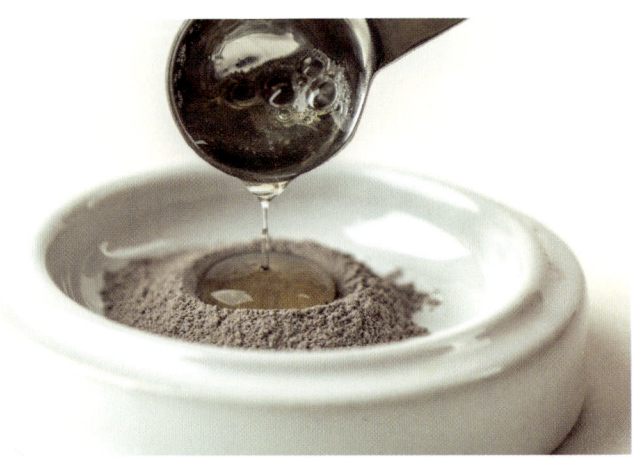

4 To make up into a paint, start with equal parts glair and refined pigment, then mix as described on page 77.

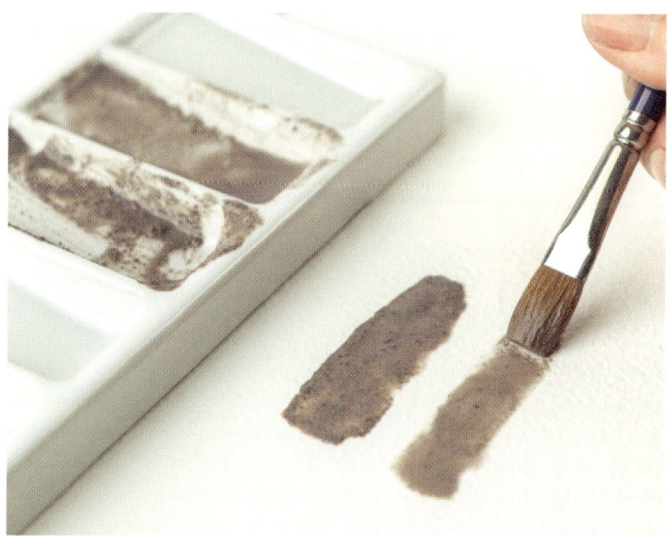

5 Add water to dilute to the required strength, then use as watercolour. Glair will keep for a couple of weeks in the fridge, but I prefer the smell of it fresh, so I use up any aging glair by making ochre grounds for drawings, rather than keep it too long.

How to use glair

I use glair for painting small, detailed work, as it runs less than watercolour but is not as glossy as tempera. When painting, if you want to make two subtly different tones from one pigment, you can use glair for a cooler effect and tempera for a warmer tone. This can be used to very good effect in a tip I learned from Daniel Chatto, with green earths (terre verte) in the background of landscape paintings, with the tempera sitting in front of the glair, giving the illusion of distance created by atmospheric conditions.

For very detailed work on a small scale, glair can be used neat, where it makes a thin cream consistency. For painting on paper I like to use it diluted, usually 1:1 glair to water, so that it handles more like watercolour. I have experimented with using it very dilute, and it binds the pigment to the paper well.

I found that glair can also be used diluted as a fixative for pastels. You can either lightly wet the whole sheet of paper before drawing with them, or use a blow diffuser or pump mister to spray the whole drawing lightly after it is finished. It doesn't discolour or smell, and is easy and non-toxic to use.

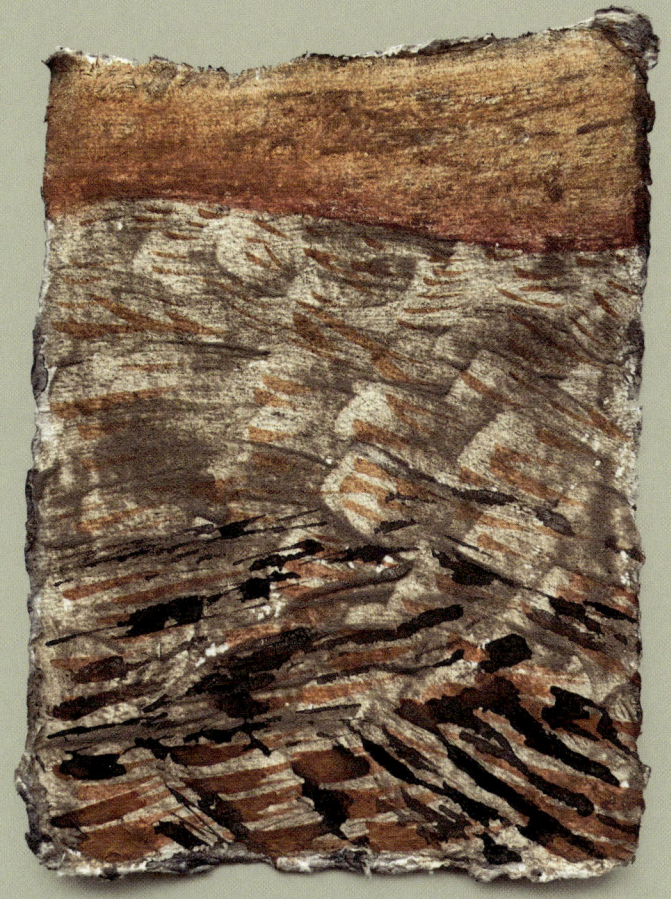

STUDY OF A PLOUGHED FIELD
Tyneham lilac, cochineal and Clearwell yellow ochre in glair medium, with iron gall ink details, on Khadi rag paper.

Veglair

With so many vegan friends and students, and a fad for aquafaba (the protein-rich water left after cooking beans or chickpeas) in the food section of my weekend newspapers, I began experimenting with vegan alternatives to eggs in my cooking in 2017. After seeing the juices from canned white beans and chickpeas photogenically whipped into peaks for vegan cooking, I was struck that the same leftover liquid could be used not only to make meringues, but to serve as a paint medium, too. After some experimentation I found that this aquafaba proved better than any of the alternatives I tried as a medium, and much faster, too.

I looked up names for what I'd made, and drawing a blank, decided to call it 'veglair', (a contraction of vegan and glair). It is a very matt medium, and intermixable with watercolours for a bit more shine. As a fine art medium, I would probably choose cherry tree gum watercolour over veglair as my matt choice, and gum Arabic as the higher gloss option. However, I have included veglair in the book to encourage you to experiment, use up what is already to hand – and to play with your food!

You will need

/ Large clean mixing bowl
/ Sieve
/ A can of white beans such as cannellini, butter beans, or chick peas
/ A storage jar with a lid
/ Whisk
/ Prepared pigment
/ Measuring jug
/ Measuring spoon
/ Artists' linseed oil (optional)
/ Paintbrush and paper

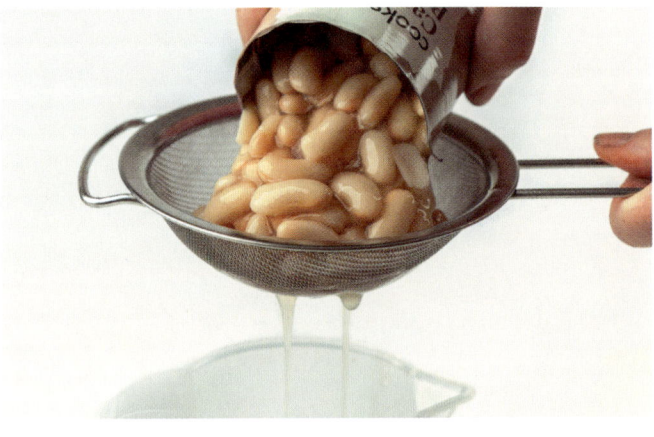

1 Pour cannellini beans through a strainer into a jug. You can use any white beans, but cannellini beans have the highest protein content, and work best.

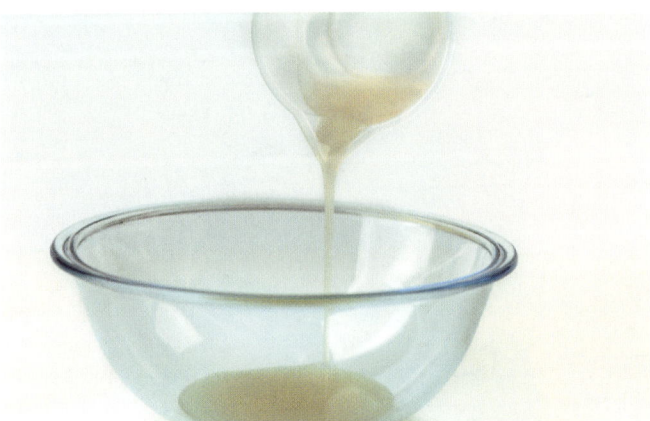

2 Leave to settle, then pour off the clear liquid into a bowl, leaving behind any particulates. This can be used as it is, but will give a very matt effect to the finished paint.

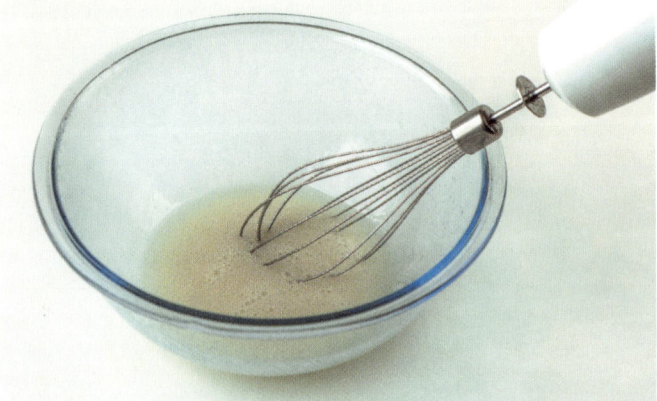

3 To add a similar gloss to egg glair, whisk in two teaspoons of artist's linseed oil; and if you'd like it to have the gloss of egg tempera, whisk in up to four teaspoons of linseed oil. The addition of the oil forms an emulsion (fat and protein in suspension); just like an egg.

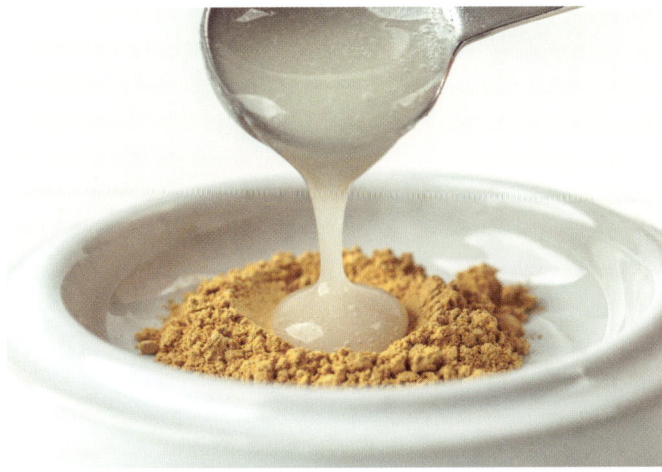

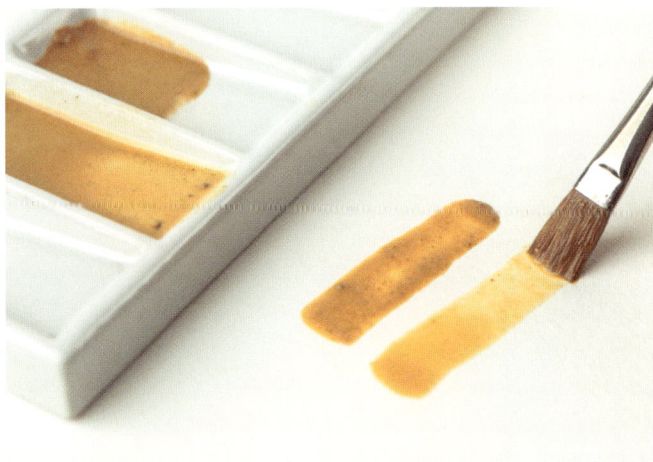

4 Combine equal amounts of veglair and refined pigment to make up into a paint.

5 Add water to dilute to the strength you require.

How to use veglair

Veglair can be used in much the same way as glair (see page 111). These notes will help your exploration:

Thickening Veglair is less binding than egg glair, so I don't dilute it much, if at all. If used too thinly, the pigment can rub off. If cooking beans at home, or if you have a couple of cans' worth of liquid, try gently simmering the liquid until it thickens and boils down somewhat. This gives the cooled resulting medium slightly better adhesion.

Additions To give a little more gloss you can add some gum Arabic solution to the mixture, or as a glaze at the end. Use an electric whisk to add a little artist's linseed oil into the veglair to add smoothness and flow to the paint; it stays in emulsion in a similar way to the oils in egg yolk. This will take a little longer to dry than neat veglair, or with added gum.

Ecologically sound As a low-impact, no-waste medium, veglair can't really be bettered, as unless used in soups and stews, it is often poured away as a waste product. I like it for its ease of use, especially with children, as much as for its matt paint effect.

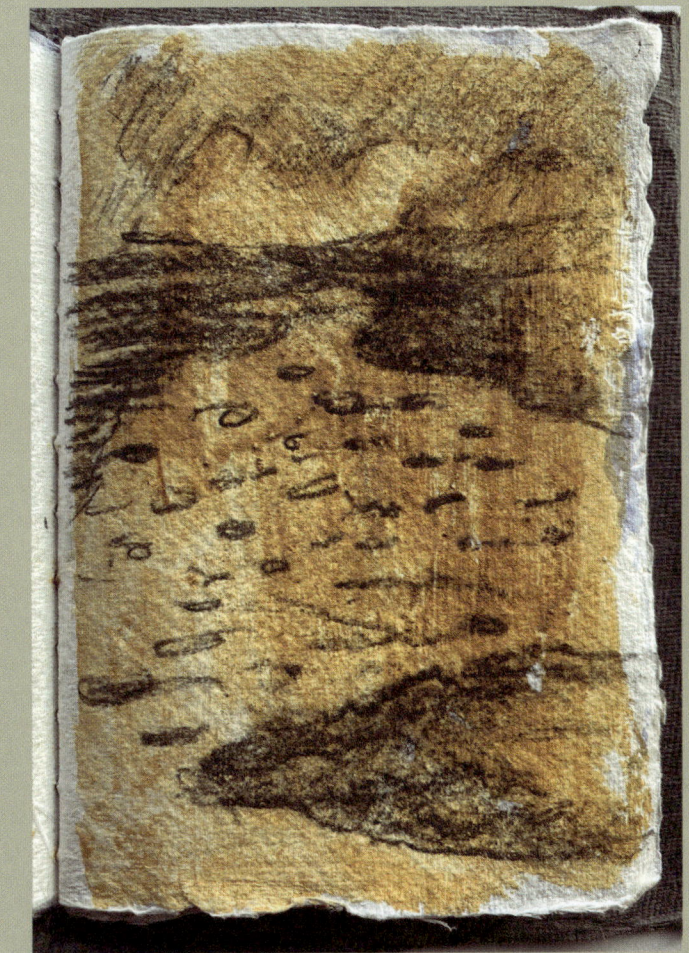

RAINY HARBOUR VIEW
This artwork, made with Dingle yellow ochre in veglair medium, shows the matt finish well. The scene has been picked out with willow charcoal.

BEYOND PAINT

In our paints, we embrace nature's complexity, steer clear of the desire for perfection, and allow the materials to express themselves by influencing our marks, colours, style and methods.

Just for a few pages, we'll look at making a simple, traditional ink. We will also explore mark-making tools and surfaces. There are also an infinite number of drawing and painting tools available to the forager. As just one example, look around during the autumn and you will find an abundance of hollow stalks, fur and hair on fences, wool shed by shaggy sheep, down from seed heads, interestingly shaped pods and teasels, all of which make great improvised brushes.

Oak gall ink

Unless we have foraged very dark carbon blacks from soot or charred materials, watercolours are never quite as deep a black as the ink we are going to make. Oak galls are very high in tannins, coloured compounds created by plants and trees. Ink made solely from galls is brown, while iron gall ink is black because the tannins react with iron, in the form of rust or iron mordant (*copperas*), to create dark, stable compounds.

You have almost certainly already seen this ink on illuminated manuscripts all over Europe, in England on *Magna Carta*, and the *Declaration of Independence* in America. Unlike in Asia and the Middle East, where carbon blacks on paper have been the norm throughout history, tannin-based inks on parchment were the historical choice in Europe.

There are countless recipes for making gall ink. Some include vinegar or wine, steeping, fermentation, and different sources of iron. We'll try two of my favourite simple methods; the first I have made even in the woods over an open fire, with no special equipment at all. The 'studio method' gives a refined ink with a smoother flow.

Because the tannin content of galls is variable, use the quantities and timings in these recipes as a guide, and adjust them as you would with a recipe for food. You can also reuse the powdered galls a couple of times to make less strong brown and sepia inks, all of which will complement your foraged paints beautifully.

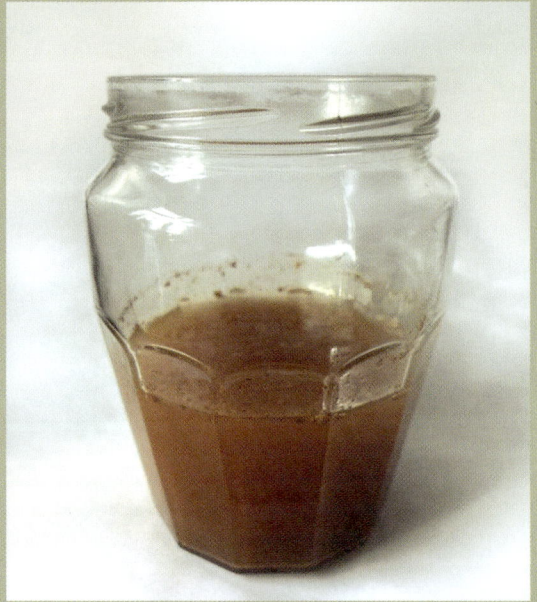

RUST PLANT

To make iron gall ink, you need some nice gunky orange rust water, which is easy to create a few weeks before you make your ink. Simply place a few rusty iron items in a glass or plastic container. Add enough water to cover most of them, but so that some of the iron is still exposed to the air. You can add a splash of vinegar and shake it gently every so often to help the iron to oxidize.

This is your 'rust plant'. Keep it sheltered but exposed to the air, and away from pets and children. A corner of the garden shed where you can safely leave it to rust away is ideal.

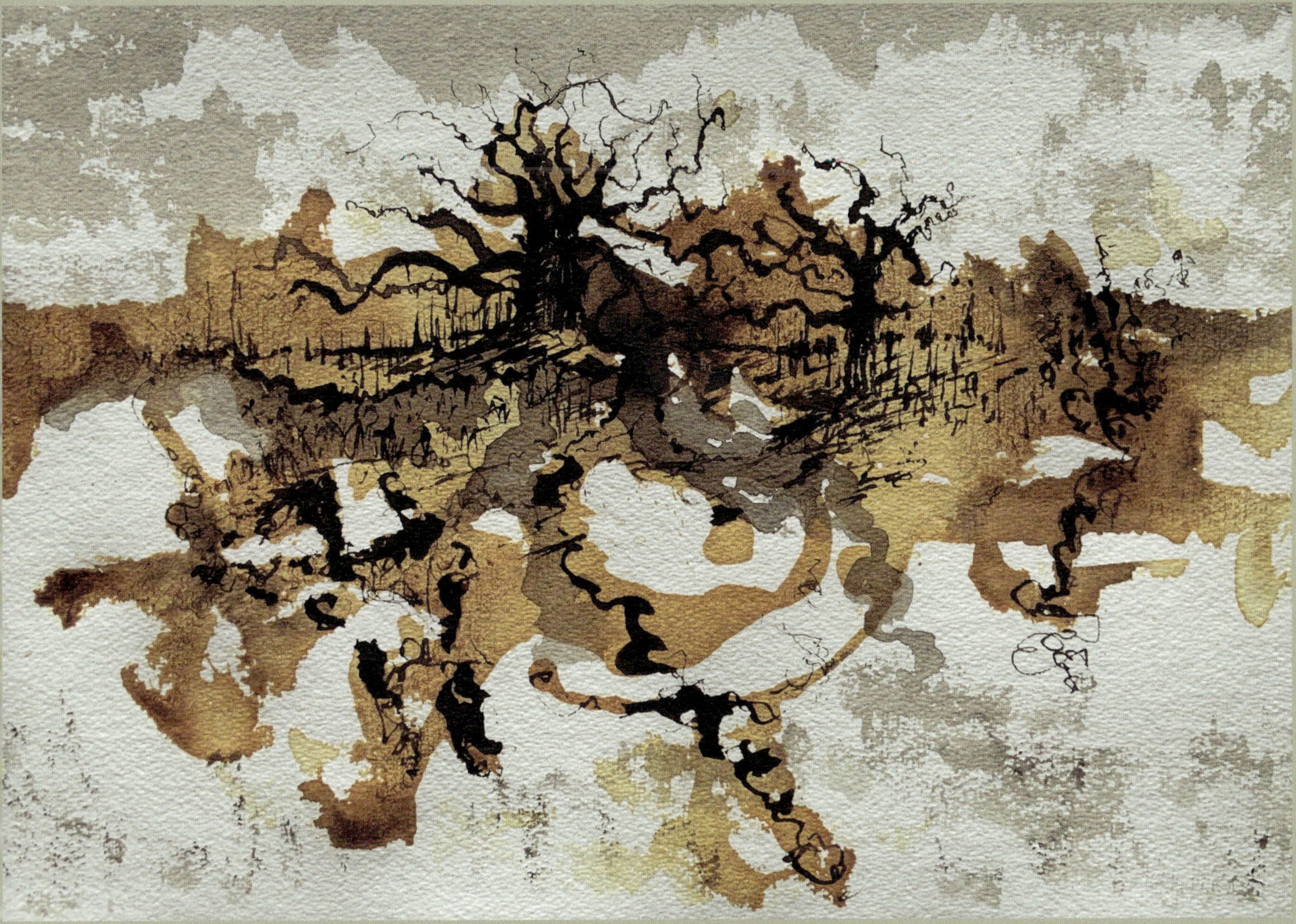

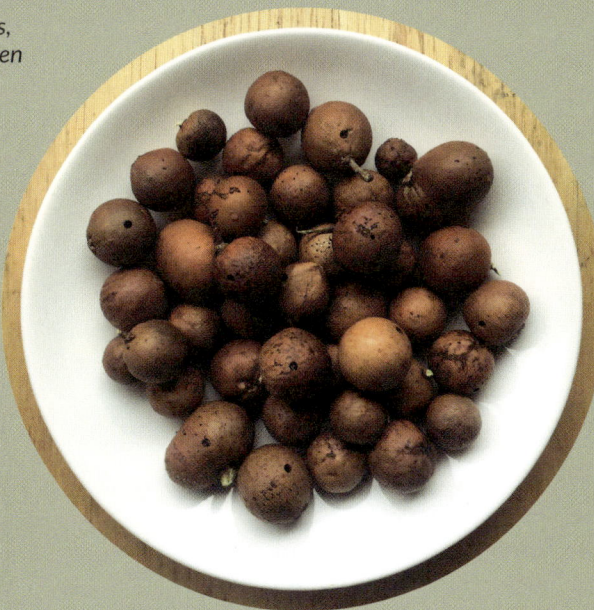

TWO OAKS 30 x 21cm (11¾ x 8¼in)

Handmade botanical inks on rag paper.

My first ink was made by just throwing rusty nails in with the cooking galls, but, though appealingly simple, this is a wasteful method as we cannot then reuse the galls. However, it made a lovely black ink.

In the collection of Nick Spahr.

Round galls are one of the many types of oak galls suitable for making ink.

Simple ink

This method results in an expressive permanent ink for use with a brush or dip pen, which is prone to granulation and interesting effects. Once dry, drawings made with this ink can be overpainted with washes of watercolour without running.

We won't know the precise strength of the gall solution or the iron – everything is done by eye and feel. You'll quickly get a sense of whether your ink will darken enough, and how to modify its colour and fluidity. You may also wish to strain it only lightly, leaving particulates in the ink, which you can mix by shaking. Spoons, sieves and pans used for making oak gall ink are best used for this only and make sure you wear old clothes or a good apron: this black ink stains formidably!

You will need

/ Smashed foraged oak galls
/ Two old saucepans
/ Rust plant (see page 114)
/ Small sieve
/ Jug
/ Funnel (optional)
/ Watercolour medium or gum solution
/ Scrap white paper and brush or dip pen for testing your ink

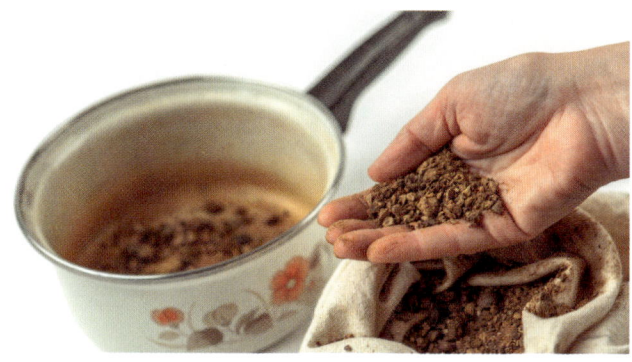

1 Place two big handfuls of smashed galls into one of the saucepans and cover with twice as much water.

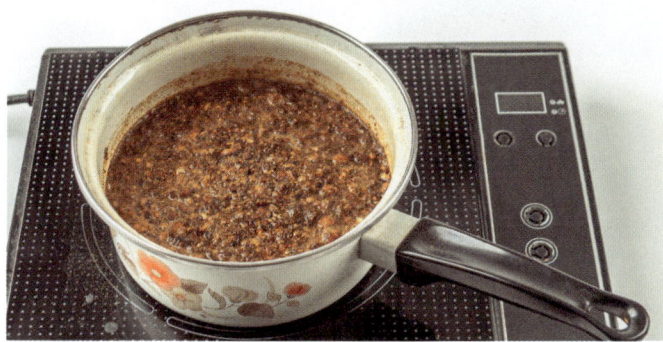

2 Simmer them very gently for up to an hour, topping up the water if it gets below the top of the galls. Test the colour every fifteen minutes by dipping a strip of paper into it. As it cooks, the brown will get darker as the tannin solution gets stronger.

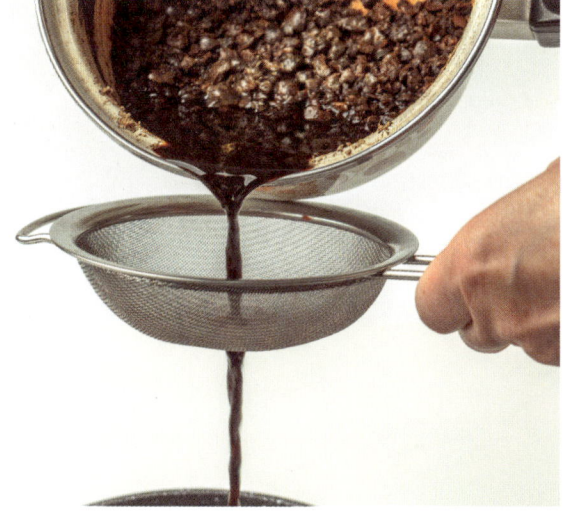

3 Once the liquor is rich and brown, take the pan off the heat and strain the liquid into the second pan. The cooked galls can be re-boiled now, or set aside for later use, as they can be reused several times. You can also freeze cooked galls to use at a more convenient time.

Tip

After straining, set aside a little of this beautiful brown oak gall ink as it is a wonderful coloured ink in its own right.

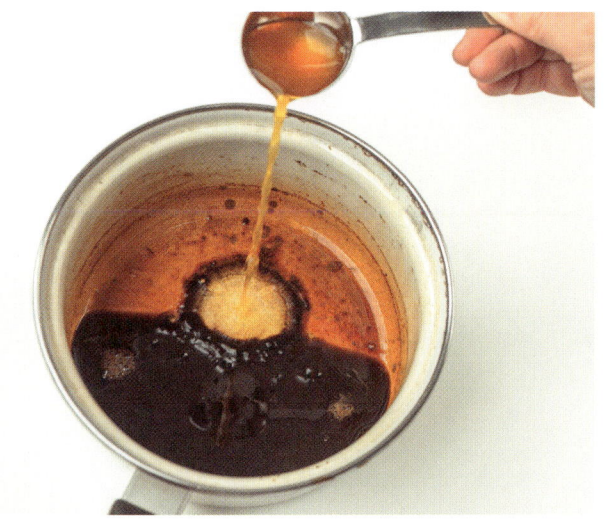

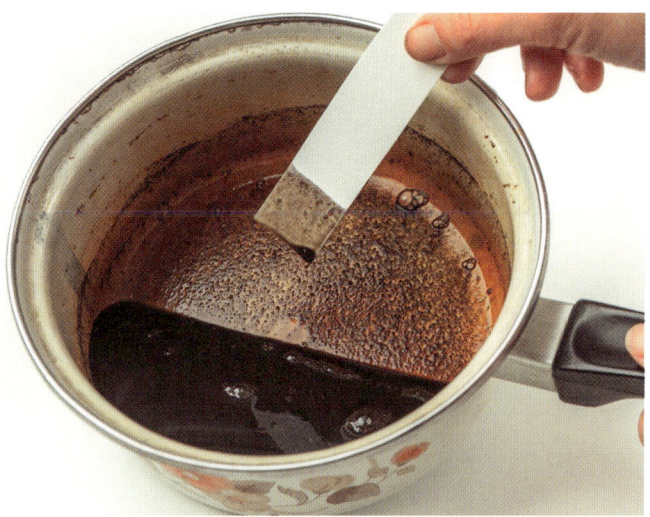

4 Add a couple of spoonfuls of the rusty water from your rust plant to the liquid. It's fine if there is sediment included, as we will strain the ink later.

5 It will start to darken almost immediately, but you may need to heat and stir the ink, if it does not go dark swiftly. Test the ink using your paper test strips. If it's too light, re-heat and reduce, or add more rust.

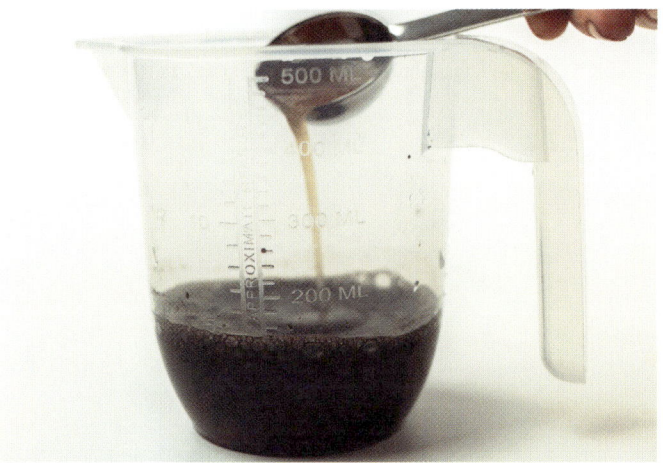

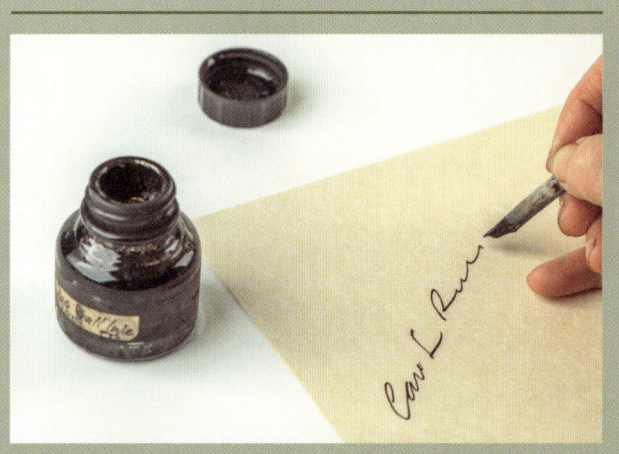

6 When it is at least very dark brown, pour it into a jug. To give fluidity and adhesion, add about 10 per cent gum Arabic or cherry tree gum solution (or your own watercolour medium) to it and to the brown oak gall liquor you set aside earlier. Your ink is ready to bottle and use. Shake before use.

How to use your simple ink

Test out your ink on paper and adjust it with the methods detailed above until it's how you like it. It darkens as it dries. Traditionally, a whole clove was placed in the jar to help prevent mould.

The ink can be used with a brush or dip pen (as shown above), but don't be tempted to fill your favourite fountain pen with it, as it may corrode or clog the pen over time.

Refined studio ink

You will need

/ Bought powdered oak galls

/ Dyer's mordant (also called ferrous sulphate, iron (II) sulphate or, in old European recipes, *copperas*)

/ Watercolour medium

/ Heatproof containers

/ Boiling water

/ Measuring spoons

/ Spoon

/ Sieve with muslin

/ Clove (optional)

This method will result in a finer but just as traditional ink. This is the ink used for the black lettering in so many historical documents such as the *Book of Kells* and *Magna Carta*. Ideal for drawing and calligraphy, it was the regular ink of much of Europe until the twentieth century.

To powder the galls, I suggest you use an electric coffee or spice grinder after smashing them. Alternatively, powdered galls can be bought from art suppliers.

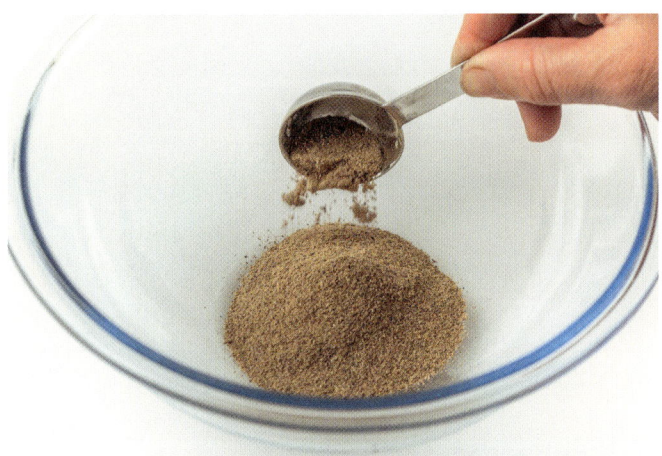

1 Place two tablespoons of powdered galls into the heatproof container.

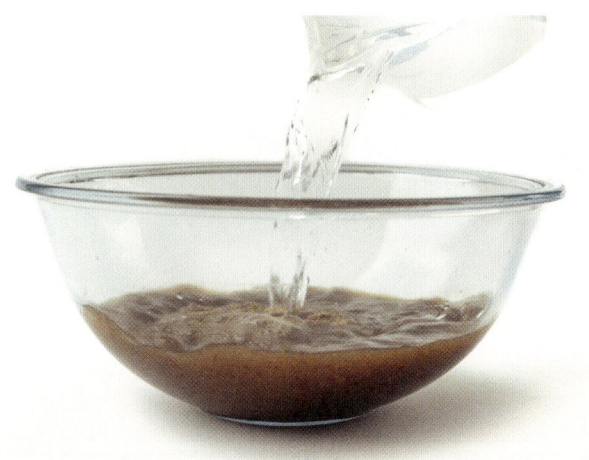

2 Cover with 500ml (16 fl oz) of boiling water and leave to steep for an hour, stirring occasionally.

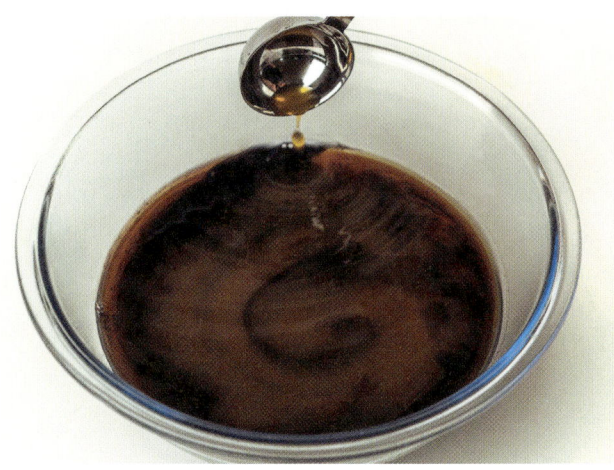

3 Add a scant tablespoon of dyer's mordant and stir to mix. It should go black very quickly.

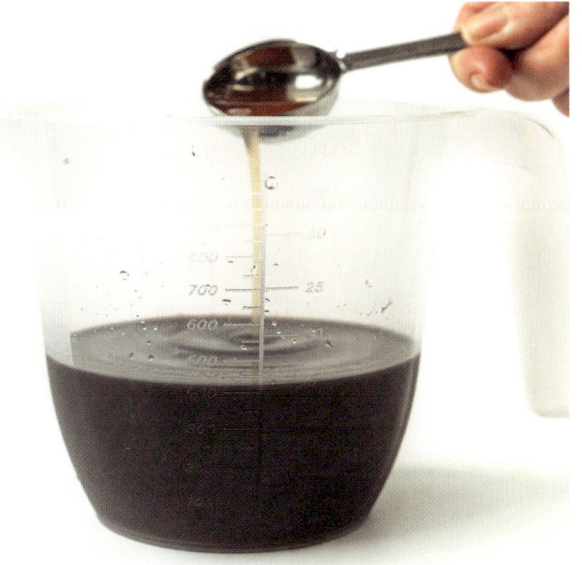

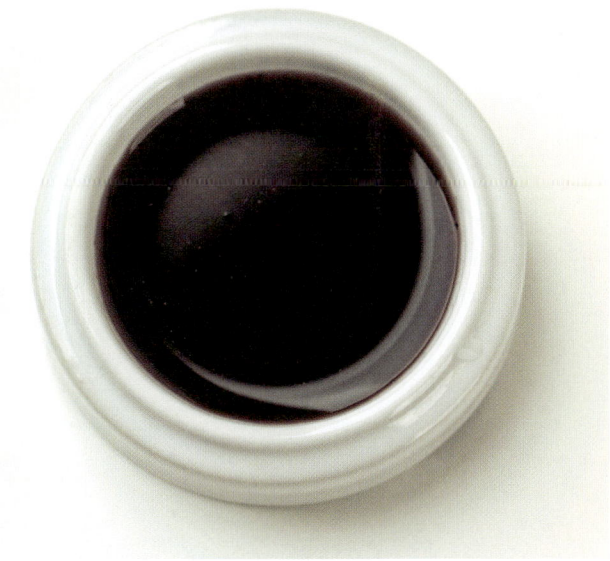

4 Strain finely into another jug or large jar, then add your watercolour medium – up to 10 per cent if based on gum Arabic, and up to 15 per cent if cherry tree gum.

5 Your ink is ready to bottle and use. You can add one whole clove if you like, traditionally used for fragrance and antifungal reasons. Shake before use.

How to use your refined studio ink

You can adjust the viscosity and flow of your ink by the amount of gum medium that you add. If the ink hasn't darkened enough, then more mordant may be needed. It is best to start with too little, and add it and gently heat the ink again.

The ink can be slightly corrosive, so it is not suitable for fountain pen use.

If you want to make the ink a thicker consistency, then you can gently reduce it down on a low heat by evaporation.

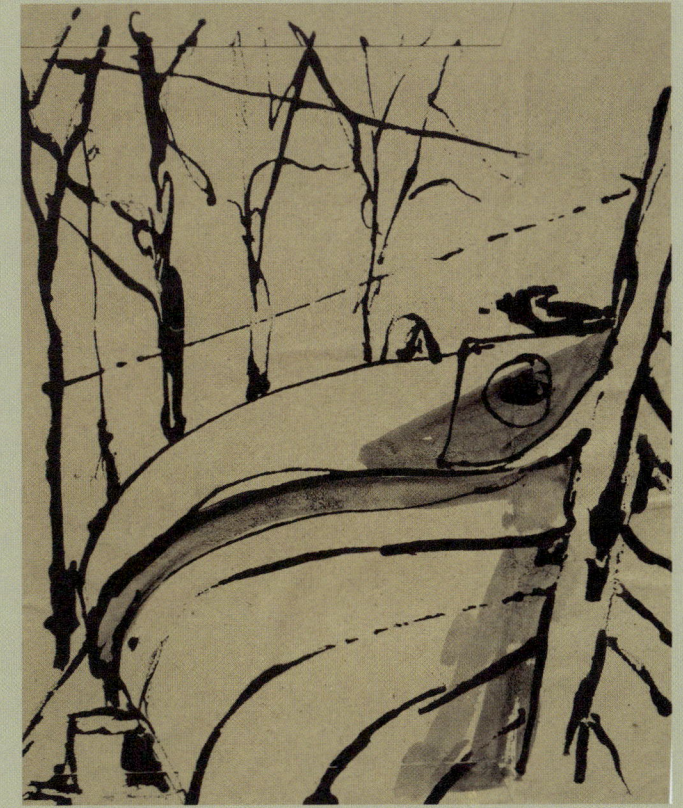

BARGE ON THE RIVER THAMES
Iron gall ink and wash on an old envelope.

Mark-making tools

Pens Found throughout history wherever the written word emerged, dip pens can be as simple as a sharp stick. Reeds, thin bamboo, hollow sticks, feathers and found objects all make superb drawing tools. Proper quill pens require us to cure (harden) feathers over time and make a few tricky cuts, a wonderful art beyond the scope of this book. But you can make an excellent pen right now without any fuss at all, as described to the right.

Instead of the uniform, machine-calibrated line produced by shop-bought pens, a dip pen creates a living line. When you first apply the freshly dipped pen to paper, it is full of ink, and as you make your mark the ink is used up, until it needs to be re-dipped. In this way it is like the breath when singing a song or telling a story. A tale intoned with a flat, even voice sounds dull. The drawings that come from dipped pens are often livelier than those made with machined tools.

Brushes We can also make paintbrushes from the materials around us. My friend Avalon in Hawai'i uses the fibrous seed pods of *hala* (*Pandanus tectorius*) to make brushes with which she paints *kapa*, the traditional bark cloth made by beating the inner bark of the *wauke* (*Broussonetia papyrifera*), a tree native to the island. These beautiful brushes inspired me to make my own brushes from local twigs and plant fibres, as we don't have such pods in the UK.

There are many woods that are used for culinary smoking or tools, such as maple, ash, birch, beech, hazel, or fruitwoods. A small pencil-thin twig from any of these can make a good brush: just chew the scraped end of a stick that you have soaked for an hour in water. Make sure you avoid toxic trees such as yew, holly and horse chestnut, and stick to deciduous rather than conifer twigs.

For those who already engage in 'nose to tail eating', and use the whole organic or wild game animal, the fur, tail, and feathers of game can be incorporated into brushes. One of my favourite stippling brushes is a hollow bone left by a fox, filled with a twist of wool from a hedgerow. Another is an empty winter stem of hogweed, stuffed with thistledown from tall weeds. We can bind our own, or our pets', hair trimmings with a little gum or glue and wrap them with thread to make an insert for a reed or hollow stick. Household finds such as trimmings, tassels, ribbons and string can all be tied into very interesting bundle brushes, perfect for washes, paint effects and expressive marks.

Once we begin to look at things as possible brushes, pompoms and decorative household trimmings falling apart seems far less sad – as this means they can become a new painting tool.

Making a simple pen

Trim a section of a reed or feather with scissors to a little longer than you'd like the finished pen. Hold it firmly in one hand, then use a craft knife to cut the thicker end at an oblique angle. Always cut away from yourself. The pen can be used as it is, or you can refine it by narrowing the side of the tip to a point for finer lines, or to a flat end for a wider mark.

Dip it in ink, draw and experiment. Wash your pens in water and dry them thoroughly before storing somewhere airy, so they won't attract mould.

Making a feather brush

Using the discarded tip of the feather with which you made your pen, trim the tip so that it fits into a thin hollow stick such as elder, reed or bamboo. A ferrule made from a section of feather shaft brings the feather tip together nicely to form a point, as shown in the top brush in the picture. Replace the brush tip as it wears out with new shapes and types of feather. Gull, corvid, swan, goose and turkey are all great, but almost any feather can make an interesting brush.

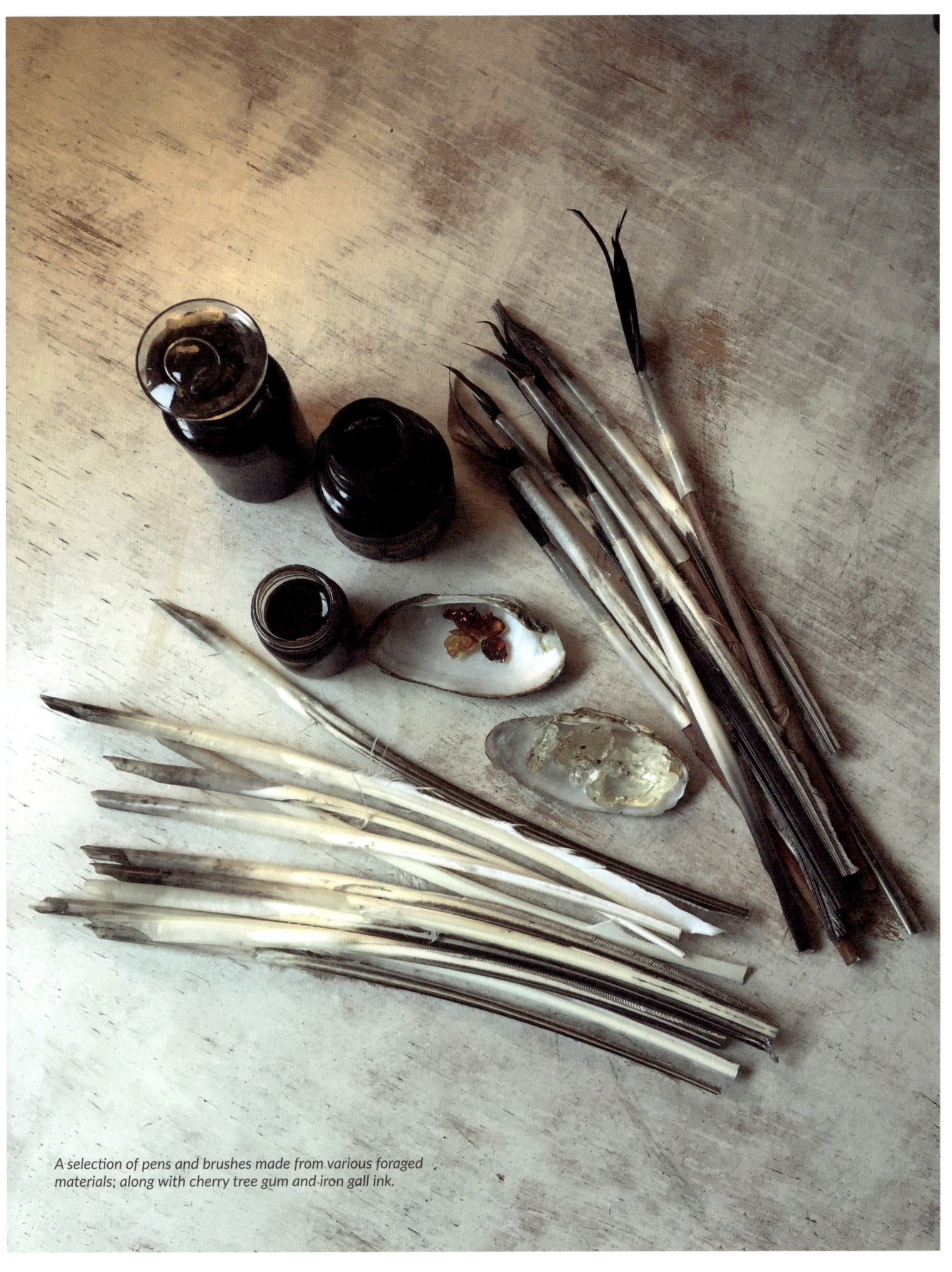

*A selection of pens and brushes made from various foraged
materials; along with cherry tree gum and iron gall ink.*

Papers, supports and surfaces

You can use your usual bought watercolour papers or pads, and you don't need to buy anything new or special to start. Heavier weight good quality watercolour paper is ideal for finished pieces using your paints and ink, as it will be strong enough to take any of the media and materials without buckling or wearing through.

There is, however, a whole world of under-used paper and natural surfaces we can work on, so let's look with a forager's eye at what else is around.

Repurposed paper Unless you need a piece to have guaranteed longevity, then repurposed paper is good enough, and anything from your recycling bin, from envelopes to book covers will provide interest in marks, shape or texture. The materials we have covered in this book are not pH sensitive, so we can be free with our choices of paper.

Birch bark As noted on page 40, this wonderful papery material can sometimes be found peeling from trees. It ranges from pure white to deep warm browns, via red and yellow, with dashes and dots in darker tones. Birch 'paper' is one of the most beautiful surfaces on which to paint and lasts indefinitely as it contains preservative natural tar.

Other bark Some trees such as London plane, some eucalyptus, and certain ornamental prunus shed or peel sections of bark naturally. The inner surfaces are paler and make beautiful supports for painting. Look out for insects or rot so as not to bring woodworm or fungi into your home.

Natural wood Slices of natural wood, once dried, make beautiful, traditional supports for painting, especially in egg tempera. Sometimes a piece of firewood is just too beautiful to burn, and with a quick sanding it can make a beautiful surface to paint on. Add a lick of diluted gelatine or dilute glair, and the surface will be even better.

Repurposed wood To prepare old wood, lightly sand the panel and wipe clean of dust. For brighter colours, prime with a pale neutral or chalk paint made with starch size, glair or gelatine, before working on top in gouache or egg tempera.

Fabrics, canvas and textiles Once glued onto a board, fabrics give a nice 'tooth' or texture for thicker media. Although the paints and inks we have made are not specially adapted to use on fabric, most will work well.

Parchment Parchment is an ideal surface for our paints and inks. For at least a thousand years, the vast majority of European books were produced this way, and it is still possible to purchase ethically sourced and manufactured parchment from artisanal suppliers.

Repurposed leather For the avid re-use fan, pale leather or suede from discarded or thrifted clothes can be transformed by drawing with iron gall ink.

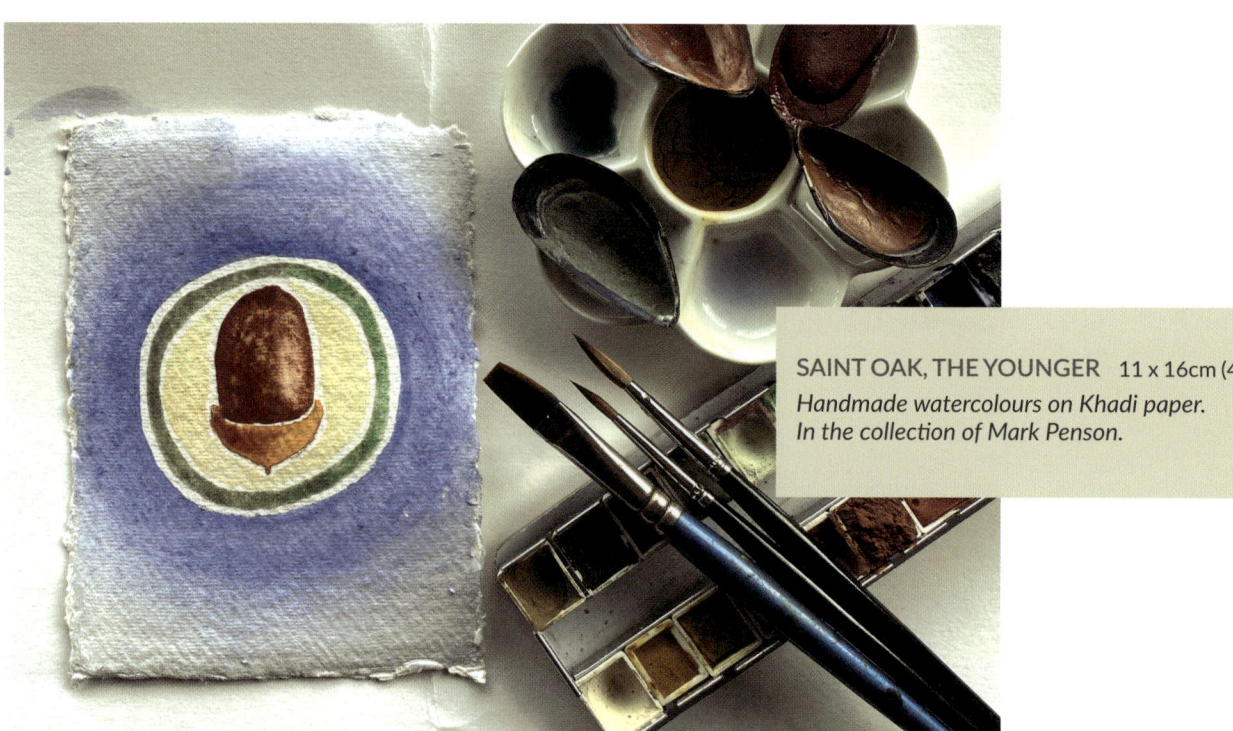

SAINT OAK, THE YOUNGER   11 x 16cm (4¼ x 6¼in)
Handmade watercolours on Khadi paper.
In the collection of Mark Penson.

Decorations

I encourage you to scavenge and experiment with surfaces to your heart's content. Take inspiration from our ancestors and decorate your walls with murals on lining paper. Banners, bunting and wall hangings can be made from paper or card, mounted fabrics or found boards. Celebrate your festivals with decorations and embellishments that bring you and your loved ones joy, without the need for plastic baubles and tinsel.

RAWHIDE RATTLE   18 x 41cm (7 x 16in)

This rattle was made by Susan Cross, and later decorated with oakleaf using homemade watercolour paint made to a thick consistency to give a relief effect.

SANCTUM   Various sizes

Produced for the Dark Mountain Project, all of these pieces were made with handmade watercolours and inks on parchment made by artist Thomas Keyes from deerskins that would otherwise be disposed of as waste.

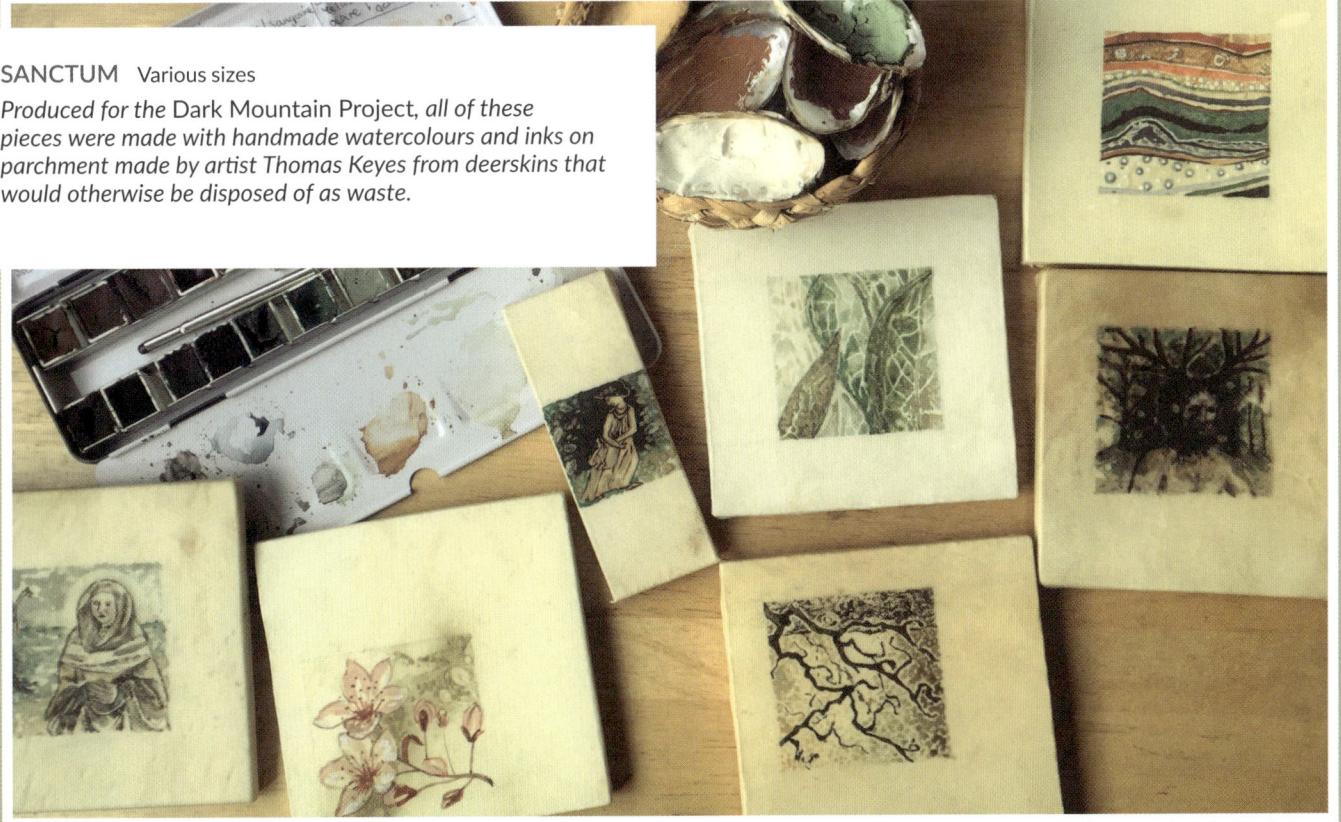

GOING FURTHER

> **There is no place on earth where people have ignored the colour under their feet.**

In the Transylvanian mountains of Romania floral designs are painted with bright ochre on whitewashed village walls. In the Indian Himalayas, gold ochre *tilak* is painted on the foreheads of those on pilgrimage through the high foothills. In Sweden, stones erected and inscribed in the Viking age are still repainted each year in bold red iron oxide, so that the longships and warriors stand out fresh as the day they were first set up. In England, locals turn over the chalk stones each spring, so that giants and horses seem to leap glowing from the green hillsides. There is no place on earth where people have ignored the colour under their feet.

Learning from the land, people, and tradition

Perhaps near you there is tremendous indigenous, traditional, or innovative new earth pigment art to be seen and appreciated, supported or protected. I encourage you to start locally, and learn what you can about your own place, whether or not your ancestors are 'from there' or arrived more recently. Working outwards, we can then spread our interest geographically, historically, or thematically, perhaps investigating a technique or material that draws us to it.

Inspiration can come from anywhere: a particular colour, a passing comment in a documentary, a book of fiction, a song.

My friend Heidi Gustafson has a great love of ochre, not simply as a source of colour or a resource for further use, but in its own right. Her research and collection is hugely inspiring to me and many pigment people. Lucy Mayes is fascinated by colour from waste streams in urban London. Her London Pigments stretch our ideas of what can be sources of colour, and encourage us to look closer at what is discarded. For me, my interest in ancient and natural pigments was renewed after reading *The Wake* by Paul Kingsnorth, a novel set around 1066CE, during the subjugation of the English by the invading Normans. I wanted to draw some of the scenes from the book, and wondered what materials were available at that time. I read about illuminated manuscripts, costumes and objects of the era, and went to see them in the flesh in museum collections. That led me to make deerskin parchment and the inks and paints to use on them, and to learn about the dyes and paints of Saxon times.

There are an infinite number of paths through foraged pigments and natural art materials. We need not appropriate anything that is not ours to take, nor slavishly search only for innovation. There is a middle way where we trust our intuition, respect and cite our sources, teachers and forebears, and make our own contribution via our art to the sum of good in the world.

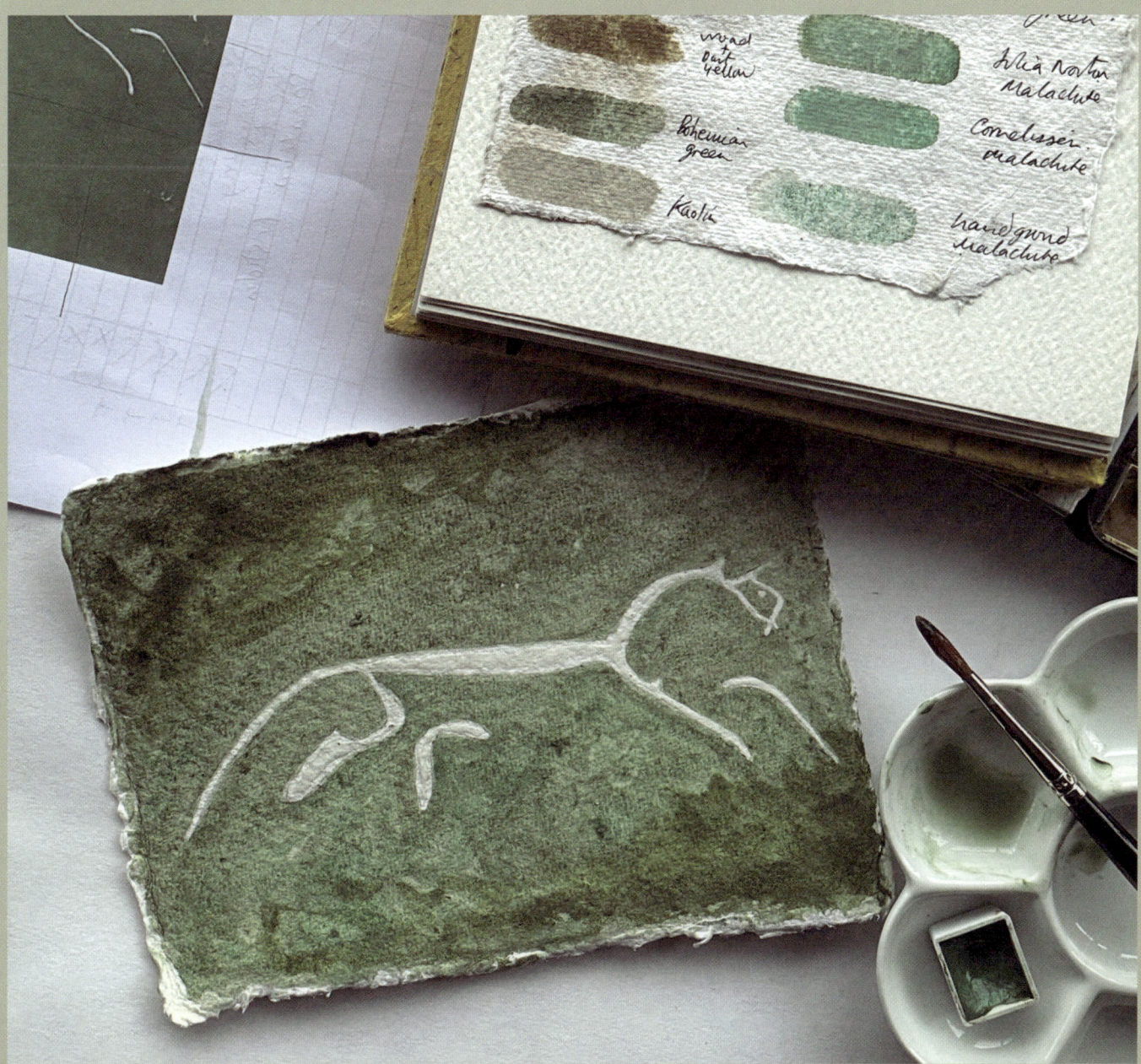

As mentioned in the introduction, the peoples of the British isles have long created monumental horses and other figures by cutting into hillsides to reveal the stark white chalk beneath the turf. Some, like the one conjured to me by my Nan, are only a few hundred years old, but others are much older – a thousand years or so for the Cerne Abbas Giant, or three thousand years in the case of the prehistoric Uffington White Horse.

STUDY OF THE UFFINGTON WHITE HORSE
40.5 x 28cm (16 x 11in)
Bohemian green ochre and malachite watercolours, buckthorn berry ink and white chalk gouache. In the collection of Stewart Lee.

GLOSSARY

Aquafaba Viscous water in which legume seeds, such as chickpeas or white beans, have been stored.

Binder Substances that hold pigment particles together to make paint.

Braying To break, pound or grind small.

Copperas Dyer's mordant, FeSO4, also called ferrous sulphate, iron (II) sulphate.

Drying oils Oils that harden to a solid film through reaction (oxidization) with air.

Dye Coloured substance that bonds chemically to a substrate.

Egyptian blue Synthetic blue pigment (calcium copper silicate) created in Ancient Egypt.

Emulsion Minute droplets of one liquid in another in which it is not soluble, e.g. fat droplets in suspension in tempera medium.

Ferrule Strengthening or joining ring, such as a section of a feather shaft used in making natural paint brushes.

Flocculation The aggregation of tiny particles that precipitate into small lumps.

Fresco Painting with water-based paints onto a still-wet freshly plastered surface.

Gelatine Water soluble protein gel from animal collagen sources used as a binder.

Gesso Mixture of plaster and glue; traditionally painted onto boards and used as a fine surface on which to paint.

Glair Water-based paint medium made from egg whites.

Glycerine Another name for glycerol, added to watercolour to allow re-wetting.

Gouache Opaque waterbased paint made from gum Arabic plus chalk or other filler. Also called poster paint.

Granulation Particles of pigment clumping together and creating attractive uneven surface effects in watercolour painting.

Gum Arabic Water soluble gum with many artistic and culinary uses. It is produced by some species of acacia tree.

Gum tempera Traditional term for watercolour paint made of pigment in gum Arabic.

Half-pan Small standardized size of watercolour paint produced by most brands. Approximately 2ml (½tsp) of paint.

Hue Colour or shade (rather than intensity or lightness / darkness of a colour).

Humectant Paint additive that allows rewetting, such as honey or glycerine.

Lake pigment Pigment made by precipitating a dye onto a substrate to create opaque particles of colour useful to make paint.

Levigation Refining pigment through grinding, washing and sedimentation processes.

Lightfast Desrcibes somethign the does not discolour when exposed to light.

Mordant Substance which fixes a dye permanently.

Muller Flat bottomed hand tool used on a slab to finely mix paints.

Mulling Refining paint by circular motions with a muller so that every particle of pigment is coated with medium until slick.

Oak gall Small tannin-rich growths forming on oak trees in response to parasitic wasps. Galls are traditionally used as a tannin source for inks.

Ochre Earth pigments containing ferric oxide.

Optical mixing Perception of a third colour formed by placing two separate colours side by side, as made popular in Pointillism.

Paint Coloured substance containing pigment and a binder.

Pestle and mortar Sturdy bowl and pounding tool commonly made of stone used since prehistoric times for grinding and mixing.

Pigment Coloured substance insoluble in water.

Size Substance applied to paper or painting surface to prepare it for painting by making it less porous or absorbent.

Spring tide Tides just after full or dark moon when there is the greatest variation between high and low water levels.

Support The material to which paint is applied, such as paper or canvas.

Tannin Plant-derived polyphenols used in tanning, ink and dye making.

Tempera Common name for water paints made using egg yolk and other additives such as vinegar.

Terre verte Green earth pigment.

Terroir Entire natural environment including soil, climate and topography.

Veglair My vegan art medium made with aquafaba and linseed oil, designed to stand in for egg-based mediums such as glair (egg white) and tempera (yolk). A contraction of the words 'vegan' and 'glair'.

Vivianite Hydrated iron phosphate mineral, which gives pigments ranging from blue to green and grey.

Watershed Area or ridge separating land that drains into different rivers or seas.

Wedging Removing air bubbles from clay by kneading and pounding.

Whiting Washed, finely ground chalk or other calcium carbonate for use in making paint or putty.

Recommended reading

The Book of Earth by Gustafson, Heidi – Abrams Books 2023

Wild Inks and Paints by Medlej, Joumana – Majnouna.com 2021

The Organic Artist for Kids by Neddo, Nick – Quarry Books 2020

Inks and Paints of the Middle East by Medlej, Joumana – Majnouna.com 2020

Make Ink by Logan, Jason – Abrams Books 2018

The Organic Artist by Neddo, Nick – Quarry Books 2015

Further reading suggestions can be found on Bookmarked (www.bookmarkedhub.com). Search for this book by title or ISBN: the information can be found under 'Book Extras'.

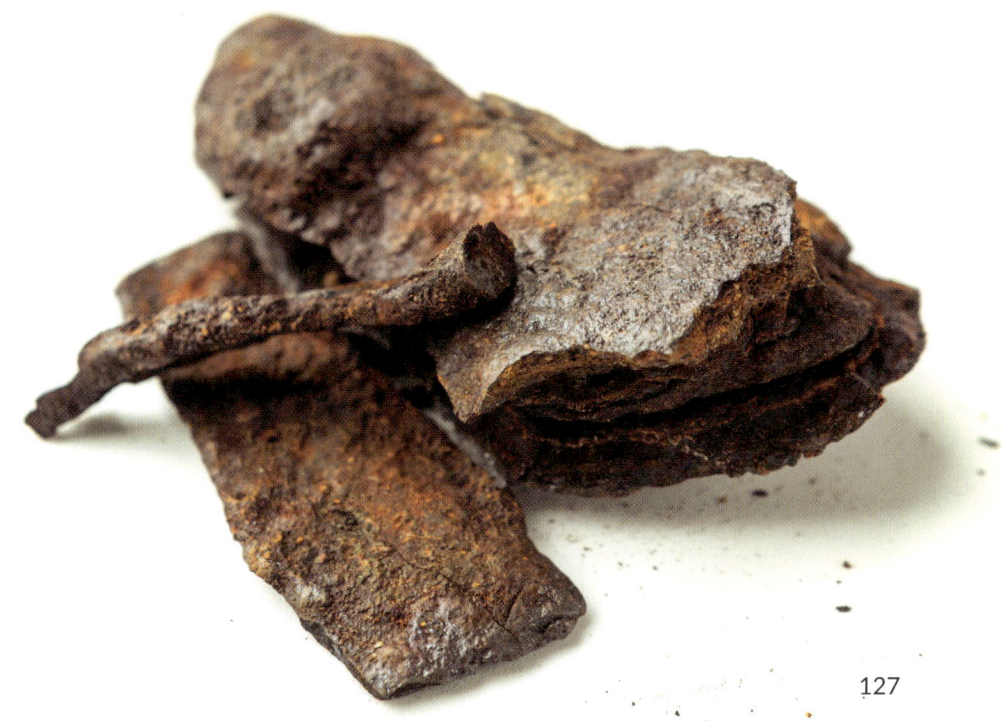

INDEX

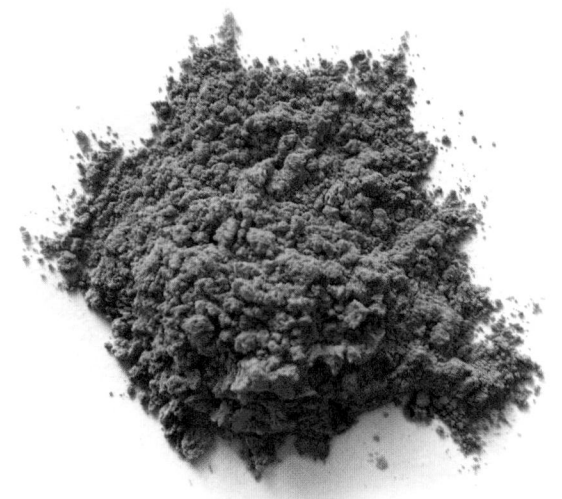